# LANGUAGE, DISCOURSE, SOCIETY
General Editors: Stephen Heath, Colin MacCabe and Denise Riley

### Series Standing Order

If you would like to receive future titles in this series as they
are published, you can make use of our standing order
facility. To place a standing order please contact your
bookseller or, in case of difficulty, write to us at the address
below with your name and address and the name of the
series. Please state with which title you wish to begin your
standing order. (If you live outside the UK we may not have
the rights for your area, in which case we will forward your
order to the publisher concerned.)

Standing Order Service, Macmillan Distribution Ltd,
Houndmills, Basingstoke, Hampshire, RG21 2XS, England.

# The Desire to Desire

## The Woman's Film of the 1940s

MARY ANN DOANE

Associate Professor, Semiotics Project
Brown University, Providence, Rhode Island

MACMILLAN

First published in the USA (Indiana University Press) 1987
First published in the UK (Macmillan) 1988

Published by
MACMILLAN PRESS LTD
Houndmills, Basingstoke, Hampshire RG21 6XS
and London
Companies and representatives
throughout the world

ISBN 0–333–45534–7 hardcover
ISBN 0–333–45535–5 paperback

A catalogue record for this book is available
from the British Library.

9   8   7   6   5   4   3   2
03  02  01  00  99  98  97  96

Printed in Great Britain by
Ipswich Book Co. Ltd
Ipswich, Suffolk

A shorter version of chapter 2 was published originally in
*Poetics Today,* vol. 6, nos. 1–2 (1985). Chapter 6 is a revised
version of an article published in *Enclitic,* 5:2/6:1 (fall 1981/
spring 1982). Portions of chapters 1, 2 and 5 appeared in
somewhat different form in *Ciné-tracts,* 11 (fall 1980) and in
"The 'Woman's Film': Possession and Address", in *Re-vision:
Essays in Feminist Film Criticism* (Frederick, Md.; University
Publications of America, 1984). A section of chapter 1 was
published in *The Quarterly Review of Film Studies,* vol, 10,
no. 4 (1987).

*Photo Credits*

Metro-Goldwyn-Mayer: Chapter 6, figures 1–32 (© 1949).
United Artists: Chapter 6, figures 33–59 (© 1940).
Warner Brothers: Chapter 4, figures 1–14 (© 1946).

FOR MY PARENTS,
*Mary R. and Ivan G. Doane*

# C O N T E N T S

# ACKNOWLEDGMENTS

I am deeply grateful to a large number of people who have made this book possible. Linda Williams, who is a tough and simultaneously very generous critic, offered valuable commentary and criticisms on a number of chapters as well as emotional support. I would also like to thank the many students at both New York University and Brown University who agreed to share my obsessions in courses on the woman's film and who contributed—frequently brilliant—insights about the films. I thank Brown University for a Wriston fellowship and the Pembroke Center for Teaching and Research on Women for a fellowship which allowed me time for research and writing. I am particularly grateful to the members of the Pembroke Seminar of 1982–83 and to Joan Scott and Elizabeth Weed, whose warm understanding and intellectual support have been invaluable to me. Thanks also go to my colleagues in the Brown Semiotics Program, Robert Scholes, Michael Silverman, and Leslie Thornton, who have been a constant source of inspiration and have made complacency impossible. Margaret Smith Weinstein gave me valuable advice about procuring films and encouraged me through her keen interest in the project. The members of a feminist reading group at Brown University—Christina Crosby, Karen Newman, Ellen Rooney, and Naomi Schor—forced me to confront the implications of my least productive contradictions and to focus my thinking about certain issues. Various forms of criticism, support, and encouragement have been provided by Janice Doane, Joan Catapano, Teresa de Lauretis, Kaja Silverman, David Bordwell, Judith Mayne, Stephen Heath, Lynn Joyrich, Deborah Linderman, Ruth Santos, and Jo Ann Putnam-Scholes. Finally, and as always, special thanks go to Phil Rosen for theoretical insights, editorial aid, and his persistent attempts to strengthen my defenses against the minor and major traumas associated with the act of writing.

The Desire
to Desire

# 1

# The Desire to Desire

## *Subjectivity and Desire: An(other) Way of Looking*

Toward the end of Woody Allen's *The Purple Rose of Cairo* (1985), there is a close-up of some duration of Mia Farrow in spectatorial ecstasy, enraptured by the image, her face glowing (both figuratively and literally through its reflection of light from the movie screen). This rapture persists despite the rather tawdry surroundings of a lower-class movie theater. What the shot signifies, in part, is the peculiar susceptibility to the image—to the cinematic spectacle in general—attributed to the woman in our culture. Her pleasure in viewing is somehow more *intense*. The woman's spectatorship is yet another clearly delineated mark of her excess. This hyperbolically intimate relation with the screen is assumed by the plot of *Purple Rose*. In the course of Mia Farrow's fifth or sixth viewing of the film of the same name, she actually catches the gaze of the male romantic lead who notices her, turns, and, drawn by her fascination, steps down off the screen to join her in the "real world." He rapidly falls in love with her, fulfilling her spectatorial dreams. What strikes me about this scenario is that, given culturally (over)determined structures of seeing, this narrative could work most convincingly only by positing a female spectator. For there is a certain naiveté assigned to women in relation to systems of signification—a tendency to deny the processes of representation, to collapse the opposition between the sign (the image) and the real. To "misplace" desire by attaching it too securely to a representation. The figure of the woman repeatedly viewing the same film (despite the principle that Hollywood movies are made to be "consumed" once) or becoming an avid reader of fan magazines is the condition of possibility of narratives based on her purportedly excessive collusion with the cinematic imaginary.

It is also critically important that *Purple Rose* is a historical film, set in the 1930s, at the beginning of a period in which the Hollywood cinema perfected its language and reached the height of its power. In the midst of the depression, Mia Farrow is clearly a member of the lower class, watching a typical '30s glossy sophisticated comedy detailing the foibles of the upper classes. For her, at least a part of the scopophiliac power of the image is that it represents money and the style associated with it. She is encouraged to align her gaze with that of the consumer.

I have lingered on this film because it demonstrates the extent to which the image of the longing, overinvolved female spectator is still with us. While it may be argued that, as a historical film, *The Purple Rose* introduces a distance between its own spectator and its represented spectator, the image retains a great deal of its effect—certainly its recognizability and even familiarity. The idea that the cinematic image functions as a lure, so forcefully elaborated in contemporary film theory, seems to apply even more insistently in the case of the female spectator who, in the popular imagination, repeatedly "gives in" to its fascination. Proximity rather than distance, passivity, overinvolvement and overidentification (the use of the term "weepies" to indicate women's pictures is symptomatic here)—these are the tropes which enable the woman's assumption of the position of "subject" of the gaze. It is, of course, a peculiarly ironic assumption of subjectivity. For, although spectatorship is thus conceptualized in terms which appear to preeminently feminize it, feminist film criticism has consistently demonstrated that, in the classical Hollywood cinema, the woman is deprived of a gaze, deprived of subjectivity and repeatedly transformed into the object of a masculine scopophiliac desire.

Yet, women would seem to be perfect spectators, culturally positioned as they are outside the arena of history, politics, production—"looking on." The iconography is quite insistent: women and waiting are intimately linked, and the scenario of the woman gazing out of a window usually streaked by a persistent rain has become a well-worn figure of the classical cinematic text. And, indeed, the rise of the novel as the most popular vehicle for the formulation of narrative is usually linked explicitly with a female reading public.[1] The greater amount of leisure time associated with the woman authorized an analysis of the "feminization" of the process of reading. Yet, although the cinema is often theorized as the extension and elaboration of the narrative mechanisms of the nineteenth-century novel, its spectator is almost always conceptualized in the masculine mode. It is as though the historical threat of a potential feminization of the spectatorial position required an elaborate work of generic containment olation. In this respect, the very fact that there is a specific genre allocated to the female spectator—the "woman's film"—is revealing. As Pam Cook notes,

One question insists: why does the women's picture exist? There is no such thing as "the men's picture," specifically addressed to men; there is only "cinema," and "the women's picture," a sub-group or category specially for women, excluding men; a separate, private space designed for more than half the population, relegating them to the margins of cinema proper. The existence of the women's picture both recognises the importance of women, and marginalises them. By constructing this different space for women (Haskell's "wet, wasted afternoons") it performs a vital function in society's ordering of sexual difference. [2]

The cinema in general, outside of the genre of the woman's picture, constructs its spectator as the generic "he" of language. The masculine norm is purportedly asexual while sexually defined seeing is relegated to the woman. Access to the gaze is hence very carefully regulated through the specification of generic boundaries.

The woman's film is therefore in many ways a privileged site for the analysis of the given terms of female spectatorship and the inscription of subjectivity precisely because its address to a female viewer is particularly strongly marked. The label "woman's film" refers to a genre of Hollywood films produced from the silent era through the 1950s and early '60s but most heavily concentrated and most popular in the 1930s and '40s. [3] The films deal with a female protagonist and often appear to allow her significant access to point of view structures and the enunciative level of the filmic discourse. They treat problems defined as "female" (problems revolving around domestic life, the family, children, self-sacrifice, and the relationship between women and production vs. that between women and reproduction), and, most crucially, are directed toward a female audience.

There is something extremely compelling about women's films—with their constantly recurring figures of the unwed mother, the waiting wife, the abandoned mistress, the frightened newlywed or the anguished mother. And this is so even today, when their images are experienced more readily as a historical memory, no longer completely culturally negotiable since they are, in an era which believes itself to be post-feminist, so strongly marked as belonging to the recent past. As Roland Barthes notes, History is "the time when my mother was alive *before me*," and, for many of us, these are the films of our mothers' time. [4] And although their images inevitably infiltrate or perhaps contaminate our cultural memories, they are already a bit defamiliarized, somewhat strange. But not strange enough. For these mythemes of femininity trade on their very familiarity and recognizability. The scenarios of the woman's film somehow seem immediately accessible in their presentation of the "obvious truths" of femininity with which we are all overly acquainted.

It is crucial to remember, then, that the genre is the outcome of Hollywood's analysis of its own market, its own grouping of films along the lines of a sexual address. Filmic narratives and mise-en-scène are organized in the service of the production of female fantasy. Thus, we have the nomenclature by means of which certain films of the '30s and '40s are situated and sold as "women's pictures," a label which stipulates that the films are in some sense the "possession" of women and that their terms of address are dictated by the anticipated presence of the female spectator. Yet, it is the precise meaning of this notion of "possession" which must be isolated and interrogated. In what sense are these films "ours"? Or should they be, somewhat forcefully, reclaimed and reoccupied by a contemporary feminist analysis? There is an extremely strong temptation to find in these films a viable alternative to the unrelenting objectification and oppression of the figure of the woman in mainstream Hollywood cinema.[5] The recent focus on issues surrounding female spectatorship and the woman's film is determined by a desire to shift the terms of an analysis of fantasy and history in favor of the woman and away from a paternal reference point. Yet, the woman's film does not provide us with an access to a pure and authentic female subjectivity, much as we might like it to do so. It provides us instead with an image repertoire of poses—classical feminine poses and assumptions about the female appropriation of the gaze. Hollywood women's films of the 1940s document a crisis in subjectivity around the figure of the woman—although it is not always clear whose subjectivity is at stake.

I have chosen to focus on the films of the 1940s (a subset of the woman's film as a genre) for a number of reasons. In the first half of the decade, due to the war and the enlistment of large numbers of young men in the armed forces, film producers assumed that cinema audiences would be predominantly female. Despite the fact that statistical analyses of audiences during the 1940s suggest that this was not ultimately the case, the anticipation of a female audience resulted in a situation wherein female stars and films addressed to women became more central to the industry.[6] Therefore, not only generic but specifically historical considerations dictate that the terms of address and the inscription of female subjectivity become more crucial in this particular group of films. Furthermore, there is an intensity and an aberrant quality in the '40s films which is linked to the ideological upheaval signaled by a redefinition of sexual roles and the reorganization of the family during the war years. The very speed of moving women into and out of the work force (the "Rosie the Riveter" phenomenon) creates ideological imperatives which are quite explicit in the films. The intensity and interest of these films is also associated with a kind of generic intertextuality which seems to characterize the period. The woman's film is frequently combined with other genres—the film noir and the gothic or horror film, even the musical. This strategy tends to expand the boundaries of what is known as the "woman's film" (which is often thought of primarily in relation to its seemingly most exemplary subgroup, the maternal melodrama).

Nevertheless, although the isolation of films from the 1940s enables an examination of not only the sexually specific but the historically specific terms of spectatorship, my interest in the films is primarily inspired by certain issues and theoretical blockages in contemporary feminist work. The insistence of their address and the forcefulness of their tropes make the women's films of the 1940s an appropriate textual field for the investigation of issues surrounding the concepts of subjectivity and spectatorship and the ability or inability of feminist theorists to align these concepts with sexual specificity. Feminist film theory has convincingly demonstrated the extent to which the woman in the cinema is imaged as deficient or lacking in her "object-hood."[7] But it is becoming increasingly evident that the construction of her "subject-hood" poses difficulties as well. One can readily trace, in the women's films of the 1940s, recurrent suggestions of deficiency, inadequacy, and failure in the woman's appropriation of the gaze. It is the very concept of subjectivity and its place in feminist theory which is in question. The predicament is specified most succinctly in the question posed by Ann Kaplan, "Is the gaze male?"[8]

Much of this important work in feminist film theory delineates a scenario which would seem to indicate the very impossibility of a genre such as the woman's film. For the figure of the woman is aligned with spectacle, space, or the image, often in opposition to the linear flow of the plot. From this point of view, there is something about the representation of the woman which is resistant to narrative or narrativization. The problematic status of a genre which purports to produce women's "stories" thereby becomes apparent. In Laura Mulvey's now classic article, "Visual Pleasure and Narrative Cinema," the woman is the object of the fixation and obsession associated with male spectatorial desires — preeminently voyeurism and fetishism.[9] The transfixing or immobilizing aspects of the spectacle constituted by the woman work against the forward pull of the narrative. While all the resources of the cinematic apparatus—including framing, lighting, camera movement, and angle—are brought to bear in the alignment of the woman with the surface of the image, the male character is allowed to inhabit and actively control its illusory depths, its constructed three-dimensional space. Similarly, Linda Williams demonstrates how, in Muybridge's contributions to the prehistory of the cinema, the male figure seems more compatible with processes of narrativization than the female figure.[10] While the man comfortably adopts "natural" poses of activity and agency, the "plotting" of the female body is more difficult. Williams outlines the lengths to which Muybridge goes in constructing narrative situations for the woman which are marked by their very lack of familiarity. With respect to a narrativization of the woman, the apparatus strains; but the transformation of the woman into spectacle is easy. Through her forced affinity with the iconic, imagistic aspects of cinema, the woman is constituted as a resistance or impedance to narrativization.

This scenario is, perhaps, most forcefully elaborated in Teresa de Lauretis's analysis of the articulation of feminism, semiotics, and cinema. In the course of a discussion of Jurÿ Lotman's semiotics of plot construction, de Lauretis claims that his description is predicated

> on the *single* figure of the hero who crosses the boundary and penetrates the other space. In so doing the hero, the mythical subject, is constructed as human being and as male; he is the active principle of culture, the establisher of distinction, the creator of differences. Female is what is not susceptible to transformation, to life or death; she (it) is an element of plot-space, a topos, a resistance, matrix and matter. [11]

The male is the mover of narrative while the female's association with space or matter deprives her of subjectivity. This has particularly problematic consequences for the notion of female spectatorship. As de Lauretis goes on to explain, ". . . each reader—male or female—is constrained and defined within the two positions of a sexual difference thus conceived: male-hero-human, on the side of the subject; and female-obstacle-boundary-space, on the other." [12] Although de Lauretis is careful to point out that Lotman himself is unaware of the sexual politics informing his theory of narrative, she does not explicitly contest the relevance of its sexual divisions.

This delineation of the a-subjectivity of the represented woman goes some way toward explaining the convolutions and complexities of the attempt to theorize female spectatorship. A sometimes confusing array of concepts—transvestism, masochism, masquerade, double identification—is mobilized in the effort to think the relation between female spectator and screen. [13] Laura Mulvey, for instance, has recourse to the notion of an "uncomfortable" transvestism in her delineation of female spectatorship as an oscillation between a passive feminine position and a regressive but active masculine position that enables the female spectator's engagement with narrative mechanisms. Identification with an active protagonist or with the linear movement of narrative is specified as masculine: "The phantasy 'action' can only find expression, its only *signifier* for a woman is through the metaphor of masculinity." [14] De Lauretis attempts to move beyond Mulvey's formulation by specifying a way in which the woman's identification with narrative process can be conceptualized outside of masculine parameters (or at least by reducing these parameters as much as possible). She refers to this operation as "double identification" or "a surplus of pleasure":

> If women spectators are "related as subject" in the film's images and movement, as Heath puts it, it is insofar as they are engaged in a twofold process of identification sus-

taining two distinct sets of identifying relations. The first set is well known in film theory: the masculine, active, identification with the gaze (the looks of the camera and of the male characters) and the passive, feminine identification with the image (body, landscape). The second set, which has received much less attention, is implicit in the first as its effect and specification, for it is produced by the apparatus which is the very condition of vision (that is to say, the condition under which what is visible acquires meaning). It consists of the double identification with the figure of narrative movement, the mythical subject, and with the figure of narrative closure, the narrative image. Were it not for the possibility of this second, figural identification, the woman spectator would be stranded between two incommensurable entities, the gaze and the image. Identification, that is, would be either impossible, split beyond any act of suture, or entirely masculine. [15]

In other words, identifications associated with narrative as a process overlay those associated with the more cinematically specific concepts of the gaze and the image. This is consistent with de Lauretis's contention that it is the Oedipal logic of narrative which decisively inflects any reading of the image. Yet, several questions remain, indicating the extreme complexity of the issues at hand. De Lauretis substantially complicates the notion of female spectatorship by activating two different sets of terms and by making the figural identifications simultaneous (rather than alternating or oscillating as in Mulvey's description). And, somehow, the second set of terms, unlike the first (active-gaze/passive-image) becomes disengendered. Is the mythical subject no longer male? More importantly, I am struck by the sheer multiplicity and dispersal of subject positions activated in the description. While it is certainly true that spectatorship is a complex and multi-faceted process, why should it be the case that processes of identification and spectatorial engagement are more complicated (if not convoluted) for the female spectator than for the male? And why does it seem essential that a masculine position appear somewhere in the delineation of female spectatorship (in Mulvey's, de Lauretis's, and, for that matter, my own formulations)?

My contention is that this apparent blockage at the level of theory (the seemingly insurmountable difficulties in conceptualizing the female gaze) does not simply indicate a disagreement among various feminist critics but a series of contradictions which are active at the level of the social/psychological construction of female spectatorship. Perhaps the female spectator—or, more accurately, the projected image of the female spectator—*is* that of a being stranded between incommensurable entities. Elsewhere in her analysis, de Lauretis refers to the association of the feminine with a masochist position defined as "the (impossible) place of a purely *passive* desire."[16] This formulation would seem to designate more accurately the appeal made to the female spectator by genres which are specifically *addressed* to her.

From this point of view it is important to specify precisely what is meant by the "female spectator" or "female spectatorship." Clearly, these terms are not meant to refer directly to the woman who buys her ticket and enters the movie theater as the member of an audience, sharing a social identity but retaining a unique psychical history. Frequently, they do not even refer to the spectator as a social subject but, rather, as a psychical subject, as the effect of signifying structures. Historically, the emphasis on issues of spectatorship in film theory derives from a psychoanalytically informed linguistics, not from a sociologically based analysis. It has been the task of feminist theory to point out that this spectator has been consistently posited and delineated as masculine. Feminist theory therefore necessarily introduces the question of the social subject, but unfortunately, it frequently and overhastily collapses the opposition between social and psychical subjects, closing the gap prematurely. There has never been, to my mind, an adequate articulation of the two subjects in theory (which is another way of saying that psychoanalysis and a Marxist analysis have never successfully collaborated in the theorization of subjectivity).

There seems to be general agreement, however, that the terms *femininity* and *masculinity*, *female spectatorship* and *male spectatorship*, do not refer to actual members of cinema audiences or do so only in a highly mediated fashion. Women spectators oscillate or alternate between masculine and feminine positions (as de Lauretis points out, identification is a process not a state), and men are capable of this alternation as well. This is simply to emphasize once again that feminine and masculine positions are not fully coincident with actual men and women. Nevertheless, men and women enter the movie theater as social subjects who have been compelled to align themselves in some way with respect to one of the reigning binary oppositions (that of sexual difference) which order the social field. Men will be more likely to occupy the positions delineated as masculine, women those specified as feminine. What is interesting, from this point of view, is that masculinity is consistently theorized as a pure, unified, and self-sufficient position. The male spectator, assuming the psychical positions of the voyeur and the fetishist, can easily and comfortably identify with his like on the screen. But theories of female spectatorship constantly have recourse, at some level, to notions of bisexuality—Mulvey's transvestism or de Lauretis's double identification. It is as though masculinity were required to effectively conceptualize access to activity or agency (whether illusory or not).

What I am interested in in this study are the ramifications of this idea, in the exploration of the specifically feminine aspects of spectatorship, acknowledging all the while that this notion of female spectatorship may be specified only by its lapses or failures, in what de Lauretis refers to as the impossible place of a "non-subject effect."[17] I hope to analyze what is, above all, a certain *representation* of female spectatorship, produced as both image and position as an effect of certain discourses specified as "belonging" to the woman. De Lauretis is careful to differentiate between her own analysis of female spectatorship and the "prevailing notion of woman's narcissistic overidentification with the image."[18] The idea of feminine overidentification "prevails" nowhere if not in the popular imagination, in the signifying structures which ground genres labeled "weepies" and "tearjerkers" and which enable the image of Mia Farrow submitting to the lure of the screen. The tropes of female spectatorship are not empowering. But we need to understand the terms of their psychical appeal more fully before we can produce an effective alternative cinema.

The female spectator (the spectator singled out and defined entirely by her sex) exists nowhere but as an effect of discourse, the focal point of an address. Sexual differentiation in spectatorship is not something to be sought after and applauded as an end in itself. In the same way, one would not necessarily embrace and applaud the conceptualization of the male spectator as voyeur or fetishist. One would hope, instead, that spectatorship could one day be theorized outside the pincers of sexual difference as a binary opposition. On the other hand, the shift in focus from the male spectator to the female spectator in contemporary film theory is a political gesture of some significance in itself. The blockage is similar to one experienced by literary theorists concerned to include women in the traditional canon. After Barthes and Foucault have proclaimed the death of the author,[19] is it feasible or desirable to isolate, identify, and honor women authors? As literary theorists ask—is it possible for the woman to relinquish the idea of the author before she has had a chance to become one?[20] In an era which is post-author, post-Cartesian subject, in which the ego is seen above all as illusory in its mastery, what is the status of a search for feminine identity?

It is for these very reasons, I believe, that we must continue to investigate the representation of female subjectivity or its failure in a variety of discourses—film, psychoanalysis, literature, law. The aim of this study is to outline the terms in which a female spectator is conceptualized—that is, the terms in which she is simultaneously projected and assumed as an image (the focal point of an address) by the genre of the woman's film. And that image is a troubled one. Here, the representations of the cinema and the representations provided by psychoanalysis of female subjectivity coincide. For each system specifies that the woman's relation to desire is difficult if not impossible. Paradoxically, her only access is to the desire to desire.

The notions of the "subject" and "subjectivity" which I have been referring to are categories of a linguistically based psychoanalysis. The subject is not synonymous with the "self," still less is it compatible with any notion of agency. The crucial role of the "I" in language has been systematically delineated by Émile Benveniste, who holds that " 'subjectivity,' whether it is placed in phenomenology or in psychology, as one may wish, is only the emergence in the being of a fundamental property of language. 'Ego' is he who *says* 'ego.' "[21] The sense of uniqueness, identity, and unity which we tend to associate with subjectivity are the effects of the ability to say "I" and to thereby appropriate language as one's own. But the dependence is reciprocal. Language is only possible because it is infused with subjectivity. The personal pronouns "I" and "you" enable the "conversion of language into discourse," in other words, the situation or instance of speech whereby language is actualized and becomes an event. The peculiarity of the cinema as a signifying system composed of heterogeneous materials (image, dialogue, music, etc.), is that it cannot produce a coherent "I." An "I" may occur in the dialogue but it is not the "I" of the film, properly speaking. Subjectivity is inscribed in the cinema in various ways—through voice-over, point of view structures, etc.—but it is always localized. This condition of the medium has led theorists such as Christian Metz to align the cinema with Benveniste's concept of history (a form of statement which conceals the source of its enunciation) rather than his concept of discourse (a statement which exhibits or foregrounds its "I"). [22] Subjectivity in the cinema (the inscription of the "I") is hence displaced from the producer of the discourse to its receiver. In film, there is a curious operation by means of which the "I" and the "you" of discourse are collapsed in the figure of the spectator.

Analyses of language which have stressed the role of subjectivity as its privileged ground and effect have also strongly asserted that the major mechanism of language is difference. Following the Saussurean dictum that language is composed of differences rather than positive terms, these analyses emphasize the extent to which loss or lack (of the referent) is the condition of possibility of linguistic systems. And since a linguistically based psychoanalysis, Lacanian psychoanalysis, makes the phallus the master representative of the lack which structures language, sexual difference is mapped onto linguistic difference—and this is not to the advantage of the woman. The woman, whose access to that signifier is problematic, finds herself in a kind of signifying limbo. [23] For the logical consequence of the Lacanian alignment of the phallus with the symbolic order and the field of language is the exclusion of the woman or, at the very least, the assumption of her different or deficient relation to language and its assurance of subjectivity. The French feminists who are repeatedly accused of situating the woman in an impossible place, outside language, are simply elaborating on the implications of such a theory. [24]

Subjectivity can, therefore, only be attributed to the woman with some difficulty. Luce Irigaray goes even further when she claims that "any theory of the subject has always been appropriated by the 'masculine.' " She specifies the a-subjectivity of the woman as an inability to maintain the gap between subject and object by posing the somewhat sarcastic question: "A 'subject' that would re-search itself as lost (maternal-feminine) 'object'?" [25] Because the feminine is the ground, the foundation of phallocentric philosophical systems, the woman must be described as "the non-subjective sub-jectum."[26]

But it is still necessary to ask what this linguistic/psychical subjectivity (which the woman is denied) amounts to beyond the ability, first and foremost, to say "I." The subject of a psychoanalytic semiotics is not endowed with the attributes of agency, identity, and coherency usually associated with, for instance, the Cartesian "I." Indeed, any notion of mastery is greatly reduced, and, as Kaja Silverman extensively demonstrates, the subject is more accurately understood as "subject to" rather than "subject of": the subject "has no meaning of its 'own,' and is entirely subordinated to the field of social meaning and desire."[27] Similarly, Jacqueline Rose problematizes the concept of subjectivity by defining it as the constant failure of identity: ". . . the division and precariousness of human subjectivity itself . . . was, for Lacan, central to psychoanalysis' most radical insights."[28] Subjectivity is characterized by the division and splitting effected by the operations of that "other scene," the unconscious. In short, the subject is no authority on its own activities. From this point of view one might be led to believe that it is, in fact, disadvantageous to be a subject.

However, this description is somewhat misleading. The attributes of agency, identity, and coherence are not absent from the definition of subjectivity but, instead, constantly referred to as fictions or illusions. The "ego" is the term which most precisely specifies the psychical locus of this illusion of mastery, and the mistake of ego psychology is its misrecognition of the unity of the ego as a reality. The function of the ego is to foster such a belief. Jean Laplanche speaks of the ego as "indeed an object, but a kind of relay object, capable of passing itself off, in a more or less deceptive and usurpatory manner, as a desiring and wishing subject."[29] It is this *illusion* of a coherent and controlling identity which becomes most important at the level of social subjectivity. And the woman does not even possess the same access to the *fiction* as the man.

Furthermore, subjectivity in its psychoanalytic formulation is always a desiring subjectivity. Desire is a form of disengagement—from need, from the referent, from the object—which is crucial to the assumption of the position of speaking subject. As Julia Kristeva points out, ". . . by overestimating the subject's having been the slave of language since before his birth, one avoids noting the two moods, active and passive, according to which the subject is constituted in the signifier. . . ."[30] It is with the Oedipal complex, the intervention of a third term (the father) in the mother-child relation and the resulting series of displacements which reformulate the relation to the mother as a desire for a perpetually lost object, that the subject accedes to the active use of the signifier. Distance from the "origin" (the maternal) is the prerequisite to desire; and insofar as desire is defined as the excess of demand over a need aligned with the maternal figure, the woman is left behind. Voyeurism, according to Christian Metz, is a perfect type of desire insofar as it presupposes and activates as its fundamental condition a spatial distance between subject and object.[31] The necessity of such a disengagement is explicitly delineated by Lacan when he distinguishes between the human and animal relations to the fascination of the lure: "Only the subject—the human subject, the subject of the desire that is the essence of man—is not, unlike the animal, entirely caught up in this imaginary capture. He maps himself in it. How? In so far as he isolates the function of the screen and plays with it."[32] The terms "man" and "he" in this description of the desiring subject should be taken literally as denoting a specifically masculine subject, while the woman is situated within the realm of the animal. Desire may be insatiable, it may entail the constantly renewed pursuit for a perpetually lost object, but at least the male has desire.

The woman's relation to desire, on the other hand, is at best a mediated one. Lacan defines the hysteric's desire as "the desire for an unsatisfied desire."[33] In a discussion of the "framework of perversions in the woman," Lacan attempts to delineate her different relation to desire and ultimately specifies it as the "envy of desire": "Far from its being the case that the passivity of the act corresponds to this desire, feminine sexuality appears as the effort of a *jouissance* wrapped in its own contiguity (for which all circumcision might represent the symbolic rupture) to be *realised in the envy* of desire, which castration releases in the male by giving him its signifier in the phallus."[34] The image of the woman "wrapped" in contiguity, deprived of the phallus as signifier of desire, has been taken up by French theorists such as Irigaray, Cixous, Montrelay, and Kofman in a sometimes hyperbolic celebration of the only picture of feminine "subjectivity" available from psychoanalysis. These theorists activate the tropes of proximity, overpresence or excessive closeness to the body, and contiguity in the construction of a kind of "ghetto politics" which maintains and applauds woman's exclusion from language and the symbolic order. In Montrelay's analysis, what the woman lacks is lack, the ability to represent for herself a distance from the body which is the prerequisite for desire. The description by these theorists of a body wrapped up in itself, too close, is effectively political only in its hyperbole or excess, for what they delineate is not a desirable place. In fact, it is a nonplace.

Nevertheless, it is the position allotted to the female "subject" both by psychoanalytic scenarios and by the cinema. A distance from the image is less negotiable for the female spectator than for the male because the woman is so forcefully linked with the iconic and spectacle or, in Mulvey's terms, "to-be-looked-at-ness." Voyeurism, the desire most fully exploited by the classical cinema, is the property of the masculine spectator. Fetishism—the ability to balance knowledge and belief and hence to maintain a distance from the lure of the image—is also inaccessible to the woman, who has no need of the fetish as a defense against a castration which has always already taken place. Female spectatorship, because it is conceived of temporally as immediacy (in the reading of the image—the result of the very absence of fetishism) and spatially as proximity (the distance between subject and object, spectator and image is collapsed), can only be understood as the confounding of desire. Similarly, the increasing appeal in the twentieth century to the woman's role as perfect consumer (of commodities as well as images) is indissociable from her positioning *as* a commodity and results in the blurring of the subject/object dichotomy (the relation between the woman, consumerism, and the commodity form will be discussed more fully later in this chapter). Situating the woman in relation to a desiring subjectivity seems to effect a perversion of the very notion of agency. Insofar as the woman is constructed culturally as the perfect spectator—outside the realm of events and actions—it is important to note that spectating is not the same as seeing. And consuming is certainly not synonymous with controlling the means of production.

The woman's film, in its insistent address to the female spectator-consumer, confronts all the difficulties and blockages outlined so far in the attempt to conceptualize female subjectivity: the woman's positioning as the very resistance to narrative, her problematic relation to language and the signifier *par excellence* (the phallus) of its major mechanism (difference), and her purportedly deficient and highly mediated access to desire. The woman's film is in many respects formally no different from other instances of the classical Hollywood cinema; its narrative structure and conventions reiterate many of the factors which have contributed to a theorization of the cinema spectator largely in terms of masculine psychical mechanisms. Nevertheless, because the woman's film insistently and sometimes obsessively attempts to trace the contours of female subjectivity and desire within the traditional forms and conventions of Hollywood narrative—forms which cannot sustain such an exploration—certain contradictions within patriarchal ideology become more apparent. This makes the films particularly valuable for a feminist analysis of the way in which the "woman's story" is told. The formal resistances to the elaboration of female subjectivity produce perturbations and contradictions within the narrative economy. The analyses in this study emphasize the symptoms of ideological stress which accompany the concerted effort to engage female subjectivity within conventional narrative forms. These stress points and perturbations can then, hopefully, be activated as a kind of lever to facilitate the production of a desiring subjectivity for the woman—in another cinematic practice.

## Freudian Scenarios and "Ours"

Spectatorship in the cinema has been theorized through recourse to the "scenario" as a particularly vivid representation of the organization of psychical processes. The scenario—with its visual, auditory, and narrative dimensions—seems particularly appropriate in the context of film theory. Given the diversified and multifaceted history of psychoanalysis, Freudian and Lacanian texts appear to be privileged at least partially for their ability to generate convincing scenarios which act as condensations of several larger psychical structures or as evocations of a particularly crucial psychical "turning point" or movement: the primal scene, the mirror stage, the "look" at the mother's (castrated) body, the *fort/da* game, etc.[35] Needless to say, many of these scenarios are chosen because they activate a specifically *visual* register. The major scenarios, those which underpin arguments about voyeurism, fetishism, and the general conditions of spectatorship required by the cinema as an institution—in short, the theory of the cinematic apparatus—are organized and defined in relation to a masculine subjectivity. Despite the fact that the primal scene, in its broad outlines, has no inherent or necessary sexual differentiation in its specification of infantile experience, the small voyeur is generally conceptualized as male. In the classical cinema, seeing is eroticized, and the privileged object of the scopophiliac drive is the female body. Even the curious gaze, which might seem to be inflected differently than the erotic gaze, is linked to a specific curiosity about the female body or to childhood theories of sexuality via Freudian formulations.

Similarly, while Freud's account of the *fort/da* game[36] might initially present itself as sexually undifferentiated—in other words, it doesn't appear to matter whether the protagonist is a little boy or a little girl—it is, in effect, a crucially sexualized scenario. For the game of throwing and retrieving a cotton reel which the little boy plays is interpreted by Freud as a means of controlling and mastering the absence of the *mother*. The implications are clearly greatest for masculine subjectivity. Yet, this psychical trajectory has been influential in the conceptualization of repetition within the classical Hollywood cinema—the repetition associated with genre as well as that of narrative structure and editing patterns.[37] Even repetition compulsion, seemingly a purely formal psychical mechanism, is closely aligned with a highly gender-specific scenario.

The Freudian scenario appropriated by film theory which most explicitly depends on sexual differentiation is that involving fetishism. The traumatic moment of the look at the mother's "castrated" body initiates a process of simultaneous affirmation and denial of the possibility of the subject's own castration, and hence the manufacture of a substitute maternal phallus in the form of the fetish. Fetishism has been particularly important in the theorization of the film-spectator relation because its scenario turns on the "glance" and on a reading of the image of the castrated woman. In the cinema, spectatorial fetishism is evidenced as a process of balancing knowledge and belief in relation to the reality status of the image. While the spectator knows that the image is merely an image and not the real (similarly, the fetishist knows that the fetish object is simply a substitute for the woman's lack), he simultaneously believes in the impression of reality produced by that image in order to follow the story (the fetishist believes in the substitute maternal phallus in order to attain sexual pleasure). [38] Because it is so intimately articulated with castration anxiety and the desire to preserve the phallus, because it relies on the image of the mutilated female body, fetishism is not available to the woman—for she has nothing to lose. Furthermore, since fetishism is a form of distancing from any immediate implications of perception (the woman's "nothing-to-see"), the assumption that the woman's gaze is nonfetishistic rationalizes the proximity, empathy, and overidentification associated with genres addressed to the female spectator.

Christian Metz's analysis of primary cinematic identification has been the most significant and influential activation of Lacan's description of the mirror phase in film theory. In Metz's analysis, the film spectator achieves a sense of unity, mastery, and control—which is analogous to that of the child in front of the mirror—by identifying with his own look and, consequently with the camera (ultimately identifying himself as a "pure act of perception"). [39] Coherence of vision insures a controlling knowledge which, in its turn, is a guarantee of the untroubled centrality and unity of the subject. This confirmation of the subject's mastery over the signifier, this guarantee of a unified and coherent ego capable of controlling the effects cf the unconscious, is, essentially, a guarantee of the subject's identity. Similarly, the mirror allows the child to conceptualize the body as a limited form and hence insures an identity.

The psychical process of identification would, once again, appear to be sexually indifferent. But the use of terms such as "all-perceiving," "all-powerful," "transcendental subject," and "ego" in the descriptions of primary cinematic identification already indicate a difficulty in this respect. [40] For the female subject quite simply does not have the same access as the male to the identity described in this manner. In the theory of Luce Irigaray, for example, the woman is relegated to the side of negativity, making her relation to the processes of representation and self-representation more problematic. Because she is situated as lack, nonmale, non-one; because her sexuality has only been conceptualized within masculine parameters (the clitoris understood as the "little penis"), she has no separate unity which could ground an identity. In other words, she has no autonomous symbolic representation. [41] But most importantly, and related to this failure with respect to identification, she cannot share the relationship of the man to the mirror. The male alone has access to the privileged specular process of the mirror's identification. And it is the confirmation of the self offered by the plane-mirror which, according to Irigaray, is "most adequate for the mastery of the image, of representation, and of self-representation." [42] The term "identification" can only provisionally describe the woman's object relations—for the case of the woman "cannot concern either identity or non-identity."[43]

Hence, the scenarios which ground the theory of the cinematic apparatus are all aligned in some way with the delineation of a masculine subjectivity. This is particularly true of those scenarios which narrativize the psychical mechanisms most dependent on the gaze—voyeurism and fetishism. However, there are, within Freudian theory, a number of scenarios which purport to describe the vicissitudes of female subjectivity—scenarios focusing on masochism ("A Child is Being Beaten"), paranoia ("A Case of Paranoia Running Counter to the Psychoanalytic Theory of the Disease"), and hysteria (scenarios of the disfigured or symptomatic body). They are inevitably subsidiary or supplementary to the major scenarios of masculinity and frequently center on a pathological condition (compare Freud on fetishism: "The significance of fetishes is not known to the world at large and therefore not prohibited; they are easily obtainable and sexual gratification by their means is thus very convenient.").[44] These scenarios of female subjectivity have generally *not* been instrumental in delineating the cinematic apparatus. Nevertheless, they are fully compatible with the scenarios of the woman's film as a genre, particularly when they concern themselves with masochism. For in films addressed to women, spectatorial pleasure is often indissociable from pain.

As noted above, identification on the part of the female reader or spectator cannot be, as it is for the male, a mechanism by means of which mastery is assured. On the contrary, if identification is even "provisionally" linked with the woman (as it is for Irigaray), it can only be seen as reinforcing her submission. From this perspective, it is not accidental that the Freudian scenarios describing identification with respect to the woman frequently hinge on the specific example of pain, suffering, aggression turned round against the self—in short, masochism. In *The Interpretation of Dreams*, it is the hysterical symptom which acts as the point of articulation for identification. Apropos of the discussion of a dream in which a woman identifies her friend with herself and then proceeds to dream of an unfulfilled wish, Freud claims that "identification is a highly important factor in the mechanism of hysterical symptoms. It enables patients to express in their symptoms not only their own experiences but those of a large number of other people; it enables them, as it were, to suffer on behalf of a whole crowd of people and to act all the parts in a play single-handed."[45] In his subsequent reference to the contagion of a hysterical spasm by all the members of a hospital ward, it becomes even clearer that, for Freud, the sign written on the body of the female hysteric is a pivot for the exchange of masochistic identifications.

While this is a relatively early account of identification, aligned with the first topography of psychoanalysis and preceding the description of the ego as a veritable sedimentation or history of object choices, later attempts to rethink identification in the context of the second topography and the intersubjective economy of the Oedipal complex retain this link between the woman and masochism. The chapter entitled "Identification" in *Group Psychology and the Analysis of the Ego* begins with a delineation of the little boy's identification with his father as an ideal—a "typically masculine" process—and its relation to the Oedipal complex. The little girl's case is resistant to a metapsychological definition, and it is as though Freud's text can only traverse and retraverse a number of scenarios. The first involves the identification of a little girl with her mother—articulated by the fact that the little girl assumes the neurotic symptom exhibited by the mother, a painful cough. The symptom, according to Freud, expresses the little girl's guilty desire to usurp her mother's place with respect to the father. And the imaginary dialogue Freud attributes to the symptom underlines its masochistic effects: "You wanted to be your mother, and now you *are*—anyhow so far as your sufferings are concerned."[46] Freud's second scenario dramatizing the relation between the little girl and identification is a simple rewriting of the scene described earlier in *The Interpretation of Dreams*— the scenario merely undergoes a change in location—from a hospital ward to a girls' boarding school. While in the case of the boy, the superego is the relay of identification, in the girl's situation, it is the symptom which becomes the "mark of a point of coincidence between two egos which has to be kept repressed."[47]

Addressing itself to a female audience, the woman's film raises the crucial question, "How can the notion of female fantasy be compatible with that of persecution, illness, and death?" In what way do these texts engage their spectator? Freud's explanation of paranoia and masochism relates them both to the assumption by the subject—whether male or female—of a feminine position. In Dr. Schreber's paranoid delusions, his body is transformed, painfully, into the body of a woman. The masochism which Freud assigns to the classical sexual pervert (usually male) is labeled "feminine" precisely because the fantasies associated with this type of masochism situate the subject in positions "characteristic of womanhood, i.e. they mean that he is being castrated, is playing the passive part in coitus, or is giving birth."[48] The economic problem of masochism, for Freud, lies in the apparent paradox of pleasure-in-pain. But this paradox is not unique to "feminine" masochism in Freud's typology, for there is a sense in which masochism is primary for the subject, and ultimately, for Freud, a manifestation of the fundamental and inexorable death drive.

Nevertheless, when confronted with concrete clinical cases where masochism is embodied in a particularly insistent fantasy—"A Child is Being Beaten"—Freud is forced to make crucial distinctions along the lines of sexual difference. For it does, indeed, matter whether the subject of the fantasy is male or female. And it is not accidental that a certain ease of interpretation characterizes the psychoanalysis of the female masochistic fantasy. The article focuses on the female manifestation of the fantasy which takes the form of a three-part transformation of a basic sentence: (1) My father is beating the child whom I hate; (2) I am being beaten (loved) by my father; (3) A child is being beaten. In the construction of the male fantasy, Freud can isolate only two sentences: (1) I am being beaten (loved) by my father; (2) I am being beaten by my mother. Although both the female and the male instanciations stem from the same origin, an incestuous attachment to the father, their psychical meaning-effects are necessarily quite different. The woman's masochism can be located unproblematically within the terms of the "normal" female Oedipal configuration, while the attribution of masochism to the man depends on the possibility of an "inverted" Oedipal attitude in which the father is taken as the object of desire. The man can, however, avoid the homosexual implications by remodeling his fantasy so that the mother takes the place of the father as the agent of the beating.

For my purposes here, there are two aspects of this sexual differentiation of the masochistic fantasy which assume paramount importance: the relationship established between fantasy and sexuality and the presence or absence of spectatorship as a possible role in the scenario. On the first point, Freud is quite explicit. In the case of the male, the erotic implications of the fantasy are acknowledged no matter what the vicissitudes of its transformation—sexuality remains on the surface. Furthermore, he retains his own role and his own gratification in the context of the scenario. The "I" of identity remains. On the other hand, the feminine masochistic fantasy, in the course of its vicissitudes, is desexualized—by means of the fantasy, "the girl escapes from the demands of the erotic side of her life altogether."[49] The fantasy, whose primary function in Freud's description is the facilitation of masturbation, becomes an end in itself. The women are prone to construct an "artistic super-structure of daydreams," fantasies which in some instances approach the level of a "great work of art" and eliminate entirely the need for masturbation. It is the fantasmatic gone awry, dissociated completely from the body as site of the erotic. But most crucially, the third sentence—"A child is being beaten"—which is significantly absent in male masochism, necessitates the woman's assumption of the position of spectator, outside the event. The "I" of the fantasy is no longer operative within its diegesis and, instead, the child who is being beaten is transformed into an anonymous boy or even a group of boys who act as the representative of the female in the scenario.[50] Confronted with Freud's insistent question, "Where are *you* in this fantasy?," the female patients can only reply, "I am probably looking on."[51] Or, in Freud's eloquent summation of the sexual differentiation of the masochistic fantasy, "the girl escapes from the demands of the erotic side of her life altogether. She turns herself in fantasy into a man, without herself becoming active in a masculine way, and is no longer anything but a spectator of the event which takes the place of a sexual act."[52] Thus, simultaneous with her assumption of the position of spectator, the woman loses not only her sexual identity in the context of the scenario but her very access to sexuality.

Masochistic fantasy *instead* of sexuality. The phrase would seem to exactly describe the processes in the woman's film whereby the look is de-eroticized. In the paranoid subgroup (analyzed in chapter five), the space which the woman is culturally assigned, the home, through its fragmentation into places that are seen and unseen, becomes the site of terror and victimization—the look turned violently against itself. In the films which mobilize a medical discourse (chapter two), where blindness and muteness are habitually attributed to the woman, she can only passively give witness as the signs of her own body are transformed by the purportedly desexualized medical gaze, the "speaking eye," into elements of discourse. The dominance of the bed in the mise-en-scène of these films is the explicit mark of the displacement/replacement of sexuality by illness.

There is a sense then, in which these films attempt to reverse the relation between the female body and sexuality which is established and reestablished by the classical cinema's localization of the woman as spectacle. As spectacle, the female body is sexuality; the erotic and the specular are welded. By deeroticizing the gaze, these films in effect disembody their spectator—the cinema, a mirror of control to the man, reflects nothing for the woman—or rather, it denies the imaginary identification which, uniting body and identity, supports discursive mastery. Confronted with the classical Hollywood text with a male address, the female spectator has basically two modes of entry: a narcissistic identification with the female figure as spectacle and a "transvestite" identification with the active male hero in his mastery. This female spectator is thus imaged by its text as having a mixed sexual body—she is, ultimately, a hermaphrodite. It is precisely this oscillation which demonstrates the instability of the woman's position as spectator. Because the woman's film purportedly directs itself to a female audience, because it pretends to offer the female spectator an identity other than that of the active male hero, it deflects energy away from the second "transvestite" option described above and toward the more "properly" female identification. But since the woman's film reduces the specularizable nature of the female body, this first option of a narcissistic identification is problematized as well. In a patriarchal society, to desexualize the female body is ultimately to deny its very existence. The woman's film thus functions in a rather complex way to deny the woman the space of a reading.

All this is certainly not to say that the woman's film is in any way radical or revolutionary. It functions quite precisely to immobilize — its obsession with the repetition of scenarios of masochism is a symptom of the ideological crisis provoked by the need to shift the sexual terms of address of a cinema which, as Laura Mulvey has shown, is so heavily dependent on masculine structures of seeing. The very lack of epistemological validity ascribed to these films—manifested in the derogatory label, the "weepies"—is an active recuperation of the contradictions which necessarily arise in attributing the epistemological gaze to the woman. For, a bodyless woman cannot see.

Hence, when one explores the margins of the major masculine scenarios informing theories of the cinematic apparatus, one discovers a series of scenarios which construct the image of a specifically feminine subjectivity and spectatorial position as well. But in both cases there are still a number of unanswered questions about the methodological implications of the use of the scenario. What, precisely, is the epistemological status of the scenario? Why are psychical trajectories represented so frequently by Freud and Lacan in narrative form? What do these narratives have in common with those of the cinema? In the analysis of the cinematic apparatus, theorists such as Metz and Baudry often appeal to these scenarios as if they were sexually indifferent, as if they described the universal and hence ahistorical condition of the human psyche. While psychical structures do have a certain autonomy in relation to social structures, the scenarios of psychoanalysis are socially and historically specific. Psychoanalytic scenarios of a masochistic femininity and the woman's film's positing of female subjectivity are not only comparable in many ways, but contiguous, that is, definable at the same level as symptoms.

This is because psychoanalysis in its delineation of sexual difference is a historical phenomenon, and, as Stephen Heath has shown, it is complicit with the novelistic and with those conceptions of the individual and of family romance associated with it.

> The 'emotional democratic period' [the period of *Madame Bovary* according to D. H. Lawrence] is that too of psychoanalysis, implicated in the same stories, the same terms of the individual. Hence the simultaneously explicit and complicit nature of psychoanalysis: Freud analyses, brings to light the specific terms of the construction of the individual and at the same time casts those terms he finds as individual and so as universal, not historical, not—in the end—specific at all. Which is then the complicity: psychoanalysis as repetition of the novel, the novelistic, and as supreme order, coping with the disorders, the pressures, the symptoms, the hysteria, all the fog in the head, making up the individual again and again, a universalizing regulation of the man and the woman in their conventional but precarious place.[53]

Freud himself remarked that "it still strikes me myself as strange that the case histories I write should read like short stories."[54] The coincidence of the birth of psychoanalysis and that of the cinema at the end of the nineteenth century has also been frequently noted by film theorists. The "stories" psychoanalysis tells, its fictions of subjectivity, are fully compatible with those proffered by the cinema. In that case, we might privilege Freudian psychoanalysis because it makes the cultural construction of femininity more legible—not because it dictates a "truth" of femininity. Reading Freud is often as strangely compelling as watching a woman's film—both entail the simultaneously pleasurable and unpleasurable effect of recognition/misrecognition of one's own cultural positioning.

Psychoanalysis is hence frequently called upon in this study of the desiring mechanisms of the woman's film. But psychoanalysis is not used in the traditional sense in which one might activate it as a pure or neutral metalanguage or methodology, a usage whereby psychoanalysis is posited as a superior, intelligent discourse of which film is only an illustration. Rather, my purpose is to trace a coincidence of cinematic scenarios and psychoanalytic scenarios of female subjectivity. The alliance between feminist theory and psychoanalysis has always been a somewhat uncomfortable one. On the one hand, psychoanalysis, due to its elaborate conceptualization of the unconscious and of femininity and masculinity as psychical rather than biological categories, is perceived by many feminist theorists (e.g., Juliet Mitchell, Jacqueline Rose)[55] as offering the most forceful analysis of the cultural construction of subjectivity and sexual difference. Insofar as it focuses on address, spectatorship, and the inscription of female subjectivity, this study also privileges a psychoanalytic critical language. On the other hand, it is also clear—and this has often been pointed out by feminist theorists—that femininity, when it is infrequently and marginally discussed within psychoanalysis, is analyzed in relation to a norm of masculine subjectivity and is inevitably found lacking or deficient. The structuring absences of psychoanalysis are therefore themselves open to critical analysis. In this sense, I do treat the scenarios of psychoanalysis as models. But they are models only insofar as they are symptomatic of a more generalizable cultural repression of the feminine. From this perspective, the cinema and psychoanalysis are the sources of entirely compatible scenarios which purport to outline the development (or nondevelopment, or deficiencies) of female subjectivity. This does not exonerate psychoanalysis.

The analysis of the relation between subjectivity and sociality has always been a difficult one, but it is a question which must constantly and insistently be broached. If it is not, we risk the assumption of a completely autonomous register of the psychical which would be just as disastrous for feminism as the notion that there is an ahistorical biological determination of sexual difference. However, the precise nature of the relation between psychical subjectivity and the social is elusive. It would seem that particular social orders are correlated with specific organizations of subjectivity and that these produce certain advantages for the speaking subject, but specifying the status of this correlation is much more difficult. In the words of Julia Kristeva,

> One might advance the hypothesis that a (social) symbolic system *corresponds* to a specific structuration of the speaking subject in the *symbolic order*. To say that it "corre-

sponds" leaves out questions of cause and effect; is the social determined by the subjective, or is it the other way around? The subjective-symbolic dimension that I am introducing does not therefore reinstate some deep or primary causality in the social *symbolic system*. It merely presents the *effects* and especially the *benefits* that accrue to the speaking subject from a precise symbolic organization; perhaps it explains what desiring motives are required in order to maintain a given social symbolics. Furthermore, it seems to me that such a statement of the problem has the advantage of not turning the 'symbolic system' into a secular replica of the 'preestablished harmony' or the 'divine order'; rather, it roots it as a *possible variant* within the only concrete universality that defines the speaking being—the signifying process. [56]

The study of discourses addressed specifically to women can contribute to the determination of what "desiring motives" are instilled in women themselves in order to "maintain a given social symbolics." The question, What do women want?, which Freud despaired of answering, is not an idle question, nor is it Freud's alone. For it has crucial implications for the organization of the social field. The rise of the classical cinema is also coincident with the emergence and rapid growth of a consumer culture and its corresponding economics of desire. The following section is an attempt to outline in broad terms the ways in which the spectatorial gaze and the consumer gaze are articulated in the cultural construction of female subjectivity. It points toward the articulation of social and psychical, which must be our ultimate concern.

### The Economy of Desire: The Commodity Form in/of the Cinema

Much of feminist theory tends to envisage the woman's relation to the commodity in terms of "being" rather than "having": she is the object of exchange rather than its subject. What is invoked here is the asubjectivity of the commodity. The woman's objectification, her susceptibility to processes of fetishization, display, profit and loss, the production of surplus value, all situate her in a relation of resemblance to the commodity form. As Fredric Jameson points out, "by its transformation into a commodity a thing, of whatever type, has been reduced to a means for its own consumption. It no longer has any qualitative value in itself, but only insofar as it can be 'used'. . . ."[57] But the status of the woman as commodity in feminist theory is not merely the result of a striking metaphor or parallel. Its elaboration is a response to Lévi-Strauss's description of the exchange of women as nothing less than the foundation of human society, of culture—the guarantee of an exogamy without which the family, and society along with it, would suffer an incestuous collapse.

The notion of the woman as the Ur-object of exchange has been taken up by theorists such as Luce Irigaray and subjected to a parodic overwriting in essays such as "When the Goods Get Together" and "Women on the Market."[58] From this perspective, Marx's analysis of value and of the commodity as the elementary form of capitalist wealth is understood as an accurate although displaced interpretation of the status of woman in a patriarchal society.

> In our social order, women are 'products' used and exchanged by men. Their status is that of merchandise, 'commodities'. . . . So women have to remain an 'infrastructure' unrecognized as such by our society and our culture. The use, consumption, and circulation of their sexualized bodies underwrite the organization and the reproduction of the social order, in which they have never taken part as 'subjects.'[59]

The erasure of female subjectivity by the commodification of the female body is, however, never quite successful. Just as Lévi-Strauss, despite his attempt to compare the exchange of women to the exchange of words, must admit that women also speak, the feminist theorist must acknowledge the fact that women also buy. Not only do they buy, but since the early years of the twentieth century the woman has been situated by a capitalist economy as the prototype of the modern consumer. In the theorization of the commodification of the woman there is, therefore, a hitch—a hitch not unlike the one encountered by Lévi-Strauss. Much to his dismay, the anthropologist discovers that the woman "must be recognized as a generator of signs."[60] But Lévi-Strauss makes an amazing comeback and recoups his losses by attaching the woman's "talent, before and after marriage, for taking her part in a duet"[61] to an intensification of the affective value of sexual relations—to that "affective richness, ardour and mystery" which originally characterized all signs-to-be-exchanged, not just the woman. This leaves the woman with a fairly heavy burden of affect. I would like to argue here that the woman's ability to purchase, her subjectivity as a consumer, is qualified by a relation to commodities which is also ultimately subordinated to that intensification of the affective value of sexual relations which underpins a patriarchal society. In other words, Irigaray's theory of the woman as commodity and the historical analysis of the woman's positioning as consumer—as subject rather than object of the commodity form—are only apparently contradictory. But this involves rethinking the absoluteness of the dichotomy between subject and object which informs much feminist thinking and analyzing the ways in which the woman is encouraged to actively participate in her own oppression.

Of course it is only insofar as consumerism is associated with a particularly maligned form of subjectivity or agency that the woman's role in such an exchange is assured. As Jameson points out, "the conception of the mindless consumer, the ultimate commodified 'false consciousness' of shopping-centre capitalism, is a conception of 'otherness.' . . . degraded consumption is assigned to women, to what used to be called 'Mrs. American Housewife.' "[62] The degradation here is linked to the idea of the consumer as a passive subject who is taken in by the lure of advertising, the seduction of the image. In other words, the phenomenon of consumerism is conceptualized in terms which are not far from those used to delineate spectatorship in the cinema. The film frame functions, in this context, not as a "window on the world" as in the Bazinian formulation, but as a quite specific kind of window—a shop window. Or, as Charles Eckert points out with reference to the short films of the first decade of the century, "they functioned as living display windows for all that they contained; windows that were occupied by marvelous mannequins and swathed in a fetish-inducing ambiance of music and emotion."[63] The relation between the cinema and consumerism is buttressed by the film's capability for representing not merely objects but objects in their fetishized form as commodities. The glamour, the sheen of the cinema and its stars metonymically infect the objects of the mise-en-scène. As Jeanne Allen claims, the spectator is encouraged to desire the possession of a material environment, an environment which "represented a standard of living promised to the viewer ideologically, but awarded only to the eye."[64] Or, as Will Hays put it in a 1930 radio speech, "The motion picture carries to every American at home, and to millions of potential purchasers abroad, the visual, vivid perception of American manufactured products."[65] It would be quite appropriate, it seems, to apply Laura Mulvey's phrase, "to-be-looked-at-ness" to the filmic object in its transformation into a commodity as well as to the woman as spectacle.

One can isolate at least three instances of the commodity form in its relation to the cinema and the question of the female spectator-consumer. The first is fully consistent with Irigaray's analysis of the woman as commodity in a patriarchal system of exchange and involves the encouragement of the woman's narcissistic apprehension of the image of the woman on the screen. The female spectator is invited to witness her own commodification and, furthermore, to buy an image of herself insofar as the female star is proposed as the ideal of feminine beauty. "Buying" here is belief—the image has a certain amount of currency. This level involves not only the currency of a body but of a space in which to display that body: a car, a house, a room filled with furniture and appliances. The second type of relation between the commodity form and the cinema is in some ways the most direct—the commodity tie-in which often involves a contractual agreement between the manufacturer and the studio. The result may be the subtle or not so subtle placement of a Coca-Cola logo or other brand name in the background of a scene. As the most explicit link between the commodity form and the cinema, this type of display has historically been subjected to a great deal of criticism. Such criticism is then deflected to some extent away from the movie industry when the commodity is "tied in" in a space offscreen by linking a line of clothing, for instance, to a particular film or associating a star with a specific product. This process serves to mediate the spectator's access to the ideal image on the screen. It disperses the fascination of the cinema onto a multiplicity of products whose function is to allow the spectator to approximate that image. Finally, the third instance of commodity form in the cinematic institution concerns the film itself and its status as a commodity in a circuit of exchange. The film in its commodity form promotes a certain mode of perception which is fully adequate to a consumer society and which, for the female spectator, initiates a particularly complex dialectic of "being," "having," and "appearing." Michèle Le Doeuff has, quite legitimately, warned us about the metaphorical use of the term "economy" in contemporary theory—the resort to phrases such as "libidinal economy," "textual economy," "classical economy," "general economy"—a usage which absolves the theorist from a confrontation with the economy "proper" insofar as it refers to such things as prices, exchanges, markets.[66] However, the injunction negates the profound connections between the different economies, a connection which is, perhaps, most visible in the cinema. The economy of the text, its regulation of spectatorial investments and drives, is linked to the economy of tie-ins, the logic of the female subject's relation to the commodity—her status as consumer of goods and consumer of discourses.

The development of the cinematic institution is frequently associated with the rise of consumerism. Overproduction toward the end of the nineteenth century, together with Henry Ford's development of "line production" in 1910 and the intensification of production during World War I, led to a situation in which there was an excess of material goods and a scarcity of consumers, a condition necessitating the perfection of advertising and marketing strategies geared toward a mass audience. Positioning the laborer as a consumer was also an effective means of countering an emerging resistance to the industrial and corporate structure on the part of workers.[67] As Judith Mayne points out in her study of immigrant audiences, ". . . consumerism offered the image of an homogeneous population pursuing the same goals—'living well' and accumulating goods. The movie theater seemed to offer an ideal space for the exhibition of this image, for workers and eventually middle-class people needed only to pay a small admission price in order to share equally in the spectacle offered on the screen."[68] And it would seem that the spectator-consumer was increasingly envisaged as female. Jeanne Allen notes how, as early as 1916, Paramount's promotional journal printed an article describing "the way in which fashionable women derive ideas for interior decoration by copying the sets presented in films."[69] Furthermore, as Allen points out, the space of the theater itself was conceived as specifically feminine:

A 1927 article in *Theatre Management*, for example, stressed the importance of women as the primary component and motivators of film attendance and argued that

> both the appeal of the film and the theater must be geared to pleasiո.ɓ
> bilities. Art works in the lobbies, attractive fabrics and designs for interior decoɩаɩɩ
> and subdued and flattering lighting were important appeals to women's tastes and to
> their desire for comfort and relaxation. [70]

Fan magazines in their earliest incarnations are linked with the purportedly female obsession with stars, glamour, gossip, and fashionability. The much sought-after address to the female spectator often seems more readily accessible in the discursive apparatus surrounding the film than in the text itself.

In an article entitled "The Carole Lombard in Macy's Window," Charles Eckert sketches the history of the cinema's links to commodity fetishism, but he is most concerned with what he refers to as "the almost incestuous hegemony that characterized Hollywood's relations with vast reaches of the American economy by the mid-1930s."[71] What is striking about Eckert's account is the amount of space he must devote to the two genres of commodities which are most strongly evocative of female narcissism: fashion and cosmetics. Indeed, Eckert suggests that the projected audience for this "showcasing" of commodities was not at all heterogeneous in relation to such factors as age, sex, ethnicity, or marital status: "Out there, working as a clerk in a store and living in an apartment with a friend, was *one girl*—single, nineteen years old, Anglo-Saxon, somewhat favoring Janet Gaynor."[72] Eckert carefully traces the vicissitudes of fashion's intimate connection with Hollywood from clothing lines such as "Miss Hollywood Junior," which exploited labels with a star's name and picture, to the brainchild of Bernard Waldman, the chain of Cinema Fashions shops, only one to a city, which sold copies of the gowns worn by stars in specific pictures. Although there were, in addition to such showcasing techniques, a very large number of commodity tie-ins which were not so gender-specific—from watches to toothpaste, to desks, typewriters, and cars—the glamour, sheen and fascination attached to the movie screen seemed most appropriate for the marketing of a certain feminine self-image.

The commodity tie-in is usually closely associated with the materials prepared by the studio's publicity department in order to market the movie, materials which are gathered together in a publication referred to as the campaign book or press book and sent to exhibitors. In an article in the *Saturday Evening Post* in 1927, Carl Laemmle speaks of the press book primarily in terms of the marketing of the film itself as a commodity:

> Three departments of advertising, publicity, and exploitation combined first on the
> preparation of the press book or campaign book. This constitutes a complete and en-
> cyclopedic guide to the local theater owner in selling the picture to his public. In effect,
> it places in the employ of the smallest theater owner in the country the services of the
> best possible advertising, publicity, and exploitation brains that we can secure. [73]

The press book even goes so far as to provide the "intimate, chatty type of copy so eagerly relished by the screen fans."[74] By the mid-1930s the press book has been perfected for the promotion not only of the movie itself but of a host of products connected in often extremely tangential ways to the film. In sections entitled "Exploitation," the studio experts isolate a particular scene, condensed onto a publicity still (an arrival scene, for example), and suggest its affiliation with the appropriate commodity (in this instance, luggage). Metonymy is the trope of the tie-in. The press book constitutes a detailed reading of the filmic text to produce the conditions of its own marketability as well as the conditions of a general consumerism which it invites and encourages. It works to disseminate the fetishism of the filmic image in a metonymic chain of commodities.

If the film frame is a kind of display window and spectatorship consequently a form of window-shopping, the intimate association of looking and buying does indeed suggest that the prototype of the spectator-consumer is female. And ultimately Eckert's argument is that the alliance between the cinema and the commodity form in a consumer conscious society generates a genre of films explicitly addressed to the female spectator. As he points out, "Consumer statistics widely disseminated in the late 1920's and early 1930's show that women made 80 to 90 percent of all purchases for family use. They bought 48 percent of drugs, 96 percent of dry goods, 87 percent of raw products, 98 percent of automobiles."[75] The confluence of three different factors—the expanding awareness of the significant economic role of the female consumer, the industry's commitment to the development of commodity tie-ins, and a star system dominated by women—opened up a space for "a steady output of films dominated by starlets—those hundreds of 'women's films' which are of such interest to feminist critics like Haskell and Rosen."[76] The conditions of possibility of the woman's film as a genre are closely linked to the commodity form.

By the 1940s the system of tie-ins and press books was fully in place, and the machinery of advertising had attained a fairly sophisticated form. Furthermore, the war served to reinforce the view that the spectator to be addressed is female. As mentioned previously, the film industry tended to operate under the assumption that the audience was composed primarily of women. In addition, audience analysis confirms that women were "usually better versed than men on movie topics."[77] Women were fully immersed in the discursive apparatus surrounding the cinema—fan magazines as well as news columns and articles on or by stars in women's magazines.

Advertising outside the context of the cinema, by this time a highly efficient machine designed to facilitate the circulation of commodities, was frequently subordinated to the ideological imperative of moving women first into and then out of the work force in a fairly short period of time (the "Rosie the Riveter" phenomenon). The commodity was at least a small part of the lure tempting the woman to take a job in the first place—the era of high consumerism had arrived, and the new assessment of "economic need" persuaded the woman to work in order to maintain her standard of living. But the commodity was also activated as the lure back into the domestic space of the home in the postwar years, when the threat of male unemployment was great. Even during the war, as Susan M. Hartmann notes, "General Electric predicted that women would welcome their return 'to the old housekeeping routine' because it would be transformed by new appliances. The Eureka Vacuum Cleaner Company praised its women on the assembly line, but promised that at war's end, 'like you, Mrs. America, Eureka will put aside its uniform and return to the ways of peace . . . building household appliances.' "[78] Advertising during the war provoked the reader to fantasize about the various types of commodities which would be available after the war—cars, houses, furniture, and household appliances.

What is amazing about advertising in this particular historical conjuncture is that it continues to operate at full force despite the absence of commodities—the scarcity of material goods imposed by a wartime economy. Undoubtedly this advertising without an object functions to insure that consumers do not forget brand names, causing advertisers to somehow lose their hold over their audience. But it also demonstrates how advertising, beyond the aim of selling a particular commodity, functions to generate and maintain an aptitude for consumption in the subject. A picture of a woman holding a Revere Copper-Clad Stainless Steel pan in front of a scene depicting an intense military battle is captioned with the apologetic statement, "Mrs. Parker's cooking utensils are making it hot for the Japs." A young woman clad only in a bra and a Lastex Real-Form panty girdle licks a food stamp and looks out provocatively at the reader beneath the phrase "Military Needs Come First."

This objectlessness of the advertising discourse frequently prompts a return to the female body as the prototypical object of commodity fetishism. "Rosie the Riveter" was conceived from the beginning as a temporary phenomenon, active only for the duration, and throughout the war years the female spectator-consumer was sold a certain image of femininity which functioned to sustain the belief that women and work outside the home were basically incompatible. The woman's new role in production was masked by an insistent emphasis on a narcissistic consumption. She was encouraged to view herself as engaged in a constant battle to protect her femininity from the ravages of the workplace with the aid of a host of products: hand lotions, facial creams, mattresses, tampons. Furthermore, it was this idea of femininity that American soldiers were fighting to protect. This notion is most explicit in an ad for Tangee lipstick entitled "War, Women and Lipstick." Alongside a photograph of a glamorous young female pilot emerging from a cockpit is the following text:

For the first time in history woman-power is a factor in war. Millions of you are fighting and working side by side with your men.

In fact, you are doing double duty—for you are still carrying on your traditional "woman's" work of cooking, and cleaning, and home-making. Yet, somehow, American women are still the loveliest and most spirited in the world. The best dressed, the best informed, the best looking.

It's a reflection of the free democratic way of life that you have succeeded in keeping your femininity—even though you are doing man's work!

If a symbol were needed of this fine, independent spirit—of this courage and strength—I would choose a lipstick. It is one of those mysterious little essentials that have an importance far beyond their size or cost.

A woman's lipstick is an instrument of personal morale that helps her to conceal heartbreak or sorrow; gives her self-confidence when it's badly needed; heightens her loveliness when she wants to look her loveliest.

No lipstick—ours or anyone else's—will win the war. But it symbolizes one of the reasons why we are fighting . . . the precious right of women to be feminine and lovely—under any circumstances.

Femininity was intimately articulated with a patriotic nationalism. It could also be argued that the Rosie the Riveter image (the original—parodic—Norman Rockwell painting on the cover of *The Saturday Evening Post* in which a Rosie with bulging muscles and a huge riveting gun across her lap crushes a copy of *Mein Kampf* beneath her heel), was chosen precisely for its effectiveness in demarcating the absoluteness of the antithesis between femininity and what continued to be considered "men's work." Traditional ideas concerning femininity were crucial to the plethora of antifeminist discourses emerging after the war, reaching their apex in Lundberg and Farnham's *Modern Woman: The Lost Sex.*[79]

This aura of a femininity fully contained by a fetishized body image and its corresponding narcissism was also promoted in the press books designed to market and exploit the films of the '40s.[80] The woman's split subjectivity as worker and wife, or masculinized worker and the embodiment of femininity, is accompanied in the press book by a doubling of female types, subsumed beneath the overpowering category of beauty. A suggested promotional scheme associated with *A Stolen Life*, a film in which Bette Davis plays twin sisters, involves setting the claim "Every Woman Plays a Double Role" next to any one of the following advertisements: "Secretary and Siren—so delightfully *both* with a make-up kit from Maxine's"; "You're bright. . . . You're blasé. . . . You're Both with Fashions from Georgia's Dress Shoppe"; etc. The press book for *Dark Victory* is insistent about its potential audience: "*Dark Victory* is definitely a woman's picture and should be exploited as such via the woman's page of your local paper and in cooperation with women's shops." The suggestions include a translation of the film's two female stars, Bette Davis and Geraldine Fitzgerald, into two feminine types with two entirely different makeup needs: medium skin with blonde hair (Bette Davis) and fair skin with dark hair (Geraldine Fitzgerald). The press book for *The Two Mrs. Carrolls* employs a similar strategy by encouraging exhibitors to set up a contest with the following angle: "All women fall into two general classifications from a beauty-point-of-view. By analyzing the attractions of two beautiful stars of 'The Two Mrs. Carrolls,' contestant should be able to evaluate her own charms at the same time." Another press book exploits the title of Irving Rapper's *Deception* to sell makeup with the expert's claim that "Most beauty is a delightful deception." The "Exploitation" page of the press book for *In This Our Life* articulates connections between the different media— magazines, radio, cinema—and underlines the status of the star as an intertextual phenomenon with its headline: "Bette Davis Story in 'Ladies Home Journal' Cues Campaign for Femme Business!" The story is about how Bette Davis manages to keep a career and hold a husband as well and is entitled "Could Your Husband Take It?"

The very familiarity and banality of such ploys should not blind us to the overwhelming intensity of the injunction to the female spectator-consumer to concern herself with her own appearance and position—an appearance which can only be fortified and assured through the purchase of a multiplicity of products. The woman's film as a genre, together with the massive extracinematic discursive apparatus, insure that what the woman is sold is a certain image of femininity. There is a sense in which the woman's film is not much to look at— the nonstyle or zero-degree style of films of the genre has frequently been noted. It is as though there were a condensation of the eroticism of the image onto the figure of the woman—the female star proffered to the female spectator for her imitation (and often this took place in extracinematic discourses—outside the context of particular filmic narratives which frequently de-eroticized the female protagonist). The process underlines the tautological nature of the woman's role as consumer: she is the subject of a transaction in which her own commodification is ultimately the object. As Rachel Bowlby points out, even when consumerism concerns the objects of the space which she inhabits, its tendency is essentially narcissistic.[81] For all consumerism involves the idea of the self-image (perhaps this is why the woman is the prototype of the consumer).

Consumerism requires a transformation in modes of perception. Looking and buying are closely linked. Wolfgang Schivelbusch argues that the development of the department store in the latter half of the nineteenth century profoundly alters the notion of the attractiveness of an item which now "results from the totality of *all* the goods assembled in the salesroom . . . . In the department store, the goods achieve more of their character *as* goods—their appearance as items of exchange value; one might say that their 'commodity-esthetic' aspect becomes ever more dominant."[82] At the cinema, the consumer glance hovers over the surface of the image, isolating details which may be entirely peripheral in relation to the narrative. It is a fixating, obsessive gaze which wanders in and out of the narrative and has a more intimate relation with space—the space of rooms and of bodies—than with the temporal dimension. It is as though there were another text laid over the first—a text with an altogether different mode of address—so that the film becomes something of a palimpsest. In this other text, the desire to possess displaces comprehension as the dominant mechanism of reading. Jameson refers to "a quasi-material 'feeling tone' which floats above the narrative but is only intermittently realized by it: the sense of destiny in family novels, for instance, or the 'epic' rhythms of the earth or of great movements of 'history' in the various sagas can be seen as so many commodities towards whose consumption the narratives are little more than means, their essential materiality then being confirmed and embodied in the movie music that accompanies their screen versions."[83] It is the sense of the film as spectacle, and desirable in its very appeal to the eye, which is consumed in the viewing.

Walter Benjamin, in his essay "The Work of Art in the Age of Mechanical Reproduction," refers to a possible history of the modes of human sense perception and to the decay of the aura which characterizes contemporary perception. This decay is associated with the development of mass culture and with the "desire of contemporary masses to bring things 'closer' spatially and humanly, which is just as ardent as their bent toward overcoming the uniqueness of every reality by accepting its reproduction."[84] The processes of reproduction and commodification have in common the leveling of differences between things and the promotion of their abstract comparability through the medium of money. Schivelbusch uses Benjamin's claim to argue that the development of the railroad as a new form of transportation and of the circulation of commodities functions in much the same way—bringing geographical locations closer and annihilating the uniqueness of the outlying regions. His argument ultimately links together the railroad, the cinema, the department store, and modernized traffic patterns in the constitution of what he calls "panoramic perception": "In the filmic perception—i.e., the perception of *montage*, the juxtaposition of the most disparate images into one unit—the new reality of annihilated in-between spaces finds its clearest expression: the film brings things closer to the viewer as well as closer together."[85]

Benjamin's conceptualization of the opposition between the effect of the aura and that of mechanical reproduction is expressed in the spatial terms of "distance" and "closeness." The aura attached to natural objects is "the unique phenomenon of a distance, however close it may be."[86] And the logic of the consumer's relation to the commodity annihilates this distance: "Every day the urge grows stronger to get hold of an object at very close range by way of its likeness, its reproduction."[87] It is not accidental that the logic of consumerism and mechanical reproduction corresponds to a logic of perception attributed to the female spectator whose nonfetishistic gaze maintains a dangerous intimacy with the image. For the woman, as outlined above, is positioned as the preeminent consumer. What we tend to define, since Marx, as commodity fetishism is in fact more accurately situated as a form of narcissism. Fetishism, in the Freudian paradigm, is a phallic defense which allows the subject to distance himself from the object of desire (or, more accurately, from its implications in relation to castration) through the overvaluation of a mediating substitute object. Narcissism confounds the differentiation between subject and object and is one of the few psychical mechanisms Freud associates specifically with female desire.[88]

Having and appearing are closely intertwined in the woman's purportedly narcissistic relation to the commodity. Commodification presupposes that acutely self-conscious relation to the body which is attributed to femininity. The effective operation of the commodity system requires the breakdown of the body into parts—nails, hair, skin, breath—each one of which can constantly be improved through the purchase of a commodity. As Stuart Ewen points out, in relation to this "commodity self," "each position of the body was to be viewed critically, as a *potential* bauble in a successful assemblage."[89] The ideological effect of commodity logic on a large scale is therefore the deflection of any dissatisfaction with one's life or any critique of the social system onto an intensified concern with a body which is in some way guaranteed to be at fault.[90] The body becomes increasingly *the* stake of late capitalism. *Having* the commodified object—and the initial distance and distinction it presupposes— is displaced by *appearing*, producing a strange constriction of the gap between consumer and commodity. The form of affect which embodies this constriction is also an affect aligned with the feminine—empathy. As Benjamin points out, "If the soul of the commodity which Marx occasionally mentions in jest existed, it would be the most empathetic ever encountered in the realm of souls, for it would have to see in everyone the buyer in whose hand and house it wants to nestle."[91] Commodity and consumer share the same attributes—appeal to the eye and an empathetic relation to the other—and become indistinguishable. Just as the category of "youth" has been expropriated by the commodity system and, as Guy de Bord maintains, "is in no way the property of those who are now young,"[92] "femininity" as a category is not the possession of women—it is not necessarily something we should strive to reclaim. The feminine position has come to exemplify the roles of consumer and spectator in their embodiment of a curiously passive desiring subjectivity.

In her desire to bring the things of the screen closer, to approximate the bodily image of the star, and to possess the space in which she dwells, the female spectator experiences the intensity of the image as lure and exemplifies the perception proper to the consumer. The cinematic image for the woman is both shop window and mirror, the one simply a means of access to the other. The mirror/window takes on then the aspect of a trap whereby her subjectivity becomes synonymous with her objectification. In the words of Irigaray: "Man endows the commodities he produces with a narcissism that blurs the seriousness of utility, of use. Desire, as soon as there is exchange, "perverts" need. But that perversion will be attributed to commodities and to their alleged relations. Whereas they can have no relationships except from the perspective of speculating third parties."[93] The female subject of the consumer look in the cinematic arena becomes, through a series of mediations, the industry's own merchandizing asset. One must ask at this point, "Whose gaze is ultimately addressed?" and "Who profits?"

## A Woman's Place/"Genre"

Mrs. Jane Frazer is—or rather was—a badly bewildered, if not frightened woman. History, in a manner of speaking, had entered her placid life. Crashed in, to be precise. Once a faintly dull classroom subject, later a vague but handy backdrop for stirring romantic novels, history face to face turned out to be a shocking apparition, a grisly visitation which had evidently come to stay. Leering, it declined to budge. . . . (Jane was a long time learning to recognize the haunting face of history.)

> "Women in Defense,"
> *Defense Digest* pamphlet
> published by the American
> Association for Adult
> Education, 1941.

The overwhelming sense of this *Defense Digest* "message" is that History must go out of its way to address the female subject, who is only called upon to recognize it in moments of crisis. And World War II was, of course, one such crisis in which the female "reserve army" of labor was called forth to fill in the gaps in industry left by the male soldiers. But this "filling in" is always perceived as temporary and somewhat uncomfortable, a potential disturbance of a rather neat distribution of sexual difference. As Michael Renov points out, while the 1930s were characterized by class conflict, the mobilization and unification spurred by World War II displaced the most perceptible differentiation from the realm of class to that of sexuality: ". . . in the context of American social life during the World War II years, it was sexual difference rather than class conflict that constituted the crucial problematic to which countless cultural artifacts and public utterances were addressed."[94] In such a context, the woman is addressed more frequently and more insistently by discourses which purport to delineate not only her duties but her desires.

The woman's film undoubtedly does not constitute a genre in the technical sense of the term, insofar as the unity of a genre is generally attributed to consistent patterns in thematic content, iconography, and narrative structure. The heterogeneity of the woman's film as a category is exemplified by the disparity between gothic films such as *Undercurrent* (1946) or *Dragonwyck* (1946), influenced by film noir and the conventions of the thriller, and a love story such as *Back Street* (1941) or a maternal melodrama such as *To Each His Own* (1946). But the group does have a coherence and that coherence is grounded in its address to a female spectator. The woman's film, quite simply, attempts to engage female subjectivity.

As Annette Kuhn has pointed out, the notions of audience address and spectator positioning are not at all synonymous.[95] "Address" refers to strategies which are conscious, explicit, and often extremely specific socially and historically. It is a category of rhetoric. Spectator positioning, on the other hand, is a theoretical concept associated with the alliance between psychoanalysis and film theory. The positions adopted by the spectator (a term which here refers more to a place or a site than to an individual) are basic, unconscious positions which establish the very coherence or readability of the text. Although the concept of spectator positioning as it has been developed in film theory is not equivalent to that of address to a specific audience, the two are not entirely unrelated. Indeed, an analysis of the interaction between the two different aspects of discursive address can contribute to a more thorough articulation of theoretical and historical approaches to the analysis of spectatorship. Spectator positioning, the inscription of a place for the reading or viewing subject within the signifying chain, has been theorized primarily on the basis of a description of the cinematic situation in general, emphasizing such factors as the darkness of the auditorium and the resultant isolation of the individual spectator; the placement of the projector, source of the image, behind the spectator's head; and the effect of the real produced by the classical fiction film. In this respect, it is impossible to draw up a list of elements specific to the woman's film in its address to a female spectator. The films are in many ways, and certainly in their general cinematic setting, no different from conventional classical films with a male address. There is nothing strikingly "feminine" about them in terms of conventions, formal strategies, point of view, etc. Yet, the sustained attempt to incorporate female subjectivity *for* a female subject-spectator introduces perturbations and discrepancies which are frequently not quite successfully contained by the narrative process. Excesses and the revelation of incoherencies and contradictions are a by-product of the films' mode of address. This is why my choice of films has been largely determined by their tendencies to activate the specifically cinematic structures of subjectivity—primarily the voice-over, point-of-view shots, and the marking of certain sequences as dreams, hallucinations, or flashback-memories—in relation to a female character. Films which attribute a narrative or story-telling agency to the woman (e.g., *Possessed, Rebecca, The Gay Sisters*) are particularly important. Because this study is primarily concerned with issues of subjectivity and spectatorship, I have privileged films which attempt to specify female subjectivity via narrative mechanisms, point-of-view, or voice-over as somehow distinct or different from male subjectivity and narrational authority.

The category of the woman's film as a whole is clearly divisible into coherent subgroups in a number of different ways, depending upon the focus of the analysis. Molly Haskell, one of the first feminist critics to isolate and analyze the woman's film, claims that its themes can be reduced to four categories: sacrifice, affliction, choice, competition.

> In the first, the woman must 'sacrifice' (1) herself for her children—e.g., *Madame X*, *The Sin of Madelon Claudet*; (2) her children for their own welfare—e.g., *The Old Maid*, *Stella Dallas*, *To Each His Own*; (3) marriage for her lover—e.g., *Back Street*; (4) her lover for marriage or for his own welfare—e.g., *Kitty Foyle* and *Intermezzo*, respectively; (5) her career for love—e.g., *Lady in the Dark*, *Together Again*; or (6) love for her career—e.g., *The Royal Family of Broadway*, *Morning Glory*. . . .
>
> In the second category, the heroine is struck by some "affliction" which she keeps a secret and eventually either dies unblemished (*Dark Victory*), despite the efforts of her doctor-turned-lover, or is cured (*The Magnificent Obsession*), by the efforts of her lover-turned-doctor.
>
> The third category, "choice," has the heroine pursued by at least two suitors who wait, with undivided attention, her decision; on it, their future happiness depends (*The Seventh Veil*, *Daisy Kenyon*, *Lydia*).
>
> In the final category, "competition," the heroine meets and does battle with the woman whose husband (fiancé, lover) she loves (*The Great Lie*, *When Ladies Meet*, *Love Story*—the forties' English version; *Old Acquaintance*). While deciding the man's fate, the women will discover, without explicitly acknowledging it, that they prefer each other's company to his.[96]

Haskell's categories are in many respects quite close to the subgroups I delineate here. However, I have attempted to align my groupings more closely with recognizable "generic" associations—for example, Haskell's "sacrifice" films are dealt with primarily as maternal melodrama here; her "choice" films become instances of the love story; her "affliction" films are translated into the "medical discourse." Other critics include "career women comedies" such as *His Girl Friday* (1940) or *Adam's Rib* (1949) within the realm of the woman's film.[97] However, despite the fact that a woman is often the protagonist of such films (although it would be more accurate in many instances to say that the protagonist is a couple), their address to the spectator strikes me as less sexually specific than that of the other categories of the woman's film. Michael Renov has proposed a quite different taxonomy of filmic representations of the woman in the 1940s, organized along the lines of the given "unities" or entities associated with female subjectivity: the female body or body part, the female subject, and the female group.[98] However, Renov is interested not so much in the address to the woman as in the *representation of her*, and many of the films (in the first group in particular) are aimed at the male spectator.

Haskell's subgroupings of the woman's film and her association of the "genre" with "wet, wasted afternoons," together with my own taxonomy and sustained appeal to psychoanalytic scenarios, can easily suggest an obsession with the more pathological aspects of the films. However, one can readily respond that there is a very real sense in which femininity within a patriarchal culture is always constituted as a pathological condition. Given the apparent "masculinization" of the very process of looking in the cinema, these films often manifest a certain convolution and instability in their attempted construction of female fantasy. The narratives assume a compatibility between the idea of female fantasy and that of persecution—a persecution effected by husband, family, or lover. There is an almost obsessive association of the female protagonist with a deviation from some norm of mental stability or health, resulting in the recurrent investigation of psychical mechanisms frequently linked with the "feminine condition"—masochism, hysteria, neurosis, paranoia. The films can be classified into a number of subgroups along these lines. *The Desire to Desire* is organized as an investigation of four subgroups of the woman's film of the 1940s: (1) films in which a medical discourse is activated and a male doctor treats a female patient suffering from either a psychical or physical disease— e.g., *Possessed* (Curtis Bernhardt, 1946), *Dark Victory* (Edmund Goulding, 1939) (chapter two); (2) maternal melodramas in which an enforced or threatened separation between mother and child tends to produce an alignment of the mother with the figures of masochism—e.g., *The Great Lie* (Edmund Goulding, 1941), *To Each His Own* (Mitchell Leisen, 1946) (chapter three); (3) the classical "love story" which investigates the feasibility of female desire—e.g., *Humoresque* (Jean Negulesco, 1946), *Back Street* (Robert Stevenson, 1941) (chapter four); (4) films heavily influenced by the gothic novel which link the woman with paranoia through a conflation of legalized sexuality (marriage) with violence—e.g., *Gaslight* (George Cukor, 1944), *Rebecca* (Alfred Hitchcock, 1940) (chapter five). The boundaries separating categories in this taxonomy are not impenetrable, and frequently one film will be discussed in the context of two different subgroups—for example, *Now, Voyager* is both an instance of the medical discourse and a love story.

Because the films all insistently trace the contours of female subjectivity, they tend to produce a more or less explicit discourse on the vicissitudes of the female gaze (the differences between the subgroups in this respect are detailed more fully in the concluding chapter). Scenes of movie spectatorship often have a prominent positon in the narrative trajectory. Near the beginning of *Stella*

*Dallas, Stella* becomes heavily involved in a movie and expresses a strong desire to be "like" the people on the screen. The opening scene of *The Spiral Staircase* details a movie projection which coincides with a murder. When movies themselves are absent from the mise-en-scène, the woman's "usurpation" of the process of looking is signaled by a frequent recourse to concrete externalizations of the gaze such as the window or the mirror. The violence associated with the attribution of a desire to see to the woman reaches its culmination in the gothic paranoid films, where the cinematic apparatus itself seems to be mobilized against the female spectator, disabling her gaze. In chapter six, I analyze two particularly intense and violent scenes of movie screenings from *Caught* and *Rebecca*. It is as though the very premise of a seeing and desiring female subject— a premise which the woman's film cannot avoid—must elicit extremely forceful, and not altogether successful, strategies of containment and discipline. There is always a manifest level of *strain*, if not caricature, in the representation of a woman looking. In *The Gay Sisters*, one of the sisters is asked why she always wears a monocle, and her reply is that the monocle is something to help you keep "a grip on yourself."

Ways of looking are inevitably linked to ways of speculating, of theorizing (derived from the Greek *theoria*—a "looking at, viewing, contemplation . . . a sight, a spectacle"—*Oxford English Dictionary*) and, ultimately, to ways of representing oneself. This is why the woman's film, in its obsessive attempt to circumscribe a place for the female spectator, is so crucial to a feminist analysis. Cultural representations are historically specific, true, but they also circulate and inflect even current understandings of female subjectivity. The figures of the women's films of the 1940s still have a certain currency. Appropriately enough, the managing director of the International Division of the Motion Picture Association wrote, in 1947, "The motion picture is one product which is never completely consumed for the very good reason that it is never entirely forgotten by those who see it. It leaves behind it a residue, or deposit, of imagery and association, and this fact makes it a product unique in our tremendous list of export items."[99] It is the purpose of this study to examine this residue and to defamiliarize the all too familiar icons and gestures of femininity associated with it.

# 2

## Clinical Eyes:
## The Medical Discourse

It's as if they [doctors] are looking at something beneath the flesh.

—Cissy's remark to Bailey about his
eyes in *Experiment Perilous*

An important component of what Michel Foucault refers to as "the fantasy link between knowledge and pain"[1] is the association, within patriarchal
configurations, of femininity with the pathological. Disease and the woman
have something in common—they are both socially devalued or undesirable,
marginalized elements which constantly threaten to infiltrate and contaminate
that which is more central, health or masculinity. There is even a sense in which
the female body could be said to harbor disease within physical configurations
that are enigmatic to the male. As is frequently noted, the word *hysteria* is derived from the Greek word for *uterus*, and the nineteenth century defined this
disease quite specifically as a disturbance of the womb—the woman's betrayal
by her own reproductive organs. The patient whose discourse is read and interpreted at the origin of psychoanalysis, as the text of the unconscious, is the female hysteric. As Phyllis Chesler points out, "Although the ethic and referent
of mental health in our society is a masculine one, most psychoanalytic theoreticians have written primarily about women."[2] It is thus as an aberration in
relation to an unattainable norm that the woman becomes narratively "interesting," the subject for a case history. A narrativization of the woman which

might otherwise be fairly difficult, as argued in the introduction, is facillitated by the association of women with the pathological.

As the example of hysteria and the more modern conceptualization of hormones and their effects indicate, the border between physical and mental illness is often of little consequence in the medicalization of femininity. Represented as possessing a body which is *over*present, unavoidable, in constant sympathy with the emotional and mental faculties, the woman resides just outside the boundaries of the problematic wherein Western culture operates a mind/body dualism. Hence the illnesses associated with women in the many films of the 1940s which activate a medical discourse are never restricted or localized—they always affect or are the effects of a "character" or an essence, implicating the woman's entire being. In the majority of the films discussed in this chapter,[3] the female character suffers from some kind of mental illness: depression, nervous breakdown, catatonia, amnesia, psychosis. Yet even in the films which focus on a physical illness or defect, such as *Dark Victory* (1939) or *A Woman's Face* (1941), which involve a brain tumor and a facial scar respectively, the discovery or the treatment of the illness initiates a radical change in the very life-styles of the women concerned. In *Beyond the Forest* (1949), Bette Davis ostensibly dies of peritonitis, the effect of a self-induced miscarriage, but her death is really caused by an irrepressible and feverish desire to leave her small town life behind and take the train to Chicago.

This blurring of the boundaries between the psychical and the somatic is predicated on a shift in the status of the female body in this group of films. When the female body is represented within mainstream classical cinema as spectacle, as the object of an erotic gaze, signification is spread out over a surface—a surface which refers only to itself and does not simultaneously conceal and reveal an interior. Such a fetishization of the surface is, of course, the very limit of the logic of this specular system, a limit which is rarely attained since it implies that there is no attribution of an interiority whatsoever and hence no "characterization" (this extreme point is most apparent in certain Busby Berkeley musical numbers). The logical limit nevertheless exemplifies the system's major tendency and entails that the body is both signifier and signified, its meaning in effect tautological. The female body exhausts its signification entirely in its status as an object of male vision. In films of the medical discourse, on the other hand, the female body functions in a slightly different way. It is not spectacular but symptomatic, and the visible becomes fully a signifier, pointing to an invisible signified. The medical discourse films, acceding to the force of the logic of the symptom, attribute to the woman both a surface and a depth, the specificity of the depth being first and foremost that it is not immediately perceptible. A technician is called for—a technician of essences—and it is the figure of the doctor who fills that role. Medicine introduces a detour in the male's relation to the female body through an eroticization of the very process of knowing the female subject. Thus, while the female body is despecularized, the doctor patient relation is, somewhat paradoxically, eroticized.

The logic of the symptom—so essential to an understanding of the films of the 1940s which activate a medical discourse—is caught within the nexus of metaphors of visibility and invisibility. For the symptom makes visible and material invisible forces to which we would otherwise have no access; it is a delegate of the unconscious. But even outside the specifically psychoanalytic postulate of the unconscious, the organization of clinical experience, as Foucault points out, demands the elaboration of a multilevel structure.

> The structure, at once perceptual and epistemological, that commands clinical anatomy, and all medicine that derives from it, is that of invisible visibility. Truth, which, by right of nature, is made for the eye, is taken from her, but at once surreptitiously revealed by that which tries to evade it. Knowledge *develops* in accordance with a whole interplay of *envelopes*; the hidden element takes on the form and rhythm of the hidden content, which means that, like a *veil*, it is *transparent*. . . .[4]

It is the task of the doctor to *see through* this series of envelopes and reveal the essential kernel of truth which attempts to escape the eye. Physiology and psychoanalysis share this system which posits a relation between different levels— a surface and a depth, visibility and invisibility. In breaking away from biology it was perhaps inevitable that Freud should do so through recourse to an illness, hysteria, in which the body is transformed into a text—enigmatic but still decipherable. In his case history of Dora (another "woman's narrative"), Freud posits a privileged relation between hysteria and the somatic. "Somatic compliance" is the concept Freud elaborated to designate the process whereby the body complies with the psychical demands of the illness by providing a space and a material for the inscription of its signs. He analyzes a case of a female hysteric whose contorted face can be read as a direct translation into physical terms of the verbal cliché for an insult—a "slap in the face." In *Studies on Hysteria*, Freud and Breuer delineate the types of symptoms which require that the body act as the expression of the illness: neuralgias and anaesthesias, contractures and paralyses, hysterical attacks, epileptoid convulsions, tics, chronic vomiting and anorexia, disturbance of vision, etc.[5]

From the nineteenth to the twentieth century, however, hysteria is subdued and the relation between mental disturbances and the space of the body is modified. In the 1940s films of the medical discourse, neuroses and even psychoses are evidenced not by contorted limbs and paralysis but by a marked lack of narcissism on the part of the sick woman. The illness of the woman is signaled

by the fact that she no longer cares about her appearance. In the beginning of
*Possessed* (1947), when Joan Crawford—clearly demented—walks the city
streets misrecognizing every man for the one she has just killed, she is represented as quite plain, in documentary-style shots, without makeup, in stark contrast to the scenes in flashback of an earlier time when she was not yet ill. Still
the victim of a psychosis at the end of the film, she never quite regains her
"looks." This despecularization of the woman is present in films such as *Now,
Voyager* (1942) and *Johnny Belinda* (1948) as well. In both films the woman's
illness is registered as an undesirable appearance. Charlotte (Bette Davis), in the
beginning of *Now, Voyager*, wears glasses, clumsy shoes, an unattractive dress,
and is presented as being overweight, with heavy eyebrows and a harsh hairstyle.
Belinda (Jane Wyman), before she meets the doctor in *Johnny Belinda*, is dirty
and unkempt, her hair uncombed. In these films, as well as in *A Woman's Face*,
the woman's "cure" consists precisely in a beautification of body/face. The doctor's work is the transformation of the woman into a specular object. Nevertheless, the woman's status as specular object of desire is synonymous with her
"health"—her illness is characterized as the very lack of that status. The narratives thus trace a movement from the medical gaze to the erotic gaze in relation to the central female figure, activating a process of despecularization/
respecularization.

   In *Lady in the Dark* (1944), the respecularization is accomplished via an
emphasis on clothing as the most explicit indicator of sexual difference. The
traumatic incident in Liza's (Ginger Roger's) childhood, uncovered by psychoanalysis, is constituted by her father's prohibition against dressing up in a blue
gown which had belonged to her dead mother. The effect of such a traumatic
assault on feminine narcissism is given by the film as Liza's ambition to assume
and retain the position of a man—as the business head of a fashion magazine.
Her clothing as an adult reflects that denial of femininity. A dissatisfied male
employee, Johnson, bitterly jokes after noting the strict lines of her business suit,
"We must go to the same tailor." Liza's psychiatrist analyzes her dreams in the
same terms: "In reality you're obviously a woman who doesn't care for feminine
adornments. A man dying of thirst dreams of water. Have you never consciously
wanted to be a glamorous and seductive woman?" Her dreams, represented as
lush musical sequences, clearly demonstrate that what the working woman desires and represses is spectacle. The effort on the part of both psychoanalysis and
the major male character to demasculinize Liza is manifested in the constant
recurrence of the phrase, "to scare the pants off of you." When Liza tells a close
friend, Maggie, about her consultation with a psychoanalyst, Maggie reacts by
referring to psychoanalysts as "bringing up things that'll scare the pants off of
you." After Liza offers Johnson a raise to keep him on the magazine, he says, "I

impress the pants off of you, don't I?" Metaphors of clothing allow Johnson and the psychoanalyst to collude in constructing Liza as the perfect image of femininity.

The lack or impairment of a narcissism purportedly specific to femininity is hence symptomatic in these films. Although Rosa Moline (Bette Davis) begins in *Beyond the Forest* with a strong desire to constitute herself as spectacle, her fever at the end of the film is signified by her misapplication of makeup as she gazes into the mirror. Her lipstick exceeds the outline of her mouth, and eyeliner is drawn on in a crooked line far from the boundary of the eye. Her dress askew as well, she is the figure of an impaired narcissism. The pathetic nature of her condition is emphasized by the fact that the signs of her excessive desire are inscribed on her body in a hyperbolic manner. Because narcissism is the convergence of desire on the subject's own body, its opposite—overinvestment in an object relation—is also symptomatic of a serious deficiency of narcissistic libido. In *Possessed*, Louise's (Joan Crawford's) illness is depicted as overpossessiveness, as a relentless desire for a man who no longer loves her.

However, the classical text also manifests a profound ambivalence on precisely this issue of the woman's narcissism. For its logic entails the possibility of a woman being overly narcissistic as well, a condition which inevitably signifies evil tendencies on her part (this is, in fact, the case in *Beyond the Forest*). The constant subtext accompanying the text of spectacle in the classical cinema proclaims that outward appearances do not matter, that an essential core of goodness may be veiled by a misleading, even unattractive exterior. The spectacular aspect of classical cinema, its concentration on visual pleasure, carries within it its own denial. Hence, too great an insistence by the woman herself on her status as image for the male gaze is prohibited—it is unseemly, wrong-headed, and potentially indicative of an illness associated with misplaced ambition. *Dark Mirror* (1946) links psychical disturbance to female narcissism and violence via the shattered mirror acting as an endpoint to its long first shot and a more general emphasis on mirrors throughout its narrative about twin sisters. In *Caught*, the medicalization of Leonora (Barbara Bel Geddes) is synonymous with her despecularization. At the end of the film, the obstetrician's final diagnosis of Bel Geddes consists of a rejection of the object which at the beginning of the film epitomized the woman's desire—a mink coat ("If my diagnosis is correct, she won't want that anyway"). Because the mink coat is associated with femininity as spectacle and image (its first inscription in the film is within the pages of a fashion magazine), the doctor's diagnosis has the effect of a certain despecularization of the female body. That body is, instead, symptomatic, and demands a reading.

Hence, there are two strong yet contradictory impulses within the classical cinema concerning the representation of the female body. The body is either fetishized as an object of beauty or de-emphasized as totally nonrevelatory, even deceptive (this is the logic of "appearances can be deceiving"). Yet the overwhelming force of the drive to specularize is manifested by the fact that the second impulse is not concretized through the representation of "ugly" or even "unattractive" women. When a woman is designated as "plain" within the classical cinema, she is not really "plain" in relation to any contemporary standards of attractiveness (Joan Fontaine in *Rebecca*, purportedly contrasted with the beautiful but significantly absent Rebecca, is a good example of this). Furthermore, instead of going so far as to actually depict a woman as having a face or body coded as unattractive (and unchangeably so) in order to demonstrate that it is the "interior" which really "counts," the classical text multiplies its figures of feminine beauty. This is particularly the case in identical twin films of the 1940s such as *Dark Mirror* and *A Stolen Life* (1946). In each film, the twin sisters look exactly alike but are essentially different. In *A Stolen Life*, the major male character refers to one twin as "cake" and the other "icing," comparing them on the basis of a distinction between substance and excess. But because the two women are identical in appearance, a specialist is often needed to allay the effects of this "double-vision" on the part of the male, to penetrate the surface. In *Dark Mirror* one of the twins has committed a murder, and the other covers up for her; one is paranoid and the other relatively healthy. Because it is impossible to differentiate between the two on the basis of appearance (both are played by Olivia de Havilland), a psychiatrist is needed to *see through* the surface exterior to the interior truths of the two sisters—in other words, to perform a symptomatic reading.

Thus the doctor is given extraordinary powers of vision which have the potential to go beyond the barrier usually posed by an exterior surface. In this branch of the "woman's film," the erotic gaze becomes the medical gaze. The female body is located not so much as spectacle but as an element in the discourse of medicine, a manuscript to be read for the symptoms which betray her story, her identity. Hence the need, in these films, for the figure of the doctor as reader or interpreter, as the site of a knowledge which dominates and controls female subjectivity. A scenario of reading is provided within the films themselves—a hermeneutics of pathology which requires that the body approximate a two-level text. The doctor's look in the cinema, because it *penetrates*, appears to be closer to what Foucault describes as the medical glance rather than the gaze. The gaze observes an exterior, it scans a field, expanding in a horizontal rather than a vertical direction; it is "endlessly modulated" while the glance "goes straight to its object."

The glance chooses a line that instantly distinguishes the essential; it therefore goes beyond what it sees; it is not misled by the immediate forms of the sensible, for it knows how to traverse them; it is essentially demystifying. . . . The glance is of the non-verbal order of *contact*, a purely ideal contact perhaps, but in fact a more *striking* contact, since it traverses more easily, and goes further beneath things. The clinical eye discovers a kinship with a new sense that prescribes its norm and epistemological structure; this is no longer the ear straining to catch a language, but the index finger palpating the depths. Hence that metaphor of 'touch' (*le tact*) by which doctors will ceaselessly define their glance.[6]

The symptomatic reading which the doctor performs in these films by means of the instrument of the glance[7] unveils a previously invisible essence—ultimately the essence of the female character concerned. The ideology which the films promote therefore rests on a particularly extreme form of essentialism.

But the logic of the symptom might be used to read the film texts differently. Althusserian theory and strategies of interpretation derived from it assume that what is invisible, what the symptom indicates, is not an essence (as in the films) but a structure, a logic—in short, an ideological systematicity which is by definition unconscious. A symptomatic reading in this sense reveals what is excluded as the invisible of a particular discourse, what is unthought or what the discourse wishes very precisely not to think: ". . . the invisible is the theoretical problematic's nonvision of its non-objects, the invisible is the darkness, the blinded eye of the theoretical problematic's self-reflection when it scans its non-objects, its nonproblems without seeing them, *in order not to look at them*."[8] The nonobject of the woman's film, what ceaselessly exceeds its grasp, is what would appear to be dictated by its own logic—the coherent representation of female subjectivity. Breakdowns and instability in the representation of female subjectivity are evident in all types of the woman's film, but in the films of the medical discourse they receive a special twist. For these incoherencies and instabilities do not remain unseen or unrecognized by the texts; on the contrary, they are recuperated as the signs of illness or psychosis. In this way, the purported subject of the discourse, the woman, becomes its object, and her lapses or difficulties in subjectivity are organized for purposes of medical observation and study. The doctor is thus a crucial figure of constraint. Nevertheless, there are leakages which are manifested as symptoms in the body of the text as a whole.

The symptom gives access to, makes readable, the work of repression and hence indicates the process of transition from one system in the psychical apparatus to another. In a way, the symptom can be seen as manifesting the severity of the repression or the force of the energy attached to the repressed idea which "breaks through" to the surface. In film theory and criticism, this scenario provides a means of accounting for perversion within the norm by positing the paradoxical possibility of the "hysterical classical text." The genre most frequently described as the site of this "return of the repressed" is the melodrama.

Geoffrey Nowell-Smith, for instance, explicitly compares certain strategies of the melodrama with the mechanism of what Freud designated as conversion hysteria. The text is seen as analogous to the body, and "the film itself somatises its own unaccommodated excess, which thus appears displaced or in the wrong place."[9] The hysteria frequently attributed to the female protagonist in the woman's film often proliferates, effecting a more general "hystericization" of the text as body of signifiers.

Such textual hysterical symptoms are, as Althusser points out, "failures in the rigour" of the discourse, the "outer limits of its effort,"[10] sites of the collapse or near-collapse of its own logic. In the films of the medical discourse, these breaking points or ruptures cluster in several different areas and concern questions of the assimilation of psychoanalysis within the Hollywood cinema, of narration and the woman's access to language and vision, of the eroticization of the doctor/patient relation and the association of sickness and passion. The films I have chosen to examine in some detail in this context, to foreground to a greater extent than others—*The Cat People* (1942), *Possessed* (1947), *The Locket* (1946), and *Beyond the Forest* (1949)—were not chosen on the basis of their "typicality," their status as average or the norm. Rather, in the spirit of symptomatic reading, they are all in some ways extreme instances, limit-texts which inadvertently reveal the weaknesses or breaking points of a contradictory ideological project (that of a classical genre addressed to a female spectator).

It is not at all surprising that the medical figure in many of these films is a psychoanalyst, a psychiatrist, or a psychologist (Hollywood often makes no distinction between these three categories). For 1940–1950 is the decade of the most intense incorporation of psychoanalysis within the Hollywood system. Films like *Lady in the Dark*, *Spellbound* (1945), *The Cat People*, *Shock* (1946), *Nightmare Alley* (1947), and *The Snake Pit* (1948) exploited a growing curiosity about psychoanalysis and psychology. This incorporation is synchronous with a more general popularization of psychoanalysis in the late '30s and '40s which was at least partially stimulated by the influx of European refugee analysts, psychiatrists, and intellectuals at this time.[11] The diffusion of psychoanalytic concepts in Hollywood narrative is strong enough to provoke a counterresponse on the part of the psychoanalytic establishment. Articles in *Hollywood Quarterly* by analysts and psychologists decry Hollywood's reductive and often fallacious representation of psychoanalytic concepts and methods.[12] The movie industry defends itself against such criticism by calling in psychoanalytic authorities and experts to act as consultants for its productions and to guarantee the authenticity of its representations. Both *Dark Mirror* and *Sleep My Love* (1948) brought in psychoanalysts as technical advisors and advertised that fact.[13]

The popularization of Freudian psychoanalysis—its social representation—tends to magnify its sexual or erotic aspects. Sexuality as Freud understood it is resisted, but the popular notion of sexuality comes to characterize, in a kind of shorthand version, the entire project of psychoanalysis. To this kind of logic corresponds the belief that, because psychoanalysis deals with perversions, it is a perverse science. The science is contaminated by the object of its investigation. Quite often this leads to a literalization of the concept of transference and a displacement of sexuality to the relationship which is established between patient and psychoanalyst. In these cases, love is often represented as the final guarantor of a cure.

The popularized version therefore rejects what Freud theorized as a polymorphously perverse sexuality which is only gradually channeled in socially acceptable ways. Instead, it uses psychoanalysis to validate socially constructed modes of sexual difference which are already in place—although potentially threatened by a wartime reorganization. Hence, it is not surprising that women far outnumber men as patients in these films (in a film like *Spellbound*, where precisely the opposite may appear to be the case since Ingrid Bergman is a psychoanalyst and Gregory Peck her patient, it can in fact be demonstrated that she is ultimately constituted as analysand—she suffers from a frigidity constantly associated with intellectual women in the cinema). When psychoanalysis *is* activated in relation to a male patient diagnosed as suffering from some form of neurosis or psychosis, the effects of the pathological conditions are often held in check, restricted and localized by linking the illness directly to a war trauma (e.g., in *Home of the Brave* and the documentary *Let There Be Light*). What is diagnosed in the women patients is generally some form of sexual dysfunction or resistance to their own femininity. In *Now, Voyager* Bette Davis suffers primarily from a sexual repression which is traceable to her mother. She is cured through a love affair. In *The Snake Pit*, Olivia de Havilland persists in claiming that she is married but has no husband. Her symptom is the erasure of the male figure but not of the social situation entailed. Psychoanalysis discovers that a deficient relation to her father when she was a child has resulted in a pathological inability to recognize or relate to her husband. Closure of the narrative and cure are simultaneously established by her acceptance of his wedding ring. The psychoanalyst in *Lady in the Dark* tells Ginger Rogers that she is afraid of competing with other women and ultimately prescribes "some man who will dominate you." Psychoanalysis is used very explicitly to reinforce a status quo of sexual difference.

This reinforcement is mapped onto the very form of the narrative. The cinematic version of psychoanalysis acts as a tropological system entailing the construction of a specific kind of cognition (it allows a particular type of knowledge about character, plot, and causal relations between events). Psychoanalysis and classical narrative are perceived as compatible in many ways. As Marc Vernet points out in an article on psychoanalysis in the Hollywood cinema, the films rely heavily on the "cure" as Freud practiced it between 1880 and 1895, in other words, the cathartic method or the "talking cure."[14] But, in the American cinema, the "talking cure" is translated into the terms of vision. The flashback structure is the means by which the character is depicted as apprehending his or her past (this is the case in *Lady in the Dark*, *The Snake Pit*, and *Love Letters* [1945]). In this mise-en-scène of memory, a matching between self and scene is accomplished and that matching generally marks the completion of the narrative. It is not the speech between psychoanalyst and patient which acts as the medium of recovery. Rather, through *seeing* her past (and presumably reliving it more intensely than one could through the mediation of language), the patient understands herself, and her own behavior is given an explanation. It is thus a certain immediacy of vision which the psychoanalytic film narrative promotes.

The psychoanalysis which the Hollywood cinema takes as its model is easily conformable with the structure of classical narrative. It provides an enigma (What is wrong with the character? What event caused him or her to be like this?), a justification for the classical device of repetition (the compulsion to reenact the trauma, the recurrence of symptoms), and a final solution (the cure, the recovery through memory of the early scene).[15] In this scenario, a strictly linear determinism is accorded to the childhood event, and the practice of the psychoanalyst, in his attempt to discover that event, is not unlike that of the detective. Psychoanalysis also provides the Hollywood film with a set of symbols and themes and an economy which governs their deployment in the narrative. The symptom—an element which is given at the beginning of the film and continually repeated—receives its final meaning only at the end of the film, when the childhood event is clarified. Psychoanalysis is thus the source of an entirely new thematic language which is nevertheless chained to the service of a classical dialectic of delay (the thematic element is unintegrated) and recuperation (the element finally finds its place as a factor which illuminates both character and plot).

While most of these films situate the psychoanalyst as a kind of epistemological hero, as the guarantor of the final emergence of truth, Hollywood is also cognizant of the potential excesses of psychoanalysis and its methods, of the other side of a science which purports to manipulate the mind. Thus the doctor in *Shock* (1946), when he discovers that the heroine has witnessed his murder of his wife, hides her away in his private asylum and attempts to force her to forget the murder by administering drugs and hypnosis. When this strategy fails he tries, at the urging of his nurse/lover/accomplice, to kill her by means of the abuse of the treatment. Similarly, the husband in *Sleep My Love* (1948) uses hypnosis and drugs in his endeavor to stimulate his wife to commit murder and suicide. The representation of the woman clearly does not benefit from this reversal of valence in relation to psychoanalysis. Her proclivity for the role of victim is simply foregrounded and intensified. In *Nightmare Alley* (1947), on the other hand, where the psychoanalyst is a woman, she out-cons a conman, a carnival spiritualist who is overly ambitious. At first collaborating with him by revealing the confidences of her patients (which she has recorded on disks—a practice which a character in *Whirlpool* refers to as "wiretapping the subconscious"), she later cons him out of the money made by this means through a demonstration of her ability to diagnose him convincingly as a psychotic with hallucinations. Psychoanalysis becomes a successful competitor with the show business aspect of spiritualism, appropriating its strategies and revealing itself as merely another "racket." Yet, *The Cat People* is by far one of the most intriguing of this group of films which investigate the unscrupulous or suspect dimension of psychoanalysis, for it elaborates and plays on two of the most important premises of the films of the medical discourse: the specification of the doctor or of the psychoanalyst as the pivotal figure linking the visible and the invisible in the construction of knowledge (about the woman), and the constitution of the female body as symptomatic and hence the vehicle of hysteria.

*The Cat People*, focusing on a woman's problem—what might even be termed a woman's domestic problem since it concerns the happiness of her marriage—is exemplary of the extent to which the horror film acts as intertext of the woman's film (although this phenomenon is, in general, more widespread among the "paranoid gothic" films discussed in chapter 5). Irena (Simone Simon) is obsessed with a legend concerning the Serbian village of her origin. This legend maintains that sexuality and/or jealousy causes the women of the village to be transformed into great cats, panthers, who take the men as their prey. According to the legend, a King John liberated the village by killing many of the cat people (Irena keeps a statue of King John on a horse, his sword raised high, impaling a cat). In America, Irena meets Oliver Reed (Kent Smith) who describes himself as a "good old Americano" and who attempts to dispel Irena's belief in the Serbian legend. Oliver falls in love with Irena and marries her; however, because Irena fears what the legend delineates as the effects of sexuality, their relationship remains platonic. Kind and understanding at first, Oliver gradually becomes tense and dissatisfied and urges Irena to see a psychoanalyst, Dr. Louis Judd. When Irena refuses to return to the psychoanalyst because he is interested in her "mind" rather than her "soul," Oliver begins to get more and more interested in the "girl at the office," Alice, who is contrasted with Irena in every way. While Alice defines love as "understanding" and "you and me," Oliver describes his feeling for Irena as an obsessive need to watch and touch her because "there's a warmth when she's in the room;" despite the fact that he admits he does not know her at all. Irena's jealousy of Alice triggers several events which convince both Alice and Oliver that Irena can and does metamorphose into a panther. The psychoanalyst, however, a supreme rationalist, resists this hypothesis and is killed by the panther Irena becomes after he attempts to kiss her. Before dying, the psychoanalyst manages to fatally stab Irena with his cane/ knife, and she dies after letting the panther at a nearby zoo loose.

*The Cat People* is, on the one hand, the dramatization of a quasi-psychoanalytic scenario—the surfacing of the invisible, chaotic forces of instinct or the unconscious.[16] On the other hand, the film demonstrates the limits of psychoanalysis and rationality in general when faced with femininity. Forcing an equation whereby the unconscious = female sexuality = the irrational, the film can claim that the impotence of psychoanalysis stems from the unfathomable nature of its object of study—the woman and her sexuality. The psychoanalyst's insistence on rationalizing entails that he cannot see the "invisible" of the woman precisely because it is coincident with the irrational and hence outside the range of his professional vision. In moving from an opening text constituted by a quote from the scientist, Dr. Louis Judd, to an ending epitaph from a poem by John Donne, the film sustains a strict opposition between science and poetry, the rational and the irrational. This opposition is mapped onto what in 1942 was necessarily another heavily loaded opposition—that between the native and the foreign, the "good old Americano" and the Serbian, the familiar (Alice) and the strange (Irena). *The Cat People* transforms the unconscious or the instinctual not only into an object which is, by definition, outside the grasp of psychoanalysis, but also into an object which incites its murderous impulses—it is ultimately the psychoanalyst's phallic cane/knife which kills Irena. Yet, her death demands that of the psychoanalyst; her death entails the death of a science which purports to include what should remain excluded: female sexuality and all that is beyond conscious reason.

Thus, the psychoanalyst, rather than acting as a link between rationality and irrationality, between visibility and invisibility, becomes the figure of their absolute disjunction. This problematic has the effect of safeguarding visibility, rationality, and the native/familiar from what is absolutely other. The film would like very much to believe that the symptom does not inhabit the norm, that visibility and invisibility, correlated with rationality and irrationality, occupy two entirely different spaces. Yet, the mise-en-scène belies the possibility of such a desire, and hence the film operates on the epistemological threshold of the classical text's organization of the seen and the unseen and the dialectic which insures simultaneously their interaction and their separation. It dwells on the mixture, the composite, the effect of a transgression of barriers.

Although the image is indubitably the register of truth in the classical cinema, the place where knowledge resides,[17] there is also a kind of truth which is invisible, which cannot be imaged. The supernatural is one instance. The truth of a person is another. *The Cat People* conflates the two in the character of Irena.

In the horror film in general, what is unseen may appear to have a greater degree of truth value than the seen. This is why the horror film emphasizes the edge of the frame as a border and exploits the phobia attached to the truth of the unseen. But this fetishization of the frame line as border guarantees that the invisible remains an external entity, excluded from a discourse which ultimately privileges the evidence of the eyes (once it is visible, the monster of the horror film can be fought and subdued). The very technology of the cinema automatically protects the realm of visibility against otherness. Yet, *The Cat People* unwittingly elaborates a formal textual logic which, paradoxically, interiorizes the frame line, constituting the division between visibility and invisibility not as a limit but as an alien internal entity. Such a strategy accomplishes what Samuel Weber claims is characteristic of the mechanism of repression—it establishes "a relation to exteriority at the core of all that is enclosed."[18]

*The Cat People* does so by consistently elaborating a discourse on barriers, a discourse on the same and the other. Such, for instance, is the significance of the scene which dwells on the chain separating Irena from the panther in the cage at the zoo. Irena, pacing back and forth in front of the chain which in a way imprisons her, is the mirror image of the panther pacing in its cage. But the film has no difficulty in visualizing either Irena or the panther. What it cannot incorporate within the terms of its image system is the transposition of one into the other. Thus, what is invisible is, logically enough, represented by sound and its absence in a well-constructed scene in which Irena, suspicious of the relation between Oliver and Alice, follows Alice at night. For, sound in the cinema—voice, music, and sound effects—generally bears a heavy load in the signification of that which is invisible, that which is just beyond the edge of the frame. But in this scene, it is the absence of sound which signifies what is not shown, what cannot be contained within the limits of the visible. As Alice walks home at night after meeting Oliver, the sound of high heels against pavement, in quick steps, echoes the sound of her own more measured footsteps. Alice traverses a frame, Irena follows. Shots of Alice's legs walking are intercut with shots of Irena's legs. The rigid parallelism breaks down, however, when Alice once again traverses a frame which is subsequently left empty at the same time that the sound of Irena's footsteps disappears. When the sound ceases, Alice becomes more and more nervous until the shriek of a bus arriving substitutes for the growl of the panther Alice knows is nearby. After Alice is safe on the bus, there is a cut to a shot of the panther and leopard in their cages at the zoo and the sound of sheep bleating on the soundtrack. Following this is a sequence of shots detailing the discovery of some dead sheep nearby. The camera, tracking independently of the gaze of any character in the film, reveals in the muddy ground the gradual metamorphosis of paw tracks into the imprints of high heels, the mark of femininity, ending with a shot of Irena, wiping her mouth with a handkerchief. On the soundtrack, the progression is a reversal of the earlier part of the scene, moving from silence to the sound of high heels.

The opposition high heels/paws is established early in the scene as equivalent to the opposition sound/silence. What is most interesting here, perhaps, is that it is the very absence of a signifier which signifies an absence (in this case, the transformation woman-into-cat which remains invisible, incapable of being contained in the image). The film nevertheless strives to image the transgression of what should be the most solid barrier of all—that separating human and animal. It strives to include as interior to the image what its own problematic has located as exteriority. A distinction which is carried by the soundtrack—an indication that the entity it denotes inhabits the realm of invisibility—is translated into the terms of vision, brought within the image as traces, the visible tracks of the transformation and hence the crossing of a barrier. In the process, the film expounds the logic of the trace, a logic which undermines the cinema's reliance on visibility as a standard of truth. For while the track/trace acts as a kind of evidence ("you can believe your eyes"), it is also potentially deceptive, unreliable, because through the introduction of a temporal delay, it disrupts the notions of presence and immediacy which are usually attached to vision. In The Cat People the camera, framing the tracks which give witness to the transformation, cannot quite "catch up" with Irena until the metamorphosis is complete—she/it is always just outside the edge of the frame. The trace, as Derrida points out, is the "erasure of a presence,"[19] and what the scene ultimately demonstrates is that only through a temporal disphasure, an absence within, can the visible become significant—that is, signifying. The logic of the trace is, in fact, the logic of the photographic image itself which is doomed to "capture" a "having-been-there." Visibility contains its own negation.

Thus, what is most true for the film is never directly imaged—the compatibility and substitutability of feline and female. The narrative is a literalization of the idea that the female body is symptomatic and hence the vehicle of hysteria. The mechanism which Freud pinpointed as characteristic of hysteria—conversion, "the translation of a purely psychical excitation into physical terms"[20]—is hyperbolized when the return of repressed sexuality demands the transformation of the woman's entire body into the symptom. The film depicts an extreme instance of "somatic compliance." And the choice of symptom is not innocent. In his article, "On Narcissism: An Introduction," Freud compares the self-sufficiency and inaccessibility of the narcissistic woman to that of "cats and the large beasts of prey" (as well as that of the child, the criminal, and the humorist). The cat is the signifier of a female sexuality which is self-enclosed, self-sufficient, and, above all, object-less. This sexuality, in its inaccessibility, forecloses the possibility of knowledge, thus generating a string of metaphors—cat, criminal, child, humorist. The Cat People designates female sexuality as that excess which escapes psychoanalysis; it is that which inhabits the realm of the unknowable. On the one hand, this is a well-worn figure (particularly in another genre of the period, film noir). On the other hand, not only does female sexuality escape the objectification of the medical discourse but, by means of psychoanalysis's own formulation—conversion hysteria—this femininity returns to kill the representative of psychoanalytic authority. The female body is entirely subsumed by the symptom. As the zoo-keeper points out, quoting the Bible, the panther is the figure of a failed mimesis: "Like unto a leopard but not a leopard." For the biblical text the panther is unnameable. Similarly, the film demonstrates that the woman, in becoming most like herself, that is, the embodiment of female sexuality, must become *other*. What we are left with is the asexual Alice, perfect and unthreatening mate for the "good old Americano."

Because the implementation of psychoanalysis in the cinema is forcefully linked to a process of revelation, to an exposure of the answer to the text's hermeneutic question, it is inseparable from issues of narration and the woman's access to language and vision—issues which are intensified within the context of the woman's film's attempt to foreground female subjectivity. The tendency in these films to organize narrative as a memory which is retrieved is evocative of Freud and Breuer's famous claim, *"Hysterics suffer mainly from reminiscences."*[21] For these films do, for the most part, contain stories of suffering and hence entail a certain violence in the forcing of narration. The study of hysteria and the films of the medical discourse are quite close in their revelation of a curious and dynamic interaction between the narrativization of the female patient and her inducement to narrate, to become a storyteller as a part of her cure. Breuer represents his relation to Fräulein Anna O. as that of listener, but it is clear that her stories are not always spontaneous.

> I used to visit her in the evening, when I knew I should find her in her hypnosis, and I then relieved her of the whole stock of imaginative products which she had accumulated since my last visit. It was essential that this should be effected completely if good results were to follow. When this was done she became perfectly calm, and next day she would be agreeable, easy to manage, industrious and even cheerful; but on the second day she would be increasingly moody, contrary and unpleasant, and this would become still more marked on the third day. When she was like this it was not always easy to get her to talk, even in her hypnosis. She aptly described this procedure, speaking seriously, as a 'talking cure,' while she referred to it jokingly as 'chimney-sweeping.' She knew that after she had given utterance to her hallucinations she would lose all her obstinacy and what she described as her 'energy'; and when, after some comparatively long interval, she was in a bad temper, she would refuse to talk, and I was obliged to overcome her unwillingness by urging and pleading and using devices such as repeating a formula with which she was in the habit of introducing her stories.[22]

Later in the analysis, when Breuer was forced to separate from his patient for several weeks, he claims that "the situation only became tolerable after I had arranged for the patient to be brought back to Vienna for a week and evening after evening made her tell me three to five stories." Without Breuer, "her imaginative and poetic vein was drying up."[23]

The woman's assumption of the position of narrator is thus constituted as therapeutic, an essential component of her cure. Furthermore, there is a compulsiveness attached to this requirement—the woman must channel all of her energy into narrativity and thus exhaust the other more aggressive or "unpleasant" tendencies she might possess. However, *Studies on Hysteria* also demonstrates, very curiously, that the woman's imagination, her storytelling capability, is not only therapeutic but disease-producing as well. For it is daydreaming which instigates the illness in the first place—an uncontrolled and addressee-less daydreaming. Freud and Breuer, referring to the hypnoid states which are associated with hysteria, claim, "they often, it would seem, grow out of the day-dreams which are so common even in healthy people and to which needlework and similar occupations render women especially prone."[24] The pathological aspect of the female relation to creativity, daydreaming, and mental productions in general is also underlined by Breuer in his introduction of Anna O. to the reader. After citing the "extremely monotonous existence in her puritanically minded family," he maintains that "she embellished her life in a manner which probably influenced her decisively in the direction of her illness, by indulging in systematic day-dreaming, which she described as her 'private theater.' "[25]

The distinction between the two types of narrativity—an excessive narrativity as one of the causes of illness and a constant incitement to narrate as a therapeutic strategy—might appear at first to rest on another distinction between two different species of narrative: story as fantasy or imagination unleashed and story as history, as an accurate reflection of past events. The opposition would thus be one between fantasy and mimesis, where mimesis would be endowed with curative powers. While this explanation might prove attractive since the dangers imputed to daydreaming reside in the fact that it is totally unanchored, unrestrained and independent of referent or reference, we know that the necessity for historical truth in fantasy was never established for Freud. *Psychical* truth was most important, and in this respect it was virtually impossible for the subject to lie, for the narrative to become *too* fantastic. Rather, the distinction between the two types of narrativity has more to do with the structuring effect of the presence or absence of a narratee—the doctor. The daydream is produced by the woman for herself. It is thus not only prone to excess and nonutility—an unnecessary by-product of "needlework and similar occupations"—but it feeds that narcissistic self-sufficiency to which women are always prey. The woman's narrative acumen is thus transformed into the symptom of illness. Her narrative cannot stand on its own—it must be interpreted. Narration by the woman is therefore therapeutic only when constrained and regulated by the purposeful ear of the listening doctor. By embedding her words within a case history, psychoanalysis can control the woman's access to language and the agency of narration. In Breuer's account the woman, "narrated-out," loses her energy, becomes pliable and subdued. The logic seems to be this: if the woman must assume the agency of speech, of narration, let her do so within the well-regulated context of an institutionalized dialogue (psychoanalysis, the hospital, the court of law). Psychoanalysis and the cinema alike present the woman with a very carefully constructed relation to enunciation.

This is why, in the films, the woman's narration is so often framed within an encompassing discourse. *The Locket* (1946), constructed as flashback within flashback—only the central one the property of the woman who is the subject of all the stories—is an extreme instance of this. And if the woman hesitates, in the manner of Anna O., she is compelled to tell, to produce an account of herself. In *Possessed*, Louise's (Joan Crawford's) illness is indicated immediately by her fixed stare and the fact that she can only repeat compulsively one word—the name of the man with whom she is in love. This situation causes certain difficulties of narration since she is the only one in the hospital room who knows and can therefore tell her own story. The dilemma receives a rather remarkable narrative solution which is, in a sense, exemplary for the woman's film. The mute Joan Crawford is given an injection by the doctor which induces cinematic narrative.[26] The thrill of her story, the pleasure of the cinema is encapsulated in the doctor's words, "Every time I see the reaction to this treatment I get the same thrill I did the first time." The woman's narrative, as a repetition of that first time, is nevertheless held in check by recurrent withdrawals from her flashback account to the present tense of the doctor's diagnosis. For instance, the first part of her story illustrates, according to one of the doctors, "the beginning of a persecution complex" indicated by the fact that there is "no attempt to evaluate the situation, to see the man's viewpoint." Within the encompassing masculine medical discourse, the woman's language is granted a limited validity—it is, precisely, a point of view, and often a distorted and unbalanced one. The quasi-magical, and at the same time scientific, ability of medicine to discover the truth is evidenced by the popularity of the notion of the truth serum in these films. In *Shock* (1946), a female victim of amnesia is also given an injection so that the doctor can discover what she knows, what she has seen (here the speech-inducing agent is scopolamine, in *Possessed* it is "narcosynthesis").

The woman's narrative reticence thus necessitates supplementary props—e.g., the injection—to elicit her story. Another such prop of narrativity is the apparatus of the courtroom. Although not confined, by any means, to the woman's film, the court and the law it embodies here collude with medicine to exert a narrational pressure on the woman—the underlying assumption being that female illness is synonymous with a form of criminality. This is most explicit in *A Woman's Face*, which is structured as a chronologically ordered series of flashbacks corresponding to the testimony of various witnesses called to the stand in a courtroom. The courtroom acts both as originary space of the unfolding of narrative and in the reconstruction of the scene of the crime. The camera at the beginning of the film transforms Anna's (Joan Crawford's) face into the enigma, the site of knowledge. Anna finally reveals, in the space of the courtroom and in response to a direct question from the judge, that the doctor was able to "correct" her face, to remove the scar. A second issue of utmost concern in the legalistic proceedings of the trial is whether or not the doctor who operated on Anna actually fell in love with her. The hermeneutic questions of the narrative are conflated with the legal inquiries of the courtroom. And the truth which ultimately emerges is Anna's desire to be an "ordinary" woman: "I want to get married. I want to have a house and children. I want to go to the market and cheat the grocer. I want to join the human race." Any vestigial criminal tendencies are domesticated.

Both *Beyond the Forest* and *Johnny Belinda* (1948) also structure their narratives in such a way that the courtroom provides a space and a mechanism for narration/revelation. But in both instances, the court or the law on its own is deficient in relation to knowledge. In *Beyond the Forest* the court exonerates Rosa Moline for a crime (murder) she actually committed. In *Johnny Belinda* the court requires the testimony of a doctor, an expert on nature and the maternal instinct, in order to rationalize its ruling that Belinda is innocent of murder on the basis of the natural instinct of a mother to protect her child. The authority of the doctor is, once again, based on his ability to see through the evidence of the surface—a skill which the Law and its representatives lack. Unlike the films noirs of this period, and with the exception of *The Cat People*, the films of the medical discourse generally do not situate their female protagonists as mysterious, unknowable, enigmatic. The site of potential knowledge about the woman is transferred from the Law to Medicine. This displacement is narrativized in *The Dark Mirror*, where the agent of the Law, the police detective, must appeal to a psychiatrist for a solution to the crime committed by one of two identical twins. Unable to differentiate between the two on the basis of vision, the detective must call in an expert reader of interiority. And when the doctor falls in love with one of the twins, the discourse of desire merges imperceptibly with the discourse of psychiatry: "The more I know about you, the more I want to know; I want to know everything about you."

A medical discourse thus allows this group of films to bracket the speech of the woman and her access to language—and in some instances to negate it entirely. The attribution of muteness to the woman is by no means rare in these films. In *Shock, Possessed*, and *The Spiral Staircase* (1946), the female character loses the power of speech as the result of a psychical trauma, while in *Johnny Belinda* she is deaf/mute from birth. But in all cases language is the gift of the male character—a somewhat violent "gift" in the case of *Shock* and *Possessed*, where the woman is induced to talk through an injection, and more benign, paternalistic in *Johnny Belinda*, where the doctor provides Belinda with sign language. In *Johnny Belinda* the fact that a regulated and controlled language with the potency guaranteed by inscription is the property of men is underlined by a proliferation of books and an emphasis on the book as embodying an accounting and hence a type of law. Belinda's father possesses a book whose marks indicate the work Belinda has to do; the shopkeeper Paquet keeps a detailed record in his book of debits and credits; and the doctor owns the book of sign language which gives Belinda access to words. Women, according to the logic of the film, have two basic types of relation to language: the silence of Belinda or the idle gossip of the older women of the town. Yet, Belinda's inability to tell her own story, to narrate, is predicated on much more than simply her inability to speak. The doctor and her father cultivate in her an innocence which is synonymous with a lack of knowledge about sexuality and its consequences. Belinda cannot produce her own narrative because she cannot link cause to effect, the rape to which she is subjected to the baby which is its result. She is totally ignorant of the logic which underlies her story—its narrative mechanism. Therefore, when she kills the man who raped her, it has nothing to do with narrative justice, but with maternal instinct.

The phenomenon of the mute woman is, however, only an extreme instance of a more generalized strategy whereby the films simultaneously grant the woman access to narration and withhold it from her. The woman's narrative reticence, her amnesia, silence, or muteness—all act as justifications for the framing of her discourse within a masculine narration. Thus, Louise's flashback narration in *Possessed* is situated by the doctors/listeners as the discourse of a madwoman. What is really at issue with respect to specifically filmic narration is not control of language but control of the image. For there is a sense in which vision becomes the signifier of speech in the cinema. Within the context of a psychoanalytic dramatization in particular, the flashback structure acts as the metaphor of speech in the doctor/patient relation. The flashback is the most explicit and frequent signifier of the process of narration in a cinema which is, in general, assumed to be narrator-less in its capture and reproduction of unfolding events. The great instability of the flashback as a signifier of narration, however, is that beyond the point of its introduction, the flashback effectively erases the subject of the enunciation in the same manner as the rest of the classical text, its organization partaking of the same material of representation. The very term "flashback" implies the immediacy of the past in the present. Flashback narration should, therefore, and often does assume the same reality effect, the same impartiality, as the framing filmic discourse.

But when the woman's illness or madness rationalizes the limited attribution of narrational authority to her, the flashback structure can easily become destabilized, uncertain, especially if her delirium is allowed to infiltrate and contaminate the image. This is the case in *Possessed*, which at a certain moment departs radically from the logic of the classical text. In the middle of Louise's flashback account, she describes a scene in which she, Carol (her stepdaughter by her marriage to a former employer), and David (the man with whom Louise is still in love) are spectators at a public concert. Carol is beginning to feel attracted to David, and for Louise this is an unbearable sight. When the pianist begins to play a song with historical reverberations for the relation between David and Louise, Louise claims she has a headache and leaves. The aural component of the following scene is highly subjectivized through an amplification of the soundtrack. As Louise sits in her bedroom and broods, various sounds— the ticking of a clock, her own heartbeat, the dripping of water on the windowsill—are magnified. Next to this obvious distortion of the level of the real, the sequence which follows can only be read as diegetic since it bears no such clearly hyperbolized signs of subjectivity. Louise closes the window just as David and Carol drive up. She then goes into the hall and hides behind a pillar, overhearing Carol say to David, "We fooled her, didn't we?" as the two kiss at the door. When Carol comes upstairs, Louise pulls her into her room and warns her about David. Carol accuses Louise not only of still being in love with him but of having killed her mother as well. Claiming that she is on her way to tell her father this story, Carol walks toward the stairs. Louise, terrified, hits Carol, and she falls down the stairs, lying still at the bottom. Suddenly her body disappears and Louise, standing behind the pillar once again, hears the door close and Carol saying goodnight to David. The scene in which Louise apparently kills her stepdaughter is situated only retrospectively and traumatically as a subjectivized scenario—the image, in effect, lies. The sequence is in no way demarcated initially as a hallucination.

*Possessed* is structured as Louise's flashback account of her life, told to two doctors and prompted by an injection. The audience of the film is thus represented within the text, the doctors taking on the role of audience surrogates or narratees. The spectator's eye becomes that of a doctor, and the spectator is given, by proxy, a medical or therapeutic role. Although the narrative is presented as subjective, the spectator always knows more than the female character, is always an accomplice of the diagnosis. The scene on the stairway just described, however, is an important exception to this rule of the narrative. The revelation after the fact that the scene is hallucinatory is jolting, for it implicates the image in a deviation from the truth. The viewer of the film is drawn into

Louise's illness, into her hallucination. The spectator is therefore no longer diagnosing but a part of what is diagnosed, forced into sharing her illness. In this way the filmic trajectory, at least momentarily, collapses the opposition between clarity and blurring of vision. An image which purportedly carries a generalizable truth and a guarantee of knowledge is undermined by the revelation that it is the possession not only of a single character but of a madwoman. As Foucault points out, in the classical paradigm "madness will begin only in the act which gives the value of truth to the image," and madness is "inside the image, confiscated by it, and incapable of escaping from it."[27] In a limited moment *Possessed* unveils, through the representation of a distorted female subjectivity, that collective and naturalized madness—the investment in an image—which supports the cinema as an institution.

It is as though these films were structured in a way which demanded a testing of the limits of filmic narrative's credibility. *The Locket*, which also situates its female protagonist as, in the end, mad, is also strongly characterized by disturbances in narrativity. The textual vertigo of *The Locket* is in part the consequence of embedding flashback within flashback with the Ur-story, that of the female protagonist, bracketed twice, by the narratives of two different male characters. On his wedding day, the future husband of Nancy (Laraine Day) is called apart from the festivities by a stranger, Dr. Blair (Brian Aherne) who insists on enlightening him about the true nature of his future wife. Dr. Blair, a psychoanalyst, claims that he was once married happily to Nancy and his flashback account details their meeting, marriage, and move to New York where he sets up a practice. However, within this flashback account, an aspiring artist, Norman Clyde (Robert Mitchum) visits the office of Dr. Blair and provides another flashback account in which he (Norman) is engaged to marry Nancy. He discovers that Nancy has an extremely strong desire to steal jewelry, and when Norman confronts her with the evidence she, in her turn, gives him a flashback account of a childhood incident in which she was wrongly accused, by her mother's employer, of stealing a valuable locket.

The textual vertigo of *The Locket* is not only a consequence of this structuration as a series of flashbacks but of the consistent interrogation of the authority of the male narrators as well, and the text's indecision as to whether the woman is mad or maddening. For Nancy is a *tabula rasa* and it appears that the men inscribe on her whatever they wish of their fantasies and desires. She is an incitement to wild narration, and each of the men recognizes this in the others but not in himself (thus Dr. Blair wants very badly to "psychoanalyze" Norman but restrains himself and merely listens). But the authority or credibility of these narratives is severely undermined by the fact that each of these men is driven mad, becoming neurotic or psychotic. Norman, after failing to convince Dr. Blair of the truth of his story about Nancy's relation to a murder and after leaving with the doctor as "fee" his portrait of Nancy as Cassandra, jumps out the window of the doctor's skyscraper office. Dr. Blair in turn relates to Nancy's bridegroom in the present a story in which he also suffers a nervous breakdown after discovering a cache of jewels Nancy had apparently stolen in the burned-out rubble of their bombed London apartment building. Nancy's bridegroom, John, however, refuses to believe these "fantastic" stories, and the narratives are only verified through a repetition of the events belonging to the flashback account attributed to Nancy at the core of the film. In the same room where Nancy was accused of stealing the locket as a child, John's mother (who turns out to be Nancy's mother's former employer—the one who initially accused Nancy) *gives* to her as a wedding present the same locket she had once been denied. During her walk to the altar, Nancy is assaulted by voices—her mother's, Norman's, Dr. Blair's—derived from the various narratives and ultimately, unable to stand the psychical torment, she has a mental breakdown, fully exhibiting the psychosis which the film now claims was hers all along. What is most interesting here is that it is the hallucinatory voices heard by a madwoman which act as a verification of the narratives told by the men. The film is structured so that her madness confirms their sanity.

The male narrators are therefore only apparently or temporarily mentally unbalanced while the woman is essentially mad. *The Locket* proves the truth of the portrait of Nancy as a Cassandra without eyes. In a way, the logic of the narrative is exactly the reverse of the scene in *Possessed* discussed earlier. For what is shocking in *The Locket*, after the embedding of flashback within flashback foregrounds the process of narration as a construction, is that the image is true, and is only apparently the support of a distorted male subjectivity. This is manifested most explicitly, toward the end of Dr. Blair's flashback account, when an extreme close-up of Nancy dissolves into the portrait of a blind Cassandra. The woman = Cassandra = the image which is endowed with the gift of knowledge but fated not to be believed. And this Cassandra herself is blind, lacking in subjectivity. Because she *is* the image of doom she cannot see it. *The Locket* offers a textual demonstration of the obsessive idea that a woman's madness is contagious and threatens to disrupt the very processes of narrativity.

The woman's problematic relation to the image thus accompanies a delineation of her failure or lack with respect to language (her muteness, amnesia, etc.) in the films of the medical discourse. And in many ways her disturbance or putting into crisis of the relation between the image and truth is potentially much more dangerous, given the epistemological framework of the classical text. The woman's deficient relation to the image disrupts filmic signification to such an extent that it is easier and safer to displace the representation of this deficient relation to the level of narrative content rather than the organization of narration. Hence the films often attribute to their female characters aberrations in seeing. As the field of the masculine medical gaze is expanded, the woman's vision is reduced. Although in the beginning of *Possessed*, extreme and extended point-of-view shots are attributed to Joan Crawford as she is wheeled into the hospital, she is contradictorily *represented* as having an empty gaze, seeing nothing, blinded by the huge lamps aimed at her by the doctors. In *Shock*, the woman is made ill by an image. Like Jimmy Stewart in *Rear Window*, the female protagonist in *Shock* looks out the window when she should not, and sees what she should not have seen—a husband murdering his wife. But unlike *Rear Window*, the woman goes into shock as a result of this sight, of this image which suggests itself as a microcosm of the cinema/spectator relation. The murderer turns out to be a psychiatrist who is called in to treat the catatonic woman suffering from what she has seen. All his efforts are directed toward making her forget the image and maintaining her in a state in which she is unable to articulate her story.

In *Dark Victory*, difficulties in vision and ultimately blindness are not the disease itself but major—and extremely significant—symptoms of a brain tumor. Judith Traherne's (Bette Davis's) visit to a brain specialist is prompted by a riding accident in which Judith misdirects the horse upon seeing three images of a fence. The scene in which the brain specialist, Dr. Steele (George Brent), examines Judith is exemplary of the way in which the force of the medical gaze ultimately renders the woman's speech meaningless. Because Judith does not like to talk about her health, Dr. Steele must utilize all his skill in observation in order to diagnose her, *despite herself*. When Judith denies that she has visual difficulties or that light bothers her, the doctor raises the blinds and watches her reaction. Or he watches her unsuccessfully attempt to light her own cigarette. He also demonstrates that her sense of touch is deficient (in contrast to his own— the doctor's expertise = his glance = his "touch," according to Foucault). With her eyes closed Judith misinterprets rough cloth as silk. The interchangeability of the psychical and the somatic in these films is manifested by the repetition of this same touch test in *Possessed*—this time acting as evidence of neurasthenia.

But in the course of Judith Traherne's examination in *Dark Victory* she attempts to resist the doctor's diagnosis, claiming, "I'm well. I'm young and strong and nothing can touch me. Neither you nor Dr. Parsons can turn me into an invalid." The course of the narrative subsequently demonstrates that the woman's resistance is only a moment in the trajectory of her illness. Similarly, when Dr. Steele shines a light into Judith's eyes, she looks back, stating, "I've been told they're a nice color." The attempt to look back in this context, to counter the medical gaze, is a type of transgressive seduction for which Judith is ultimately punished—with blindness. The first sign of Judith's impending death from her brain tumor, toward the end of the film, is a dimming of her sight, then blindness. But because her doctor-turned-husband is planning to attend a conference to present his medical discoveries—a conference which meets only twice a year—she must pretend to be able to see so that he will not remain with her and retard medical science by six months. Judith's heroism, then, is delineated as her ability to mime sight, to represent herself as the subject of vision.

In *Shock*, the female protagonist is dazzled by an image; in *Dark Victory*, she points out, to her doctor-husband, a shining brightness which is only a signifier of her blindness; and in *Possessed* the woman, totally confused, is dispossessed of a focused gaze. The films of the medical discourse activate the classical paradigm wherein, as Foucault points out, madness is understood as dazzlement, an aberration of seeing: ". . . delirium and dazzlement are in a relation which constitutes the essence of madness, exactly as truth and light, in their fundamental relation, constitute classical reason."[28] To be dazzled is not to be blinded by darkness but by too much light—to possess too fully the means of seeing but to lack an object of sight. The doctor, on the other hand, as the figure of classical reason itself, always possesses not only a limited and hence controllable light, but an object to be illuminated—the woman. Over and over in these films, the scenario of a doctor training a light on a woman, illuminating her irrationality with his own reason, is repeated—in *Dark Victory*, *Lady in the Dark*, *The Cat People*, *Possessed*, *A Woman's Face*. In *The Snake Pit*, Dr. Kik demonstrates the mechanism of psychoanalysis to his female patient with a dark room and a light switch analogy: "If you know where the switch is, you don't even have to know how it works." Light is the figure of rationality in these films. But light also *enables* the look, the male gaze—it makes the woman specularizable. The doctor's light legitimates scopophilia and is the mechanism by means of which the films of the medical discourse insure the compatibility of rationality and desire.

For desire is not absent from the doctor/patient relation. On the contrary, that relation is eroticized in many of the films. In *Dark Victory*, *A Woman's Face*, *Dark Mirror*, and *Johnny Belinda*, a benevolent and paternalistic relation of doctor to patient is almost imperceptibly transformed into an amorous alliance. The romanticism attached to medicine as an intellectual adventure bleeds over onto the doctor/patient axis. The prophetic status of a doctor's offhand comment in the beginning of *Dark Victory* ("To go inside a human being's skull and tinker with the machinery that makes the whole works go—that *is* romance, isn't it?") is proven when Dr. Steele, shortly after performing brain surgery on Judith Traherne, falls in love with her. Yet, the association of disease and passion, illness and sexuality is clearly not specific to the films of the 1940s but constitutes a rhetorical configuration with its own history. One of the four phases of hysteria isolated by Charcot was labelled *attitudes passionnelles* and illustrated in *Iconographie Photographique de la Salpêtrière* by hysterical women assuming poses of ecstasy, appeal, and eroticism.[29] Frailty and chronic illness were, in the nineteenth century, perceived as signs of a superior sensitivity, and tuberculosis, in particular, was exploited well into the twentieth century through an immense connotative network which linked it to passion and hypersensitivity. As Susan Sontag points out,

> Fever in TB was a sign of an inward burning: the tubercular is someone "consumed" by ardor, that ardor leading to the dissolution of the body. The use of metaphors drawn from TB to describe love—the image of a "diseased" love, of a passion that "consumes"—long antedates the Romantic movement. Starting with the Romantics, the image was inverted, and TB was conceived as a variant of the disease of love. . . . As a character in *The Magic Mountain* explains: "Symptoms of disease are nothing but a disguised manifestation of the power of love; and all disease is only love transformed."[30]

To illness were attributed powers of transfiguration (as in the final shot of *Dark Victory*)—women, in particular, are never so beautiful as when they are dying—and "consumption was understood as a manner of appearing."[31]

Passion, however, is not limited to physical diseases, where a wasting away of the body acts as a measure of the grandeur of the soul. Passion is always potentially maddening, and its conceptualization, in fact, acts as the "basis of the possibility of madness."[32] As affect or emotion gone wild, passion always contains within it excess and a potential deviation from normalcy and constraint. In *Possessed*, Joan Crawford as Louise loves excessively and wildly, and the result is psychosis. In *Guest In The House*, Evelyn (Anne Baxter) suffers from an exorbitant, although strangely desexualized (she contrasts herself to "vulgar women" with their "dirty desires") passion which is exhibited by a transgressive diary writing and the repetitive playing of a record of Liszt's "Liebestraum." Passion and delirium go hand in hand, and at the end of the film, provoked by Aunt Martha who quite properly represses her own passion for her nephew, Evelyn's hallucinations of birds drive her over a cliff into the sea.

Nevertheless, these films on the whole tend to subdue excessive passion by institutionalizing it in a relation, first between doctor and patient and then between husband and wife. Rather than lending to the woman a heightened sensitivity and hence an elevated subjectivity, illness intensifies and rationalizes her status as an object of a medical discourse. Any passion is regularized and legitimized as the doctor's process of looking, his examination and pursuit of truth. What the language of medicine, and psychology in particular, give to the classical text is a new strategy of characterization, a means of linking knowledge and authority to character. As disease becomes more and more psychologized,[33] the role of the medical figure is intensified. As Foucault points out, the whole modern experience of madness is commanded by the notion of the medical personage, and "alienation becomes disalienating because, in the doctor, it becomes a subject."[34] The doctor is not merely the practitioner of an objective science—he acts as the condensation of the figures of Father, Judge, Family, and Law, and his "powers borrowed from science only their disguise, or at most their justification."[35] He is, in short (and this is certainly the case in the films), a wise man of unlimited capabilities. His function is of a moral and social order. In this relation between doctor and patient and the structure it assumes

> were symbolized the massive structures of bourgeois society and its values: Family-Child relations, centered on the theme of paternal authority; Transgression-Punishment relations, centered on the theme of immediate justice; Madness-Disorder relations, centered on the theme of social and moral order. It is from these that the physician derives his power to cure; and it is to the degree that the patient finds himself, by so many old links, already alienated in the doctor, within the doctor-patient couple, that the doctor has the almost miraculous power to cure him.[36]

As Foucault stresses, the doctor and the patient form a "couple" in complicity against disease and madness.

It was perhaps inevitable that this complicity should be mapped onto a heterosexual relation within a classical cinema which depends so heavily on the couple for its narrative configurations and its sense of closure. The language of medicine and the love story become interchangeable, as in *Dark Victory*—she: "I'm no longer in your care"; he: "You'll always be in my care." In both *A Woman's Face* and *Johnny Belinda* the doctor constructs his patient as a woman (in *A Woman's Face* through plastic surgery, in *Johnny Belinda* through dressing her up and domesticating her) and proceeds to fall in love with her.[37] Although the medical discourse is central to films like *Dark Victory*, *Johnny Belinda*, and *A Woman's Face*, it also informs and inflects the subgroup of "paranoid woman's films" discussed in chapter seven—films which depend rather heavily on the tableau of the sick woman in bed, effecting the transformation of a site of sexuality into a site of illness and pain. In *Dragonwyck*, *The Spiral Staircase*, and *Dark Waters* the heroic male figure, a locus of wisdom and safety as well as eventual romance, is a doctor.

Sexuality or the erotic relation is thus given scientific legitimation in the figure of the doctor who acts simultaneously as a moral and social guardian. A woman's illness may be defined in many ways by the classical text, but it is never simply illness. More often than not it is a magnification of an undesirable aspect of femininity or a repudiation of femininity altogether. If the disease is excessive, it invariably necessitates punishment—in the interests of a legible sexual differentiation. But there is also a sense in which the filmic delineation of a woman's illness is always punitive. For, as Sontag points out, "Nothing is more punitive than to give disease a meaning—that meaning being invariably a moralistic one."[38]

By disturbing the structure wherein the couple is medicalized, perverting its figures, *Beyond the Forest* unveils the punitive nature of illness in the classical text and in some ways acts as a negation of the medical discourse. The charitable humanitarianism of a doctor-husband is refused by a patient-wife whose sexuality and desires cannot be contained but, instead, act as a fever which ultimately consumes her. Rosa Moline (Bette Davis) rejects the benevolence of her doctor-husband, knocks the medicine out of his hand, and acts out her illness as an exaggerated narcissism. The film activates a classical city/country opposition in which Rosa's major desire—to take the train to Chicago and leave behind what she perceives as the boredom and claustrophobia of small-town life—is embodied in the soundtrack's insistent repetition of the song "Chicago, Chicago." Rosa puts on her best clothes and walks to the station every day simply to *watch* the train departing for Chicago, simultaneously becoming a spectacle herself for the gaze of the townspeople (a woman in the post office claims, "Even in high school she was different from everybody else"). Her fascination with the train is a fascination with its phallic power to transport her to "another place." When she finally gets to Chicago in the middle of the film, Rosa is repetitively insulted in an extremely violent scene in which she is rejected by her lover, evicted from a bar because she has no "escort," and taunted by a woman from a balcony as she walks through the rain. Despite the fact that Rosa is forced to take the train back to Loyalton, Wisconsin, her desire persists. It is a desire which reverses the trajectory of a film like *Dark Victory*. In that film, the terminally ill Bette Davis is morally uplifted and prepared for a "beautiful and fine" death by leaving behind the city and her frivolous high-society life in order to provide emotional support for her husband, who pursues his medical research in a rustic house in the country.

*Beyond the Forest* begins by distancing the spectator from its female protagonist with a title of warning: "This is the story of evil. Evil is headstrong—is puffed up. For our soul's sake, it is salutory for us to view it in all its ugly nakedness once in a while. . . ." An unidentified and disembodied male voice-over, with a documentary effect, reinforces that distance. The voice introduces the town, Loyalton, Wisconsin, and describes it as a factory town whose major source of income, a sawmill, is constantly visible in the background. Noting the unrelenting image of the "hot glow of sawdust," the voice-over refers to the sawmill's "flickering which burns through the eyelids at night if the shades aren't pulled down" (an "if" of the narration which becomes a *scene* in the narrative when Rosa, unable to sleep, is forced to remind her husband to pull down the shade). Shots of the sawmill's flame abound in the film, and the fire and the heat are associated with a repressed sexuality. Rosa's problem is that she cannot maintain the repression, cannot channel her energies into the family ("You certainly go in for mass production, don't you?" Rosa tells a woman who has just had her eighth child, and Rosa refers to her own pregnancy as a "mark of death"). She is the epitome of excessive female desire: "Think of all the things I could have," she tells her husband, and, in a shot of her studying a book of Accounts Receivable in her drive to get money, the only segment of her body in frame is a hand with painted nails. Rosa's usurpation of the position of desiring subject is also evidenced by the fact that she is specified as having a "good eye"— she can shoot, both pool and guns. The film constructs a clearly legible metonymic chain connecting fire, heat, passion, desire, fever, and death. Rosa figuratively burns up, is consumed by a fever at the end of the film: unrepressed female sexuality leads to death.

Rosa's uninhibited passion ultimately leads her to murder a man for having threatened to tell her lover (who has finally agreed to take her away and marry her) that she is pregnant with her husband's baby. Thus, the film opens with a trial in which Rosa is situated as the spectacle of criminality, as the object of a gaze which here is delineated not only as a masculine gaze but as the Look of the community, commanding a precise morality and transforming her into a freak of uncertain sexuality (she doesn't want what other women want, and, as the narrator points out, the women of the town are all at the trial "wondering if at last they're going to hear the secret of Rosa's life."). Her freakish nature, in the course of the film, is visualized more and more explicitly by the increased mobilization of the garish and grotesque aspects of the iconography of Bette Davis's later years as an actress. Furthermore, the evil and undesirability of Rosa Moline is echoed, doubled in the depiction of her look-alike, the Indian maid, Ginny, who is slovenly and fails to obey Rosa's orders. Although Rosa is mistakenly exonerated for the murder, she commits an even more atrocious crime against her own womanhood by a self-induced abortion—the crime for which she is punished by fever and death.

Rosa's death walk to the train at the end of the film is, in a sense, a parody of her earlier walks in which spruced up, dressed in her fanciest attire, she is clearly pleased to elicit a masculine whistle. But this time it is spectacle gone berserk—feminine spectacle deprived of a masculine spectator. Having knocked the medicine out of her husband's hand, thus forcing him to travel a large distance for more, Rosa dresses herself up, with the help of Ginny, in order to catch the ten o'clock train to Chicago. Maddened by the fever and with an unquenchable thirst, Rosa misapplies lipstick and eyeliner, producing a grotesque image of herself, and unsteadily walks toward the train station. Just short of her desire, there is a cut and the camera assumes a position on the other side of the tracks. The whistle blows, the train begins to pull out and Rosa's dead body, outstretched toward the train, can be seen between sets of wheels.

In *Beyond the Forest*, the woman's desire to desire is signified by a fever, in other words, a symptom—a symptom which, as in *The Cat People*, consumes and destroys her. The symptom for the woman, as sign or inscription on her body, gives witness to a dangerous overcloseness which precludes the possibility of desire. For the mechanism of symptom formation as it is described in relation to femininity differs markedly from that attributed to masculinity. While Freud refused to define hysteria as a disease which afflicted only women (there were male hysterics as well), he nevertheless aligned it closely with femininity, producing a binary opposition of types of neuroses: "There is no doubt that hysteria has a strong affinity with femininity, just as obsessional neurosis has with masculinity. . . ."[39] The mechanisms for effecting repression and hence symptom formation are significantly different in the two types of illnesses. In hysteria the mechanism is that of "*conversion* into somatic innervation" (somatic compliance), while obsessional neurosis makes use of the "method of *substitution* (viz., by displacement along the lines of certain categories of associations)."[40] In hysteria, in other words, the body is in compliance with the psyche, while in obsessional neurosis the body can be bracketed or elided altogether by a displacement along a line of psychical representations. Foucault speaks of a theme common to hysteria and hypochondria: "Diseases of the nerves are diseases of corporeal continuity. A body too close to itself, too intimate in each of its parts, an organic space which is, in a sense, strangely constricted. . . ."[41] Because desire is constituted by the operations of substitution and displacement in relation to an object, the female hysteric, her symptoms inscribed on her body, is denied any access to a desiring subjectivity. She can only futilely and inelegantly, like Rosa Moline in *Beyond the Forest*, desire to desire.

There are thus two major aspects of hysteria which are relevant to the woman's incorporation within a medical discourse in these films: (1) hysteria is characterized by the mechanism of conversion and uses the body as the space for the inscription of its signs, and (2) it is strongly linked to narrativity, both in relation to its cause (excessive daydreaming) and its treatment (the "talking cure"). Narrativity and the body—the narrativization of the female body is by no means specific to the genre of the woman's film in the Hollywood cinema. But in this group of films the female body is narrativized differently. The muteness which is constantly attributed to the woman is in some ways paradigmatic for the genre. For it is ultimately the symptoms of the female body which "speak" while the woman as subject of discourse is inevitably absent. The female body thus acts as a vehicle for hysterical speech. The marked ease of the metonymic slippage in these films between the woman, illness, the bed, muteness, blindness, and a medical discourse indicates yet another contradiction in the construction of a discourse which purportedly represents a female subjectivity. If the woman must be given a genre and hence a voice, the addition of a medical discourse makes it possible once again to confine female discourse to the body, to disperse her access to language across a body which now no longer finds its major function in spectacle. Yet, despecularized in its illness, that body is nevertheless interpretable, knowable, subject to a control which is no longer entirely subsumed by an erotic gaze. If interpretation is not possible, if the medical figure is incapable of relating a surface to a depth, of restoring an immediacy of vision so that the surface matches the interior, then the disease is invariably fatal. In *Guest In the House*, the woman is unassimilable because her illness is constituted by a disjunction between image and reality. A character whose knowledge is guaranteed by his exteriority to the household compares Evelyn's entrance into the "House of Proctor" to that of a Sarah Bernhardt. Her actions and gestures are divorced from her truth; this is why the major male character, an artist, is incapable of painting her as St. Cecelia. The deficiency is not his as an artist but hers, and it is a deficiency which is ultimately incurable for she is beyond representation.

With the exception of *Dark Victory* and *Now, Voyager* perhaps, the films of the medical discourse do not encourage or facilitate spectatorial identification with their diseased female protagonists. Rather, they take the form of a didactic exercise designed to produce a knowledge about the woman. If female spectatorship is constituted as an oscillation between a feminine and a masculine position,[42] the films of the medical discourse encourage the female spectator to repudiate the feminine pole and to ally herself with the one who diagnoses, with a medical gaze. Identification with a female character is then allowable to the extent that she and the doctor form a "couple" as the condition of a cure. But the "properly feminine" aspect of spectatorship is not altogether lost—it is instead represented *within* the films across the female body in its illness.

Female spectatorship is generally understood in its alignment with other qualities culturally ascribed to the woman—in particular, an excess of emotion, sentiment, affect, empathy. That is why women's films are often referred to as "weepies." From this perspective, the female gaze exhibits, in contrast to male distance, a proximity to the image which is the mark of overidentification and hence a heightened sympathy. But the concept of sympathy is a physiological/medical one as well, of particular interest to the female subject. The meaning of "sympathy" in physiology and pathology is, the *Oxford English Dictionary* tells us, "a relation between two bodily organs or parts (or between two persons) such that disorder, or any condition, of the one induces a corresponding condition in the other." Sympathy connotes a process of contagion within the body, or between bodies, an instantaneous communication and affinity. In female spectatorship, it is a capitulation to the image, an overinvestment in and overidentification with the story and its characters. Unable to negotiate the distance which is a prerequisite to desire and its displacements, the female spectator is always, in some sense, constituted as a hysteric. And yet, the films of the medical discourse, precisely by encouraging the female spectator to ally herself with the one who diagnoses, attempt to de-hystericize their spectator, to "cure" her.

By activating a therapeutic mode, the films of the medical discourse become the most fully recuperated form of the woman's film. The therapy put into effect in relation to the spectator completely forecloses the possibility of a feminine position, freezing the oscillation between feminine and masculine poles which is characteristic of female spectatorship. The clinical eye is a most masculine eye. The female spectator, in becoming de-hystericized (distanced from the female character who suffers from the disease of femininity), must also become defeminized, must don the surgical gown. The marginal masochism which remains—linked to the pleasure of being "under the knife"—is subsumed beneath the overwhelming need to appropriate the only gaze which can see: the medical gaze which knows and can diagnose.

Nevertheless, the connotations attached to female spectatorship—a heightened sympathy, constriction and overcloseness, the immediacy of the process of contagion—are not lost in these films. Rather, these mechanisms are represented within the texts as elements of the disease. This process of narrativizing female spectatorship is parallel to the strategy discussed earlier, whereby the woman's purportedly deficient relation to the image is internalized by the texts and thematized as the blindness—actual or metaphorical—of the female protagonist. The internalization and narrativization of female spectatorship constitutes an extremely strong process of recuperation, containing the more disruptive aspects of female spectatorship by specifying them as pathological. The illness of the female character is not accidental but essential, implicating her entire being. For this reason, her body becomes the privileged site for the representation of sympathy as an overcloseness, a disorder of contagion. The war trauma of the male patient is localizable, often easily reducible. The trauma of the woman is total. This is why the woman's illness is so frequently a disease of the nerves, a psychical disturbance which manifests itself through the body. The sympathy usually activated in the film/spectator relation in the woman's picture is, in these films, reflected and reinscribed in the medical mapping of the woman's body, *within* the text—a mapping which ultimately owes more to the nineteenth century than to the twentieth. According to Foucault,

> diseases of the nerves are essentially disorders of sympathy; they presuppose a state of general vigilance in the nervous system which makes each organ susceptible of entering into sympathy with any other. . . . The entire female body is riddled by obscure but strangely direct paths of sympathy; it is always in an immediate complicity with itself, to the point of forming a kind of absolutely privileged site for the sympathies; from one extremity of its organic space to the other, it encloses a perpetual possibility of hysteria.[43]

Always on the verge of hysteria, the female character in the films of the medical discourse is placed under the care and constraint of a medical gaze.

In hysteria, the paradigmatic female disease, the body is in sympathy with the psyche to the extent that there is no differentiation between them. Illness affects and defines her whole being. The ease with which the woman slips into the role of patient is certainly linked to the fact that the doctor exercises an automatic power and mastery in the relation, which is only a hyperbolization of the socially acceptable "norm" of the heterosexual alliance. The doctor/patient relation is a quite specific one, however, which unrelentingly draws together power, knowledge, the body, and the psyche in the context of an institution. Therein lies its force in convincing the woman that her way of looking is ill.

# 3

## The Moving Image: Pathos and the Maternal

There is a scene in *Mildred Pierce* (1945) in which Mildred attempts to convince her daughter Veda to give up her job as a singer in a rather seedy nightclub and return home. When Mildred visits Veda in her dressing room backstage, one of Veda's coworkers comments upon learning Mildred's identity, "I didn't know you had a mother." Veda replies, "Everyone has a mother." In a similar scene in *The Reckless Moment* (1949), the blackmailer, Donnelly, referring to Mrs. Harper's daughter Bea, remarks, "She's lucky to have a mother like you." Mrs. Harper's immediate response is, "Everyone has a mother like me. You probably had one, too."

Everyone has a mother, and furthermore, all mothers are essentially the same, each possessing the undeniable quality of motherliness. In Western culture, there is something *obvious* about the maternal which has no counterpart in the paternal. The idea that someone might not have a mother is constituted as a joke; it is articulated in the mode of the ridiculous or absurd.[1] For the suggestion questions the unquestionable, and the status of the unquestionable is, of course, the natural. Paternity and its interrogation, on the other hand, are articulated within the context of issues of identity, legality, inheritance—in short, *social* legitimacy. To generate questions about the existence of one's father is, therefore, to produce an insult of the highest order.

The semantic valence, the readability, of the two functions is closely associated with an epistemological construction. Knowledge of maternity is constituted in terms of immediacy (one only has to look and see). Knowledge of paternity, on the other hand, is mediated—it allows of gaps and invisibilities, of doubts in short. It therefore demands external regulation in the form of laws governing social relations and the terms of inheritance. Maternity is self-regulating, it has its own internal guarantees. The logic of the sexual division of labor in relation to the upbringing of children derives its force, more than any other aspect of sexual difference, from a purported fidelity to the dictates of the biological. Although the connotations of the maternal as social position far surpass its biological aspects, the biological nevertheless infuses it with meaning and is activated as an anchor to prevent any slippage of the concept. The biological fact of motherhood is utilized to reduce all argumentation to the level of the "obvious," to statements (e.g., "Men cannot have babies") which, in their sheer irrefutability, block or preclude all analysis. These "obviousnesses" then lend credibility to another level, a different order of interpretation of sexual difference which assigns fixed positions to mother, father, and child—positions authorized by the weight of a primal configuration.

A discourse of the obvious thus grounds an understanding of the maternal in terms of the sheer ease of its readability. It is therefore not surprising that the privileged form in the cinema for the investigation of issues associated with maternity is melodrama. The dilemmas of the mother are rarely tragic; they are much more frequently contextualized in the mode of melodrama. Melodrama and the maternal: two discourses of the obvious which have a semiotic resonance. Both are inscribed as sign systems which are immediately readable, almost too explicit. Peter Brooks traces the historical origins of melodrama as a popular form and claims that it is "radically democratic, striving to make its representations clear and legible to everyone."[2] Arguing that melodrama, in its desire to "say everything," breaks down the mechanism of repression, Brooks locates its meaning on the surface, in terms of primal psychic integers.

> To stand on the stage and utter phrases such as "Heaven is witness to my innocence" or "I am that miserable wretch who has ruined your family" or "I will pursue you to the grave" is to achieve the full expression of psychological condition and moral feeling in the most transparent, unmodified, infantile form. Desire triumphs over the world of substitute-formations and detours, it achieves plenitude of meaning. . . . In the tableau more than in any other single device of dramaturgy, we grasp melodrama's primordial concerns to make its signs clear, unambiguous, and impressive.[3]

In its striving for a directness in the relation to the spectator, melodrama's semiotic straining is evidenced as a form of excess, a will-to-transparency which is self-negating through its very obviousness. In this sense, the form is inherently contradictory. For the term "melodramatic" in colloquial language connotes excess, the artifice of theatricality.

It is certainly arguable that the term "melodrama," given its vagueness and the range of its potential and actual applications (particularly in relation to the cinema), is virtually useless for analysis. While the label "melodrama" has most recently been activated primarily in the criticism of '50s family melodrama, it has also been applied in discussions of Griffith and silent cinema, crime films and film noir, and even the Western (to which it is also frequently opposed). Moreover, some critics have gone so far as to claim that the cinema itself is essentially melodramatic,[4] basing the argument on the cinema's unique organization and direction of affect, together with its orchestration of a heterogeneous group of signifying materials. Nevertheless, critical essays such as Thomas Elsaesser's "Tales of Sound and Fury: Observations on the Family Melodrama," and the *Screen* "Dossier on Melodrama"[5] demonstrate that, whether or not the term melodrama is capable of defining and delineating a specific group of films, it does pinpoint a crucial and isolable signifying tendency within the cinema which may be activated differently in specific historical periods.

Some of the characteristics of the melodramatic mode, according to Elsaesser, are: the nonpsychological conception of the characters (". . . significance lies in the structure and articulation of the action, not in any psychologically motivated correspondence with individualized experience.");[6] the consequent externalization of internal emotions and their embodiment within the mise-en-scène or decor; the claustrophobia of the settings, which are most frequently domestic and/or limited to the small towns of middle America; a concentration on the rhythm of experience rather than its content, a strategy linked to the "foreshortening of lived time in favor of intensity" which is characteristic of melodrama; and the activation of the psychical mechanisms of condensation and displacement which underlie the frustrations emerging when desire is attached to an unattainable object. The contradiction between the notion that melodrama deals with a nonpsychological conception of character and the resort to psychical categories (such as condensation and displacement) for their explanatory power is only apparent. For it is not the psychical dimension which is negated by the films but interiority which is eschewed. The narrative conflict is located *between* characters rather than *within* a single mind. As Robert B. Heilman points out, the latter situation (internal conflict), is typical of tragedy; in melodrama, on the other hand, "dividedness is replaced by a quasi-wholeness, and we find the security of an ordering monopathy."[7] The drama is thus played out within a complex nexus of relationships and the characters' major activity is that of reading, constantly deciphering the intentions, desires, and weaknesses of other characters. In the closed world of melodrama, as Elsaesser claims, the "characters are, so to speak, each others' sole referent."[8]

Hence, melodrama does have its own specificity in relation to characterization, temporality, setting, and the organization of affect. But even more importantly, for the purposes of this study, the melodramatic mode is often analyzed in terms which situate it as a "feminine" form, linking it intimately with the woman's film in its address to a female audience. Thus, Geoffrey No-well-Smith, in the *Screen* dossier, contrasts the melodrama with the Western:

> Broadly speaking, in the American movie the active hero becomes protagonist of the Western, the passive or impotent hero or heroine becomes protagonist of what has come to be known as melodrama. The contrast active/passive is, inevitably, traversed by another contrast, that between masculine and feminine. . . . [The melodrama] often features women as protagonists, and where the central figure is a man there is regularly an impairment of his "masculinity"—at least in contrast to the mythic potency of the hero of the Western.[9]

The difference is inscribed as a spatial one as well: while the wide open spaces of the Western suggest a range of options and freedom of action, in the melodrama alternatives appear to be closed off and limited by a constricting domestic sphere. The impairment of masculinity or castration which Nowell-Smith points to is generalizable—whether the character is a man or a woman, "suffering and impotence, besides being the data of middle-class life, are seen as forms of a failure to be male."[10] While Elsaesser does not explicitly delineate the (negative) feminization of the protagonist as Nowell-Smith does, he describes the major character in terms which denote passivity and impotence: the protagonist fails to act in "a way that could shape events," the characters are "acted upon," and melodrama "confers on them a negative identity through suffering."[11] More specifically, as Jacques Goimard maintains, pathos—the central emotion of melodrama—is reinforced by the disproportion between the weakness of the victim and the seriousness of the danger so that, as Goimard points out and Northrop Frye emphasizes, "the pathetic is produced more easily through the misfortunes of women, children, animals, or fools. . . ."[12] Melodrama closely allies itself with the delineation of a lack of social power and effectivity so characteristic of the cultural positioning of women.

From this point of view, it is not surprising that the social function most rigorously associated with femininity—that of motherhood—should form the focus of a group of films which exploit the pathetic effect and which bear the label *maternal melodrama*.[13] Maternal melodramas are scenarios of separation, of separation and return, or of threatened separation—dramas which play out all the permutations of the mother/child relation. Because it foregrounds sacrifice and suffering, incarnating the "weepie" aspect of the genre, the maternal melodrama is usually seen as the paradigmatic type of the woman's film. Already a popular genre in the 1920s, (*Way Down East* [1921], *Stella Dallas* [1925], *Madame* X [1920, 1929]), it reaches its American apotheosis in the 1930s with films like the 1937 version of *Madame X*, *Blonde Venus* (1932) and, perhaps most importantly, King Vidor's 1937 remake of *Stella Dallas*. In a study of the maternal melodrama from 1930 to 1939, Christian Viviani isolates the thematic matrix of the form:

> A woman is separated from her child, falls from her social class and founders in disgrace. The child grows up in respectability and enters established society where he stands for progress. . . . The mother watches the social rise of her child from afar; she cannot risk jeopardizing his fortunes by contamination with her own bad repute. Chance draws them together again, and the partial or total rehabilitation of the mother is accomplished, often through a cathartic trial scene. [14]

Although this thematic matrix is modified or inflected in various ways by particular films, all of the texts bring into play the contradictory position of the mother within a patriarchal society—a position formulated by the injunction that she focus desire on the child and the subsequent demand to give up the child to the social order. Motherhood is conceived as the always uneasy conjunction of an absolute closeness and a forced distance. The scenario of "watching the child from afar" thus constitutes itself as a privileged tableau of the genre, and it is clear why *Stella Dallas* has become its exemplary film.

While King Vidor's version of *Stella Dallas* (1937) does not, strictly speaking, fall within the time period analyzed in this study, its significance as a model of the form makes it evident that it warrants some detailed attention. [15] Viviani's investigation of '30s maternal melodrama demonstrates that the films tend to establish an intimate relationship between the problems of the mother and issues of social class and/or economic status. Motherhood is marginalized, situated on the cusp of culture (it is more compatible with nature)—looking in from the outside as it were—because it is always a source of potential resistance to the child's entry into the social arena. Thus, as Viviani points out, the child often stands for some sort of social "progress," in contradistinction to the mother. The mother's negotiation of a relation to her child is placed in opposition to his/her social or even economic recognition—according to the logic of the films the two must be incompatible. The price to be paid for the child's social success is the mother's descent into anonymity, the negation of her identity (quite frequently this descent is justified by the narrative on the surface by making her an unwed, and hence explicitly guilty, mother). She must be relegated to the status of silent, unseen and suffering support. As Viviani points out, this is a particularly cruel fate in the '30s: ". . . the mother now pays for her fault no longer through a veritable degradation but by being condemned to anonymity, the true curse in the Hollywood thematics of the Thirties, totally geared to the success story and the rise to fame." [16] Stella Dallas (Barbara Stanwyck) pathetically incarnates this fate at the end of the film when she is deprived of even the frills and jewelry, the excesses in clothing which mark her identity throughout the film. Her presence is not recognized by any of the participants of the drama she watches through the window.

Stella is the victim of desires which exceed her social status. The film prefigures its own ending by situating Stella very early as a movie spectator, but this time a dissatisfied one who measures the distance between herself and the figures on the screen and would like to collapse that difference. As Stephen and Stella leave the movie theater, Stella tells him about her dreams of social mobility, "I want to be like all the people you're around—educated and, you know, speaking nice." When Stephen urges her to be "like herself," Stella objects—"No, I don't want to be like myself, like the people around here. I want to be like the people in the movie—you know, do everything well-bred and refined." What Stella desires is movement, process, a change in the social status represented by her own working class family and, in particular, her mother, who is represented as devoid of energy or even desire. The trajectory of the film, however, succeeds in situating her in her "proper" place, as contented and passive spectator, weeping but nevertheless recognizing and accepting her position on the margins of the social scene, in a space outside.

*Stella Dallas* demonstrates that "being what you are" involves *not* mimicking those of another social class, allowing them to remain "on the screen." What Stella is, naturally, is a mother. But her downfall is directly linked to her desire to be what is forever outside her grasp since it is inconsistent with her social origins—a refined and respectable lady. Her inability to assume that position is represented as a process of misreading. Stella, misunderstanding what is involved in refinement and respectability, overcompensates, views her access to a higher social position as a matter of excess, addition, *more* of everything—more jewelry, more frills, more perfume. Calling attention to itself, her dress is aggressive, lacking the proportion necessary to refinement. And this tendency gains momentum as the film progresses, until Stella, weighted down by the burden of an inordinate amount of jewelry and accessories, is caricatured by her daughter Laurel's friends and labelled a "Christmas tree." As Viviani points out, the Americanization of the maternal melodrama is in part accomplished by transforming the mother's "moral sin" of the European version into the more typically American "social error."[17] Stella does not commit a social error, she *is* that social error. Consequently, it is embarrassment rather than guilt and punishment which is at stake. Although soon after Stella becomes obsessed by her maternal duties she largely forgets her earlier social aspirations, displacing them onto Laurel, her excesses in dressing remain as the trace of forbidden desires of social mobility.

And the separation between mother and child is ultimately predicated upon this lack of proportion on the part of Stella, the fact that she is an embarrassment to Laurel, who has outstripped her mother in the social arena (inheriting her refinement, no doubt, from her father). Stella's displacement of her desires onto her daughter is revealed as a constant need to dress Laurel (a major function of mothering in *The Reckless Moment* is also insuring that the child is well-clothed). While Laurel's father sends her books as a birthday present, Stella works at the sewing machine to produce a birthday dress and complains that books are free at the library but a fur coat is not. Although Laurel accepts the dress with pleasure (in contrast to Veda in *Mildred Pierce* whose refusal of a dress is the first sign of a difficulty in the mother/daughter relation), her greatest degree of refinement is evidenced by her rejection of the frills which are specific to her mother's pleasure. Mrs. Morrison, whose dress is more careful, basic, and proper, represents a more appropriate mother for Laurel.

The incredibly pathetic effect of *Stella Dallas* is in part the result of the fact that Stella is the embodiment of the very mechanism of pathos—disproportion (between means and ends, desires and their fulfillment). Her separation from Laurel is the consequence of her misunderstanding or denial of what is "proper" insofar as that word connotes the sign which is fully adequate to, "right" for, its referent. This is particularly regrettable since what is "proper"—propriety—is supposed to be an attribute of women, especially mothers, who must see to it that their children are properly dressed, have the proper manners, etc. Stella's signifiers are askew—they do not match the signifieds for which they are intended. She is a misplaced spectacle. But Laurel does not really perceive this until she sees her mother via the mediation of the instrument of the proper so closely associated with female narcissism—the mirror.

A mirror is always a proper representation of its referent, and the specular relation is one to which women are expected to adhere. Laurel's gradual disengagement from her mother is figured in two separate scenes in which a mirror dominates the mise-en-scène and acts as a relay of glances. In the first, Stella applies cold cream to her face and peroxide to her hair as Laurel speaks admiringly of Mrs. Morrison. Concentrating on her image in the mirror, Stella inadvertently smudges with cold cream the photograph of Mrs. Morrison which Laurel shows her. Laurel reacts with a kind of horror which is the effect of the radical divergence between the photograph, reflecting an easy and composed attractiveness, and the mirror image of Stella, revealing through curlers and cold cream the straining, the excessiveness of her cumbersome narcissistic machinery. In a subsequent shot both mother and daughter are reflected, side by side, in the mirror. Looking at her mother via the mediation of two images—photographic and specular—Laurel sees her differently. The mirror, site of identity and narcissism, initiates the disjunction between mother and daughter. The second scene that stages a specular mediation of the daughter's gaze at the mother takes place at a soda fountain. Laurel and her date are sitting slightly apart from a crowd of young people, facing a large mirror, when Stella walks in in her "Christmas tree" attire. Laurel's friends begin to whisper and make mocking comments about Stella. Presently, Laurel looks up, sees her mother reflected in the mirror, and runs out of the shop, acutely embarrassed. Her gaze mediated via the gazes of others and the mirror, Laurel finally recognizes an accurate, or "proper," reflection of her mother's disproportion. It is as though the closeness of the mother/daughter relation necessitated the deflection of the gaze, its indirection, as a precondition for the establishment of difference.

*Stella Dallas* is exemplary as a maternal melodrama because Stella figures so blatantly the psychical import or trajectory of mothering. The mother, as a mother, represents a fullness, a presence, a wholeness and harmony which must ultimately be broken. Although the film appears to isolate the issue of Stella's excessiveness in dress and manners from the issue of her mothering, to assume that there is no pertinent relation between the two, her disproportion does stand in direct opposition to the harmonious wholeness associated with motherhood. The "good mother" sacrifices herself for her child because she cannot possibly sustain that impossible image of wholeness. Stella's sacrifice/separation is made more extreme by the fact that she literally *embodies* this inability as excess, a disproportion of parts. Although her behavior toward Laurel is that of the "good mother," her image is not. Yet, Stella is simply a hyperbolization of all mothers, who are inevitably deficient in relation to this image of unity and perfection. As Linda Williams points out, "The device of devaluing and debasing the actual figure of the mother while sanctifying the institution of motherhood is typical of 'the woman's film' in general and the subgenre of the maternal melodrama in particular."[18] All mothers share the same predicament. This is why Mrs. Morrison empathizes so strongly with Stella. In the scene in which the two women meet, the distance between them is gradually reduced as Mrs. Morrison moves closer and closer to Stella, her spatial proximity signifying an increasing amount of empathy. The communication between them is almost instantaneous and eschews linguistic foundation: when Stephen reads the letter from Stella which claims that she no longer wants Laurel, Mrs. Morrison demands, "Couldn't you read between those pitiful lines?" Mrs. Morrison is the perfect reader of this text (or of its empty spaces), and, being a perfect reader, she recognizes another—it is Mrs. Morrison who insures that the curtains are left open so that Stella can see her daughter's wedding.

Stella is a lesson for the female spectator in more ways than one—what she learns and figures at the window is distance. But the position of the distanced spectator can be assumed by her only at the cost of an identity, of recognition. Nevertheless, Stella, at the window, is not, cannot be, a voyeur despite the policeman's exhortation to move on (and hence the suggestion of the illegality of her vision). Her visual pleasure is not (at least explicitly) a sexual one—it must be mixed with tears and suffering. Although much of my analysis of the woman's film stresses the refusal to attribute the gaze to the woman in a nonproblematic way, there is also a sense in which the woman is socially positioned as a spectator—asked to assume a place *outside* the "real" arena of social relations and power, with all the connotations of passivity, waiting, and watching normally attached to the function of spectatorship. But, in *Stella Dallas*, the production of a distanced spectatorial position for the woman is synonymous with her own negation as mother, at least in any material sense. Her sacrifice, her very absence from the scene, nevertheless insures her transformation into an Ideal of Motherhood.

When the policeman tells Stella to "move on" at the end of the film, she pleads with him, "Oh please let me see her face when he kisses her." What Stella desires, as spectator, is a close-up. When she walks away smiling, toward the camera and into close-up, she becomes that close-up for the spectator, who empathizes with her fate. The distance achieved by Stella is collapsed at an entirely different level. Through the insistent invitation to overidentify with the female protagonist, the maternal melodrama becomes a ritualized mourning of the woman's losses in a patriarchal society.

But this is the classic '30s articulation of maternal melodrama. In the '40s, the form is witness to a number of aberrations. In fact, the maternal melodrama loses much of its coherence as a subgenre, as a structural and iconographic logic which supports a grouping of films. Instead, a sustained effort to conceptualize the maternal surfaces in a number of different types of films—from those which closely resemble overt propaganda (*Tender Comrade* [1943], *Since You Went Away* [1944]), to films informed by the iconography of film noir (*Mildred Pierce* [1945], *The Reckless Moment* [1949]), to the biography of the "great woman" (*Blossoms in the Dust* [1942], *Lydia* [1941]), in which mothering is institutionalized as the founding and directing of an orphanage. Coincident with a wartime reorganization of sexual roles and the corresponding introduction of ambivalence about mothering, the maternal becomes a fractured concept in the '40s, necessitating its dispersal in different genres. Only a few films (e.g., *To Each His Own* [1946], *The Great Lie* [1941]) explicitly and intensively activate the classic figures of the '30s form. The separation which is most frequently narrativized is that dictated by the war: the separation between a husband and his wife and family. As the literalism of the title of *Since You Went Away* indicates, the narrative's time is telescoped into the "meanwhile" of the husband's absence, the points between his departure and return. Mother and child, far from being separated, remain together as a demonstration that the home front is a united front.

The war, quite predictably, mobilizes the ultraconservative aspects of the cultural construction of motherhood. Ann Hilton's (Claudette Colbert's) major duty as a mother in *Since You Went Away* is to maintain things "as they are." Hugging the empty bathrobe which signifies her husband's absence, she sobs, "I'll try to keep all the good things as they were. I'll keep the past alive. Like a warm room for you to come back to." The maternal is appropriated as a signifier for all that American soldiers are fighting for. Nazimova, playing a newly arrived working-class immigrant, presents Mrs. Hilton with a speech about the significance of the Statue of Liberty and then tells her, "You are what I thought America was." The identification of America with the ideal wife and mother allows a political discourse to expropriate an entire constellation of connotations associated with the maternal—comfort, nurturance, home, containment/stasis, community, closeness, affect—in the service of a nationalistic cause.[19] This process enables the naturalization of the political cause through a kind of contamination effect. For maternal characteristics are given as the most natural thing in nature. This strategy of imbricating the concept of the maternal with that of a nationalistic patriotism also succeeds in giving the woman a significant position in wartime which does not constitute a threat to the traditional patriarchal order—a symbolic role which counteracts the effects of the woman's new and necessary role in production. Thus in *Since You Went Away*, Ann Hilton's employment as a welder is an afterthought of the narrative structure, and in *Tender Comrade*, the only shots of the women actually working in a large airplane hangar are denaturalized through the use of a rear projection process which uncannily introduces a division between the woman and the space of production.[20] The sheer weight of the symbolic role of motherhood offers a strong resistance to the potentially profound implications of the socioeconomic roles now accessible to women in production. Material reality yields to melodrama, which becomes a historical document.

The mirror, which in *Stella Dallas* mediated a traumatic deflection of the gaze between mother and daughter, in *Since You Went Away* intensifies the relation between the mother and an absent husband whose representation enables her own. After Ann Hilton ascends the stairs, clasping two photographs of her husband, she stops at the door of their bedroom. Her voice-over, addressed to the absent husband, fixes her nonidentity—"You know I have no courage"—and there follows a cut to an empty mirror on the dressing table, reflecting nothing, accompanied by the continuation of the voice-over, "and I have no vision." The camera moves slightly forward toward the mirror as Ann moves into its frame and places the two pictures of her husband on either side of it, framing her own reflection. Deprived of vision and a narcissistic identification, maternal subjectivity is annihilated in the movement which brackets the woman's mirror image between the memories of the absent male. In an earlier section of this opening scene the camera hysterically documents the traces of the paternal presence and the signifiers of an impending wartime absence—the imprint of a body in a favorite soft chair, a sleeping bulldog at its foot, a carton labeled "Military Raincoats," a Western Union telegram containing instructions to proceed to camp, mementos of the couple's wedding trip and their children.

The scene activates the construction of a loss which haunts the entire narrative. References to and representations of absent males (husbands and sons) abound in *Tender Comrades* as well—each of the women keeps a photograph of an absent husband next to her bed so that the all-female house is laced with reminders of male presence. And in *Since You Went Away*, a huge mural depicting men fighting overshadows and dwarfs a group of young women (including the Hilton daughter) who are taking a nurse's aide oath. Yet, these images of men have a different valence or inflection than those of women in the classical Hollywood text—absence and hence photographability do not connote the erotic. Rather, the photographs (and other images) act as memory traces of authority-in-absence—an authority which is just as, if not more, powerful in its absence.

In the '40s, the issues of social class so important to the maternal melodrama of the '30s are repressed or marginalized (with the exception, perhaps, of *Mildred Pierce*, where Mildred's problems are a direct result of her desire to move up the social scale). The families of *The Reckless Moment* and *Since You Went Away* are decidedly middle class. Yet, while social class is made to appear insignificant given the democratic tendencies of the films, social inequalities emerge on the sidelines, in the use of black servants. In this respect, it is significant that there is a '30s version of *Imitation of Life* and a '50s version, but no '40s remake. Racial issues are too central to the film—in the '40s maternal melodramas these issues are present but marginalized. Black servants haunt the diegeses of films like *The Great Lie*, *Since You Went Away*, and *The Reckless Moment*. Furthermore, black servants are frequently used to buttress central ideologies and to invalidate any claims of racial inequality through their representation as essential and legitimate (unquestionable) appendages of the nuclear family. Female black servants in particular act to double and hence reinforce the maternal function. In *The Reckless Moment*, the black maid, Sybil, consistently occupies the background of shots which chronicle the family's dilemma. As the locus of otherness and an instinctive and unspecifiable form of maternal knowledge, she can distinguish between those who will ultimately protect the family structure (the blackmailer Donnelly played by James Mason) and those who threaten it (Donnelly's less sentimental partner, Nagel). Sybil assumes a maternal function in relation to Mrs. Harper (constantly questioning her as to whether she's had enough to eat, etc.) and hence becomes a kind of meta-mother. This representation—and others in the films—are fully consistent with psychological theories of the 1940s which held that the black woman symbolized "the primitive essence of mother-love."[21] Perceived as closer to the earth and to nature and more fully excluded from the social contract than the white woman, the black woman personifies more explicitly the situation of the mother, and her presence, on the margins of the text, is a significant component of many maternal melodramas.

Because the films tend to posit an ideal of democracy and hence to deny any functional differences based on either class or race (at the level of their manifest discourse), they also tend to situate any sociopolitical differentiation in the realm of pure ideology divorced from material constraints. The most "propagandistic" of the films—*Tender Comrade* and *Since You Went Away*—present, primarily through dialogue, a war of ideologies which are linked in curious ways to forms of sexuality. For instance, in *Tender Comrade* the character (Barbara) who articulates and advocates an isolationist policy is also represented as sexually promiscuous. A discussion about whether or not Barbara should be dating other men while her husband serves in the Navy (Ginger Rogers: "I should think that with Pete out there on a ship you might play it straight.") is linked syntagmatically to an argument about the political implications of hoarding. Barbara, who is excessive in the realm of sexuality, also desires what the film, upholding a wartime economy of scarcity, posits as an excessive desire for material goods, a tendency toward overconsumption. She situates herself as a proponent of isolationism by complaining about "shipping butter to foreigners" and "fighting for a lot of foreigners." In *Since You Went Away*, the character who unpatriotically hoards goods is excessive in the register of speech—she is the town gossip. Veda's negative characterization in *Mildred Pierce* as a type of consumer vampire ("There are so many things that we should have and haven't got," she complains to Mildred) echoes this excessive relation to commodities. Economics and sexuality are inextricably linked in this algebra whereby a wartime economy of lack or scarcity is seriously threatened by excessive female sexuality.

But from our point of view the most interesting aspect of this political economy is its relation to the register of the maternal. In this respect, promiscuous sexuality is comparable to excessive mothering—both are dangerous aspects of femininity, and both are represented as maintaining a close affinity with a detrimental politics of isolationism. The mother who is too close to her son strives to keep him out of the arena of world affairs. In *Tomorrow is Forever* (1946) and *Watch on the Rhine* (1943), the mother's desire to prevent her son from enlisting or fighting for democracy is clearly stigmatized as an isolationist tendency. It is worth stressing that these films frequently articulate an anti-isolationist politics with a maternal ideology. In other words, the historical articulation of the maternal obligation to surrender the son is merged with an anti-isolationist politics. A careful balancing of closeness and distance within the nuclear family is crucial to the maintenance of democratic nationalistic ideologies.

What the maternal melodramas of the '30s and '40s demonstrate, almost inadvertently, is that motherhood, far from being the simple locus of comfort and nostalgic pleasure—a position to which a patriarchal culture ceaselessly

and somewhat desperately attempts to confine it—is a site of multiple contradictions. In the '40s these contradictions are reduced to a single governing opposition which polarizes maternal possibilities. Figured spatially, the
oppositional terms are an overcloseness between mother and child which signals, on the political plane, the dangers of isolationism (in *Tomorrow is Forever*
and *Watch on the Rhine*) and, conversely, the maintenance of a dangerous distance from and hence neglect of the child (in other words, the situation of the
working mother in films like *Mildred Pierce* or *To Each His Own*). The maternal
is represented as its two excesses which are controlled and contained through
their narrativization.[22]

Yet, the films of the '40s simply effect a historical specification of a more
generalizable psychical configuration associated with patriarchy. As Monique
Plaza points out, "Responsible for too much or not enough, the Mother is submitted to contradictory injunctions which are a function of the representation
that the theoreticians make of the child, and of the well-adjusted adult."[23] The
mother is allowed no access to a comfortable position of moderation. Rather,
the polarization of the two maternal excesses creates a textual problematic quite
conducive to the manipulation of simple moral absolutes or primal psychic integers which Brooks claims is characteristic of melodrama. In this sense, the
films conform to what he labels the "logic of the excluded middle."[24] Nevertheless, this polarization acts as a kind of decoy to distract attention from an entirely different kind of fear associated with the maternal. It is an ideological
strategy for defusing, minimizing the effects of another diametrically opposed
understanding of the maternal as the site of the collapse of all oppositions and
the confusion of identities. This conceptualization of the material is elaborated
in detail in much contemporary feminist theory, including the work of such
writers as Irigaray and Kristeva.

Luce Irigaray is perhaps the most insistent spokesperson for the necessity
of delineating a female specificity—an autonomous symbolic representation
for the woman. The difficulty of such a project is, however, evidenced by the
constant production of figures which are by no means autonomous but gain
much of their force in direct (and thus dependent) opposition to patriarchal representations of masculinity. Thus, in the text where she confronts most directly
the question of the maternal—"And the One Doesn't Stir Without the
Other"[25]—the specification of a maternal space clearly opposes itself to and
hence departs from a notion of paternal law as the site of separation, division,
differentiation. The essay is constructed as the pre-Oedipal daughter's lament
to the mother, and in this context the mother is represented as all-powerful, engulfing, paralyzing. The suffocating closeness of the relation is exacerbated by
its anticipation of a future in which the daughter is doomed to assume the mother's place, to repeat the configuration in relation to her own daughter. In this

sense, the essay is a dramatization or theatricalization of the Freudian scenario of the mother/child relation. The plenitude and nondifferentiation associated with the maternal space is evidenced by the constant slippage and confusion of the shifters designating mother and daughter (the "you" and the "I") in the essay.

From its opening statement, "With your milk, Mother, I swallowed ice," Irigaray's essay situates the process of mothering by tracing the figures of orality. The maternal space is the realm of pure need, and mothering is obsessively linked to nurturing, feeding, the provision of an object for the oral drives. But nurturing here does not receive a positive valence as it does in much American feminist theory. The child is not simply satiated but glutted by the mother's milk/love, which is always in excess. In overinvesting her desire in the child, the mother becomes herself the perverse subject of the oral drive—the agent of an engulfing or devouring process which threatens to annihilate the subjectivity of the child. In this respect, Irigaray's analysis approaches that of Julia Kristeva in *Powers of Horror*. Kristeva associates the maternal with the abject—i.e., that which is the focus of a combined horror and fascination, hence subject to a range of taboos designed to control the culturally marginal.[26] In this analysis, the function of nostalgia for the mother-origin is that of a veil, a veil which conceals the terror attached to nondifferentiation. The threat of the maternal space is that of the collapse of any distinction whatsoever between subject and object. Within the Freudian schema, incorporation is the model for processes of identification (between "subject" and "object," mother and child) which have the potential to destroy the very notion of identity.

Kristeva elsewhere emphasizes a particularly interesting corollary of this aspect of motherhood: the maternal space is "a place both double and foreign."[27] In its internalization of heterogeneity, an otherness within the self, motherhood deconstructs certain conceptual boundaries. Kristeva delineates the maternal through the assertion, "In a body there is grafted, unmasterable, an other."[28] The confusion of identities threatens to collapse a signifying system based on the paternal law of differentiation.

It would seem that the concept of motherhood automatically throws into question ideas concerning the self, boundaries between self and other, identity. Perhaps this is why a patriarchal society invests so heavily in the construction and maintenance of motherhood as an identity with very precise functions—comforting, nurturing, protecting. The horror of nondifferentiation is suppressed through a process of attaching a surplus of positive attributes to the maternal. It might also explain why there exists a specific genre—maternal melodrama. The films of this genre play out the instabilities of maternal identity in order to locate it more solidly.[29] In films like *The Great Lie*, *To Each His Own*, and *Stella Dallas*, biological maternity and social maternity may not coincide, but the true function and responsibilities of the mother are made quite clear.

The mother must be present (as both *The Great Lie* and *To Each His Own* demonstrate) and she must be an adequate mirror for the child (the failure of Stella Dallas). The constant return in the films to the themes of mistaken identity, distance and separation, knowledge and recognition indicates the obsessiveness of a compulsion to repeat which strives to allay, through a kind of slow erosion, any danger associated with the potentially radical aspects of the maternal.

Above and beyond all other specifications, the true mother is defined in terms of pure presence: she is the one who is *there*. In *To Each His Own*, after a traumatic confrontation with the child who does not recognize her as his mother, Jody tells her friend and secretary, "I'm not his mother, not really. Just bringing a child into the world doesn't make you that. It's being there always, nursing him . . . all the things I've missed." Although presence does not exhaust the attributes essential to motherhood—in itself it is not sufficient—it is absolutely necessary for adequate mothering. Paternal power, on the other hand, often manifests itself more strongly through absence (this is the case in films like *The Reckless Moment* and *Since You Went Away*). In *The Great Lie*, Bette Davis makes use of assumptions based on the association of presence and mothering to sustain her husband's belief that the child is actually hers. In this way she manages to manufacture a lie (the "great lie") from an iconic system. Yet, it does not have the affective valence of a lie—after all, Bette Davis is *there*, while Mary Astor is not. And the (rather abrupt) closure of the film affirms the spectator's sense that Bette Davis is the "true" mother.

Circumscribed in this way, the concept of the maternal is compatible with the language of melodrama—the two discourses support one another through a mutual reinforcement of certain semes: presence, immediacy, readability. According to Peter Brooks, the melodramatic mode strives to resuscitate an originary language theorized in the eighteenth century by writers such as Diderot and Rousseau in terms of a notion of gesture as an unmediated sign and its corresponding attributes of purity and presence. In Diderot's aesthetic theory, gesture and cry signify more fully because they are the language of nature and hence accessible to all. [30] The nostalgia implicit in such a formulation is apparent in Rousseau—as Brooks points out, "Gesture appears in the *Essai* to be a kind of pre-language, giving a direct presentation of things prior to the alienation from presence set off by the passage into articulated language." [31] And according to the *Encyclopédie*, gesture is "the primitive language of mankind in its cradle." [32] This "originary language" is, of course, theorized as a maternal tongue. Although Brooks does not explicitly indicate this, references to "nature," a "pre-language," "mankind in its cradle," forcefully connect the primal language he delineates to a maternal space. The "feminine" connotations attached to melodrama are no doubt at least partially derived from this tendency.

The desire of melodrama to recover an originary language which is not structured through difference is manifested in the genre's strategy of deflecting signifying material onto other, nonlinguistic registers of the sign—gesture, looks, music, mise-en-scène. In this group of films, little is left to language. The texts, in fact, exhibit a distrust of language, locating the fullness of meaning elsewhere. At the end of *The Reckless Moment*, the bars of the staircase which appear to imprison the mother (Joan Bennett) undermine the forced optimism of her telephone conversation with the absent husband. The memory-flashback which structures the bulk of the narrative in *To Each His Own* is constituted as the repudiation of a casual remark made by a young woman to Jody as she waits in the train station for the arrival of her son: "You can't imagine what it's like to be in love with a flier." Jody proceeds to imagine/remember this and more in the production of the film's narrative. The pathetic quality of the scene in which Jody fails to disclose her secret to her son is encapsulated less in the dialogue whereby she denigrates her own right to claim the status of motherhood than in the prominence accorded an absurd balloon in the shape of a horse (Carol, the Queen of the the Corral) within the mise-en-scène. The constant presence of the horse which haunts and doubles her own image underlines the futility of her desire. Insofar as gesture is concerned, in *Johnny Belinda* the full force of the mute Belinda's maternal desire is conveyed by her constant repetition of the sign language signifiers for the phrase, "I want my baby" (signifiers which include the gesture of rocking an imaginary baby back and forth in one's arms).

But the register of the sign which bears the greatest burden in this yearning for a full language is that which authorizes the label "melodrama"—music. Music marks a deficiency in the axis of vision. Because emotion is the realm in which the visible is insufficient as a guarantee, the supplementary meaning proffered by music is absolutely necessary. The cinematic relation between music and the image is explicitly spelled out in *Lydia* when a blind pianist teaches children colors through music and produces an entire concerto as a "description" of Lydia's face. As the pianist maintains, "No one can really see what he loves," and music marks the excess. The incessant recourse to music in maternal melodrama and its heightening effect suggest that the rationality of the image is a disadvantage.[33]

In this sense, the melodramatic discourse aims to do what Brooks claims psychoanalysis accomplishes in relation to the unconscious—to recover for meaning what is outside meaning. Gesture, music, and mise-en-scène are deployed to represent that which is unrepresentable—the "ineffable." The project of the maternal melodrama is from the beginning an impossible one insofar as it strives to retrieve that which is fundamentally contradictory—a language of presence. Doubly impossible insofar as it strives to represent the maternal as a form of pure presence. And because the imaginary signifier of the cinema, as Metz has shown, is based on absence to a greater degree than other languages which activate multiple sensory registers, the melodramatic film has a greater stake in masking this absence. It does so by intensifying and displacing the presence, immediacy, and closeness which purportedly characterize the connection between sign and referent onto the relation between film and spectator. The film invests in the possibility of immediate understanding, and the immediacy of its communication is evidenced by the unthought, uncontrollable tears which it produces. The form of affect associated with maternal melodrama, pathos, connotes a violent sentimentalism.

This pathetic effect is facilitated, as mentioned earlier in the analysis of *Stella Dallas*, by a sense of disproportion—between desires and their fulfillment or between the transgression (e.g., the "sin" of the unwed mother) and the punishment associated with it. As the nurse in *To Each His Own* tells Jody, "You've sinned. You'll pay for it the rest of your life." And she does. *To Each His Own* exemplifies the classic maternal melodrama insofar as its rapid plot reversals and convolutions, its blockages of communication, all seem to serve the same function—to construct and maintain an unbridgeable distance between the female protagonist and the object of her desire, a distance which is rationalized by her originary transgression. From this perspective, it is worth exploring *To Each His Own* in some depth.

In the beginning of the film, which is predominantly structured as a flashback, Jody Norris (Olivia de Havilland) is a middle-aged American woman in London who happens to save the life of an Englishman, Lord Desham, when he falls off a roof during air raid maneuvers. When Lord Desham in gratitude takes Jody to dinner, she has a chance encounter with a soldier from her hometown who informs her that someone else from the same town is arriving on the train that night. Because that "someone else," as the spectator later learns, turns out to be Jody's son, she rushes to the train station only to find that the train has been delayed. The bulk of the film's narrative takes the form of a flashback memory which fills the time of her waiting at the train station.

As mentioned earlier, the flashback is a response to (and a repudiation of) a young woman's casual remark to Jody, "You can't imagine what it's like to be in love with a flier." In the first scene of her memory-flashback, Jody discourages one potential beau (Max, a slick salesman) in the name of her desire for "true romance" and turns down the marriage proposal of another (Alec, who marries another woman, Corrine, on the rebound). But then Jody meets a romantic young flier who descends from the sky seemingly for the sole purpose of making love to her and fulfilling her dreams and then ascends once more only to be shot down in a battle. From their one night of romance, she becomes pregnant. The speed with which the love story of the first section of the film is displaced by the maternal melo of the second is rather remarkable. As Wolfenstein and Leites point out in their description of the film, "A recurrent theme in these films of the heroine and her son is the absence of the father, who may descend from heaven in an airplane to beget the child and then fly off never to be seen again (*To Each His Own*)."[34] Wolfenstein and Leites interpret the film as an instance of Otto Rank's myth of the birth of the hero which "reduces the relation of the mother and father to a transient contact" and "gratifies the son's longing to exclude the father and have the mother to himself."[35] This analysis is, however, based on the premise that the film should be interpreted from the point of view of the son—a premise which has little credibility given the organization of affect in the film and the terms of its address.

Both Jody's pregnancy and her motherhood are riddled with problems. When the doctor tells her she is pregnant he also informs her that she is sick and either must have an operation in which she will lose the baby or die. Jody is preparing to go to New York and have the operation when she hears the news of her flier's death. This turn of events prompts her to have the baby regardless of the threat to herself in order to preserve the father's memory. Despite the doctor's warning, the baby and Jody are both healthy after the delivery in New York City. Jody devises a scheme whereby she has the baby left on a doorstep in her hometown (the doorstep of a woman who already has eight children) and plans to intervene herself with the offer to adopt the baby. But the plan miscarries when Alec and Corrine, whose first child has just died, find out about the foundling and adopt it before Jody can make her claim. Jody sees how happy Corrine is with the baby in her arms and leaves him with her, although she visits him constantly. Tension develops between Corrine and Jody over both the baby and Alec, who ultimately admits that he still loves Jody. When Jody's father dies, she asks Corrine if she can act as the baby's ("Griggsy's") nursemaid. When Corrine jealously refuses, Jody decides to tell her that the baby is hers and produces a birth certificate (a recurrent sign in scenes of recognition in melodrama). But Corrine and Alec have had the baby legally adopted to protect themselves against such a possibility, and Jody has no legal right to the child.

Upon hearing this news, Jody leaves her hometown and goes to New York to work. She becomes rich and influential as the president of Lady Vyvyan cosmetics. Several years pass and Alec occasionally brings Griggsy to New York so that Jody can get a glimpse of her son. Jody learns that Corrine and Alec are on the verge of bankruptcy and literally blackmails Corrine into giving her Griggsy. However, the little boy (who is now approximately five or six years old) soon misses his "mother" (Corrine), and in a poignant scene Jody recognizes this and is forced to let him return to his adoptive family. Hoping to displace all her energies from motherhood to work, she tells an associate, "Let me go to London. Find me fourteen hours of work a day."

Thus ends the flashback portion of the film as Jody still waits at the train station for her now fully grown son who has become, like his father, an air force pilot. Jody, of course, recognizes him immediately (perhaps because the same actor—John Lund—takes the roles of both father and son). The son now has a girl, however—a WAC who is also on leave—and he is more concerned with her and with the obstacles to their desire to get married than with "Aunt" Jody. But Lord Desham, arriving for a date with Jody, learns about the situation and by means of his high-level contacts arranges a wedding and longer leaves for the young couple. In the last scene the son, primarily through the intervention of his girlfriend (who says of Jody: "I saw her watching you. Anyone would think you were her only son."), finally recognizes that Jody is his real mother. The son approaches Jody and says, "I think this is our dance, mother."

I have delineated the plot of *To Each His Own* in such extended detail in order to specify the various ways in which the narrative structure meticulously constructs blockade after blockade against maternal desire. Even at the end of the film, when recognition finally takes place, it does so only through the mediation of a father figure (Lord Desham) and in the context of a ritual whereby the son is passed on to another woman. Despite the absence of a literal father in much of the film, father figures do play a crucial role in the narrative trajectory. Not only does Lord Desham almost miraculously provide closure, but Jody's father, earlier in the film, determines to a large extent the course of events. When Corrine and Alec decide to adopt the child found on the doorstep early in the film, Jody prepares to tell them that the child is really hers. But her father intervenes claiming, "He's my grandchild, he's not going to be brought up a marked child. Can't you hear people whispering, 'He hasn't a father—never had one.'" The lack of a father and its social consequences are determinant in the initiation of Jody's trajectory of pain and suffering. When her own father dies, Jody tries to retrieve the child but it is too late (her timing is off), and the birth certificate she produces as proof of the child's identity is now useless. From this point of view, it is quite significant that recognition takes place at the end of the film via a stand-in (Lord Desham) for the absent father. The separation between mother and son, that is, the movement of the son into the social order, must be insured before any possibility of reunification of the two can be acknowledged.

This is why the presence of Liz—the girlfriend—is so crucial at the end of the film. She effectively blocks a process which had been gaining momentum throughout the film—the eroticization of the mother/son relation—and which culminates in the use of the same actor to play the roles of both lover and son. This eroticization is registered primarily as a scopophiliac relation. Jody keeps a scrapbook filled with photographs of her son and frequently looks with longing at these photos. Caught in the act of doing so by her former beau, Max the salesman (who does not see the subject of the photographs), she has a lengthy conversation with him based on his misunderstanding that the object of her gaze is a beau (Max asks her about "obstacles" to their marrying). When "Griggsy" comes to live with Jody briefly in New York, she can't keep her eyes off of him until Griggsy finally asks, "Is my face dirty? You keep looking at it so hard." Absence and distance only intensify that love which is doomed to failure. *To Each His Own* seems to dramatize most explicitly the Freudian notion that a woman's love is always mistimed, always subject to a displacement from father to son (a psychoanalytic thematics which will be discussed more thoroughly later in this chapter). Jody must witness and accept her replacement as object of desire by Liz at the end of the film.

*To Each His Own* also dramatizes what Elsaesser refers to as the impotency of displacement as a method of attaining emotional ends in melodrama.[36] The money stockpiled by Jody for her son only increases the pathos of her failure to relate to him. When she learns that Corrine and Alec have adopted her son she substitutes hard work and economic success for the joys of mothering. Many of the maternal melodramas of the '40s elaborate this type of binary logic whereby mothering and economic success are opposed to one another and, in most cases, constituted as absolutely incompatible. In this way the films manage to effectively demarcate and separate the realms of production and reproduction. This is the case in *To Each His Own*, *Mildred Pierce*, and *The Reckless Moment*. In *The Reckless Moment*, Mrs. Harper is so absorbed by the processes of mothering that she finds herself entirely excluded from the language of economics. When she attempts to get a loan in order to pay off her daughter's blackmailer, she stumbles over the words ("I'd like to *make* a loan. . . . *get* a loan.").

The pathetic effect of the scene in which Jody, having literally bought Griggsy from Corrine and Alec, finds that she cannot satisfy his desire for his mother, is a result of this absolute disjunction between the maternal and economic activities. Jody's large, well-decorated house only underlines Griggsy's loneliness and the extent to which he misses the woman he believes to be his mother. In an earlier scene, Alec had taken Griggsy to a rodeo in order to provide a situation in which Jody could see and talk to her son. At the rodeo it becomes clear that Griggsy would like to have a ridiculous-looking balloon that the peddler refers to as "Carol, the Queen of the Corral." Jody attempts to buy the balloon but the peddler informs her that this particular balloon is not for sale since it is used as a "come-on." Later, when Griggsy has come to live with her, Jody tells him that she has a surprise for him. The little boy becomes very excited when the surprise is referred to as a "lady," but is dismayed to find that it is "Carol, the Queen of the Corral." When Jody asks him why he is so sad he replies, "I thought maybe it was my mother" and runs into a bedroom. In the following shot of Jody, "Carol, the Queen of the the Corral"—the balloon that was not for sale—occupies the background as a grotesque reminder and caricature of Jody's deficiency as a mother.

At this point, Jody's friends urge her to tell Griggsy that she is his real mother, and there follows a scene which is one of the most moving of the film, based as it is on an almost total blockage of communication and Griggsy's non-recognition of his mother. When Jody attempts to reveal her identity, he misunderstands and, thinking that she is referring disparagingly to the fact that he is adopted (a situation Corrine has clearly warned him about), he runs crying into the bathroom. As Elsaesser points out, "Pathos results from non-communication or silence made eloquent. . . ."[37] Jody can only walk over to the mirror, whose reflection seems to confirm her nonidentity as a mother. For the function of a mother, as Jody defines it, is "being there always." The slippage between the mirror image and what she desires also mirrors the female spectator's relation to the text of pathos.

Of the various subgenres of the woman's film, the maternal melodrama is the one which appears to fully earn the label "weepie." The plight of the mother with respect to her child, the necessary separations, losses, and humiliations she must suffer are always moving and often "move" the spectator to tears. The films obsessively structure themselves around just-missed moments, recognitions which occur "too late," and blockages of communication which might have been avoided. In this sense, the pathetic text appears to insist that the gap between desire and its object is not structural but accidental and therefore to reconfirm the possibility of a fullness in signification—a complete and transparent communication. Tears testify to the loss of such a fullness but also to its existence as a (forever receding) ideal.

But what activates crying as the spectatorial response to (or defense against) a text? For Franco Moretti it is a matter of timing, and in some cases it is even possible to locate a precise textual moment which triggers the tears. Although Moretti's investigation of "moving literature" focuses on boy's literature ("texts with 'boys' both as their protagonists and as their ideal readers"),[38] the pathos associated with this genre has a great deal in common with that of the woman's film. For both boys and women are "presubjects"; they are denied access to the full subjectivity bestowed on the adult male within a patriarchal culture. Occupying the margins of the social field, they are both allowed to cry. There is a difference of course. The projected future of the boy always assumes an access to subjectivity—he must simply wait. The woman, on the other hand, is always a "pre-subject"—she will always wait for that moment (scenarios in which the woman *waits* abound in the woman's film). "Boy's literature" represents for its addressee a form of preparation for the assumption of full subjectivity within society. As Moretti points out, the texts thus enact a mourning for the narcissistic losses which must inevitably accompany such an access to subjectivity. They can therefore be analyzed with reference to the *Bildungsroman*. Not so the maternal melodrama in which no *Bildung* takes place.

The moving effect is generated by what Moretti describes as a "rhetoric of the too late." All literary narrative is characterized by shifting points of view which are ultimately submitted to a process of hierarchization in the text's resolution. This is the moment of agnition or recognition. What is specific to "moving" literature is not the hierarchization of points of view or the device of agnition itself but the *timing* of that agnition—"Agnition is a 'moving' device when it comes *too late*. And to express the sense of being 'too late' the easiest course is obviously to prime the agnition for the moment when the character is on the point of dying."[39] Pathos is thus related to a certain construction of temporality in which communication or recognitions take place but are mistimed. Moving narratives manifest an unrelenting linearity which allows the slippage between what is and what should have been to become visible. What the narratives demonstrate above all is the irreversibility of time.

> And this irreversibility is perceived that much more clearly if there are no doubts about the *different direction* one would like to impose on the course of events.
>
> This is what makes one cry. Tears are always the product of *powerlessness*. They presuppose two mutually opposed facts: that it is clear how the present state of things should be changed—and that this change is *impossible*. They presuppose a definitive estrangement of facts from values, and thus the end of any relationship between the idea of *teleology* and that of *causality*.[40]

The "moving effect," then, is tied to a form of mistiming, a bad timing, or a disphasure. This is perhaps most visible in a woman's film which is not, strictly speaking, a maternal melodrama, but is a "weepie" nevertheless—*Back Street*. In the 1941 version of this film, the female protagonist literally misses the boat, and her bad timing insures that her fiancé will leave and ultimately marry another woman. That one missed moment will determine her future, relegating her to the back street of his life until she dies. The film goes so far as to provide the spectator with a means to measure the distance between what was and what should have been by supplying the missing image of their encounter at the boat landing—after both of the characters have died.

Maternal melodramas, on the other hand, favor a specific form of mistiming which allows the films quite often to corroborate Freud's theories about maternal love and the relation between the sexes. For Freud, the most perfect human relationship is that between mother and son. In his lecture on "Femininity," he notes the importance of the pre-Oedipal period in the formation of the future mother. The psychical characteristics acquired by the woman in this period later attract the man who sees in her his own mother. Freud's interpretation is somewhat despairing: "How often it happens, however, that it is only his son who obtains what he himself aspired to! One gets an impression that a man's love and a woman's are a phase apart psychologically."[41] This disphasure is echoed in Lacan's formulation, "There is no sexual relation." In the maternal melodramas, the son (or sometimes a daughter) often quite blatantly assumes the place of the father in the mother's sexual life. In films like *Tomorrow is Forever* and *Watch on the Rhine*, the son's desire to enlist or to become active in world affairs renews the threat of a lost love. The timing of the two world wars—a generation apart—allows for the narratives' exploitation of repetition in the relation between a woman and her husband and that between a woman and her son (*To Each His Own, Tomorrow is Forever, Watch on the Rhine* are examples of this tendency). In *Letter from an Unknown Woman* or even *Now, Voyager* the child takes over the space of the absent lover. The most striking example is *To Each His Own*, discussed earlier, in which a series of mistimings results in the separation between mother and son and the subsequent eroticization of the mother's (scopophiliac) relation to the son (whose role, it is worth repeating, is taken by the same actor as the now dead father). In this sense, weepies trace the outline of an inevitable mistiming or disphasure which is constitutive of feminine sexuality in a patriarchal culture.

This alleged "fault" or "flaw" in female sexuality (the woman's misdirected desire—her insistence on striving after the "wrong" object) is given extensive representation within the maternal melodramas. Maternal desire is frequently revealed as actively resistant to the development of a love story. In *Mildred Pierce*, a potential love relationship between Mildred and Monty is aborted almost before it begins by Mildred's growing involvement with a business venture designed to satisfy her daughter Veda's desires. In *The Reckless Moment*, the most aberrant and even, at times, subversive of maternal melodramas, Mrs. Harper (Joan Bennett), concentrating on the protection of her daughter, does not even recognize that she is involved in a love story with the blackmailer Donnelly until it is too late. As the editors of *Framework* point out in their insightful analysis of the film, motherhood is delineated as the repression of desire (Mrs. Harper's strict regulation of her daughter's sex life) and the body (she is constantly telling her son to put on more clothes—"Pull up your socks," "Put on a shirt," etc.).[42] An inordinate amount of film time is spent on a scene in which Mrs. Harper laboriously and in silence (there is no music on the track, only the sound of lapping waves) drags Darby's body down the beach to the boat in order to take it away and conceal it—in what is basically a literalization of the "maternal function" of hiding (or repressing) the body. A mother's instinct to protect the fully legalized institution of the family is, interestingly enough, itself outside of the law.

Particularly pertinent, then, is *The Reckless Moment*'s presentation to its female spectator of a fantasy of flirting with otherness, represented in the film by the underworld. Although the *Framework* article treats the film primarily as a family melodrama which, riddled with tensions and contradictions, tends to subvert the stability of the family as a structure, the film is based on a short story from *Ladies' Home Journal*,[43] and its mode of address is partially codified by the demands of this form. Much of its appeal lies in its status as a story of a forbidden or illicit love and the attraction of a character played by James Mason—an attraction which is strengthened by his association with illegality and the underworld. The spectator's knowledge or awareness of the love affair exceeds that of the female protagonist, who is totally oblivious to the "female fantasy" aspect of the film—being loved by a blackmailer—until the end when she must recognize it as a lost object. In this sense, the film laboriously constructs that loss for her.

When the blackmailer Donnelly first appears in the film he functions, structurally, as an erotic replacement for the absent father. The sustained tracking shot which follows Mrs. Harper down the stairs (the pivot of the mise-en-scène in the film) to meet Donnelly for the first time echoes that in which she descends the stairway in order to talk to her husband on the phone. During Mrs. Harper's conversation with Donnelly, her son enters and the camera placements emphasize a triangular spatial relationship between the three figures—mother, son, and, structurally, "father." Furthermore, it is almost as though all communications addressed to the husband-father were intercepted by Donnelly. Early in the film, Mrs. Harper writes a letter to her husband, censoring a version in which she details her anxieties about her daughter and substituting for it the standard clichés of a love letter. Several scenes later, as though the letter had reached the wrong destination, Donnelly reads to her the clichéd love letters which were, in fact, written by her daughter. The "real" father in the film is never imaged; he is represented only as a voice at the other end of the line, and that voice is merely implied, never actually heard. But Donnelly literally takes his place at the other end of the line. When he speaks with Mrs. Harper on the phone, he is given both an image and a voice.

Yet, it becomes clear fairly quickly that Donnelly's status as lover-husband figure is only an apparent one. For, what he is actually seduced by is the maternal. As Mrs. Harper fully assumes the maternal function, becoming more and more concerned about her family, Donnelly is progressively more attracted to her. The film is, in a sense, a fantasy about the power of mothers—even criminality is confounded and subdued by the maternal. In the drugstore scene, Donnelly provides Mrs. Harper with change for the phone, carries her packages, and even buys her a present (which she does not recognize as such). Later, he goes so far as to offer her his half of the blackmail money. The blackmailer is fully domesticated. At the end of the film this transformation of the potentially erotic into filial devotion is evidenced most fully by a speech in which Donnelly admits that Mrs. Harper invokes in him the memory of his own mother ("My mother wanted to make a priest out of me. I never wanted to do a decent thing until I met you. . . . Don't make the same mistake my mother did.") It is the image of the mother, not the woman, which prompts desire and reformation.

Mrs. Harper is not even aware of the possibility of another type of relationship with Donnelly—or of the possibility that she might perform a role different from that of the maternal—until she loses him when he sacrifices himself for the family she sought to protect throughout the film. But here the mother's desire for something outside of or other than the family (a desire which the spectator possesses long before Mrs. Harper) is thwarted by the process of its inclusion within that familial structure. The blackmailer, tinged with the excitement of the illicit, the underworld, is reduced to a son, paying homage to a maternal ideal. This inclusion of the external object of desire within the closed web of the family is marked by lighting. Throughout the film, a uniformly lit and clear image is associated with the inside of the Harper house and the activities of the family, while film noir lighting characterizes the scenes external to the house—on its fringes or in the boathouse, scenes associated with the intrusion of the underworld. But in the final section of the film, film noir lighting invades the household, contaminating the bedroom—site of Mrs. Harper's lost desire—as she lies on the bed, crying violently. This collapse of the opposition between inside and outside in relation to the family exemplifies the status of the maternal as a closed circuit of desire. Donnelly is a pivotal figure here insofar as he explicitly demonstrates the slippage whereby a lover figure becomes a son. Mrs. Harpers' tears testify to the pathos associated with this inevitability. In the final scene of the film, the image of Mrs. Harper sobbing, as she carries on a banal phone conversation with her husband about the color of the family Christmas tree, is not only framed by the bars of the staircase which verify her imprisonment within the family, it is also haunted by the presence of her son, finally and fully dressed, occupying the background of the image.

In films like *The Reckless Moment*, pathos is generated by a situation in which maternal love becomes a sign of the impossibility of female desire, which must remain unfulfilled precisely because it is "out of synch" with the proper order of generations. In more "standard" maternal melodramas, such as *To Each His Own* or *The Great Lie*, *Stella Dallas* or *That Certain Woman*, pathos is associated with the actual or potential separation between mother and child. Nevertheless, given the variety of instanciations of pathos and the generality of a definition linking it to a fundamental split between causality and teleology, it is difficult to support any claim which would make pathos a specifically feminine signifying strategy. And yet it is also clear that the "moving" and the maternal maintain an intimate relationship. Furthermore, it is important to keep in mind that words etymologically related to "pathos"—e.g., sympathy, empathy—are evocative of the culturally constructed understanding of the woman's relation to the other.

The maternal melodrama is maintained as a feminine genre by means of its opposition to certain genres specified as masculine (e.g., the Western, the detective film, the boxing film)—an opposition which in its turn rests on another, that between emotionalism and violence. But theories of scopophilia, the imaginary relation of spectator to film, and the mirror phase all suggest that aggressivity is an inevitable component of the imaginary relation in the cinema. In the Western and detective film aggressivity or violence is internalized as narrative content. In maternal melodrama, the violence is displaced onto affect—producing tear*jerkers*. Its sentimentality is, in some respects, quite sadistic.

This sadism generates metaphors within the critical discourse surrounding melodrama which are fully informed and inflected by ideologically complicit understandings of sexual difference. Claude Beylie, for instance, in an article entitled "Propositions on the Melo," attempts to describe the peculiarly melodramatic effect and it is not accidental that he arrives at the metaphor of rape: "The Greeks had a word for designating this, the art of captivating immediately and violently a public apparently reticent, in reality complicit (like a masochistic girl, who adores, at bottom, being violated): the word *pathos*."[44] Pathos, then, is a kind of textual rape and it is understandable from this point of view that it should frequently be perceived as lacking a certain aesthetic legitimacy. The opposition emotion/violence can be maintained at the level of generic content only by collapsing it in the film's terms of address and producing a violent emotionalism. Insofar as the spectator is feminized through pathos (transformed into a "masochistic girl"), the film is perceived as cheating or manipulating its viewer. The cultural denigration of the "weepies" is complicit with an ideological notion of sexually differentiated forms of spectatorship. From this perspective, it is not at all surprising that the maternal melodrama tends to produce the uncomfortable feeling that someone has been had.

# 4

## The Love Story

The "love story" is, paradoxically, both central to and a marginal discourse within the classical Hollywood cinema.[1] It is central insofar as the couple is a constant figure of Hollywood's rhetoric and some form of heterosexual pact constitutes its privileged mode of closure. Its marginality, on the other hand, is associated with its status as a feminine discourse—the "love story" purportedly "speaks to" a female spectator. While the horror film, as Linda Williams points out, prompts the little girl (or grown woman) to cover her eyes,[2] the sign of masculinity in the little boy, when confronted with the "love story," is the fact that he looks away. The cinema loses its captivating effect, its function as a lure. This exclusion of the male gaze would appear to be fatal in the context of an institutionalized discourse which foregrounds the inscription of masculine subjectivity. And indeed it is, at least as far as critical reception is concerned. The filmic narrative whose proairetic and hermeneutic codification are exhausted in the delineation of a love motif is frequently consigned to the ghetto of film history.

Of course there are exceptions, those films labelled "great love stories"— narratives which are usually buttressed by the weight of History and the authority of its mise-en-scène, films such as Gone With the Wind, Reds, Dr. Zhivago. The activation of history insures an immediate meaning effect, an area in which the love story, due to its fetishization of affect, is inevitably lacking. The ordinary love story, rather than activating history as mise-en-scène, as space, inscribes it as individual subjectivity closed in on itself. History is an accumulation of memories of the loved one, and the diachronic axis of representation generates a relation governed by only one set of terms—separation and reunion. Situated outside the arena in which history endows space with meaning, the ordinary love story is perceived as opportunistic in its manipulation of affect in an attempt to fully engage the spectator, binding him/her too closely to its discourse.

Symptomatic of this apparent overreliance on unbounded affect is the exaggerated role of music in the love story. Music is the register of the sign which bears the greatest burden in this type of text—its function is no less than that of representing that which is unrepresentable: the ineffable. Desire, emotion— the very content of the love story—are not accessible to a visual discourse but demand the supplementary expenditure of a musical score. Music takes up where the image leaves off—what is in excess in relation to the image is equivalent to what is in excess of the rational. Music has an anaphoric function, consistently pointing out that there is more than meaning, there is desire. To music is always delegated the task of pinpointing, isolating the moments of greatest significance, telling us where to look despite the fact that the look is inevitably lacking.

Nevertheless, there is always something horrifying about pure affect seemingly unanchored by signification. The heightening effect of music, its straining to direct the reading of the image, is paradoxically highly visible and risks spectatorial repudiation. It is as though music continually announces its own deficiency in relation to meaning. Complicit with the excessive emotionalism associated with the love story, music no doubt contributes to its denigration. This at least partially explains a very strong tendency within the genre of the love story to motivate an apparent overemphasis on music by situating its major male character—the object of female desire—in the role of a musician. In films like *Letter from an Unknown Woman, Deception, Interlude, Intermezzo, Humoresque,* and *When Tomorrow Comes,* the male lead is a pianist, a cellist, a composer, or a violinist. By transforming music into a substantial component of their content, displacing it from the level of the extradiegetic to the diegetic, these narratives provide a rationalization of their own form insofar as it involves an overreliance on a desemanticized register of the sign. Furthermore, the specification of the male character as a musician has a surplus benefit. In the love story, the male undergoes a kind of feminization by contamination—in other words, he is to a certain degree emasculated by his very presence in a feminized genre. As Roland Barthes claims, there is always something about the lover which is "feminized": "in any man who utters the other's absence *something feminine* is declared."[3] The scandal of such a masculine femininity is partially mitigated through the construction of a strong bond between the male character and the only culturally sanctioned and simultaneously "feminized" activity: Art. The subgenre effectively recoups some of the male's inevitable losses in the love story by making him into a respected artist, a musician.

Of the above listed films, *Humoresque* (1946, Jean Negulesco) is perhaps the most excessive in its reliance on music as the privileged signifier of affect. It includes three extended concert scenes; in two of these the only other signifying register which is foregrounded outside music is a highly meaningful relay of glances between characters. In the third and final, very long, concert sequence, crosscutting between the male violinist's rendering of "Tristan and Isolde" in a concert hall and the female character's suicide through drowning results in the construction of her death as a type of spectacle. The music of the performance becomes the soundtrack of her death scene; her last moments coincide with the last notes of the concert and are succeeded by the applause of the audience. The amount of narrative time used up, exhausted by music is unusual, even within this subgenre.

Hence, there are extended segments of *Humoresque* which stake out a space of signification almost totally outside language—language in any form, whether dialogue, voice-over, or graphics. The signifying supports of the sequences—music and image—as analogical semiotic systems, are generally regarded as discourses of pure affirmation. As the Group $\mu$ points out, in their work toward a general rhetoric, "negation (or contradiction, or contrarity) do not exist in the analogical," and iconic signs are analogical insofar as they "are definable, in their theoretical purity, as non-discrete (continuous), non-arbitrary (motivated) and not structured by binary oppositions."[4] The lack of explicit and stable demarcations, the fluidity of the system as it were, indicate an ontological inability to produce a "no" or a "not." Or, as Peter Wollen points out in a discussion of Godard's scratching or marking the surface of the film in *Wind from the East*, Godard "is looking for a way of expressing negation. It is well known that negation is the founding principle of verbal language, which marks it off both from animal signal-systems and from other kinds of human discourse, such as images."[5] The image is an indicator of presence and affirmation—in Metz's terms, an image of a revolver always means, at the very least, "Here is a revolver."[6] The love story, doubly dependent on image and music, would appear to be a doubly affirmative discourse.

Yet, *Humoresque* as a whole is characterized by a work of active denial of the female gaze and consequently a negation and punishment of the female spectator. And because it contains extended sequences in which the only signifying materials activated are music and the image, it offers particularly instructive instances of the rather strained attempt to operate negation within an iconic system. Or perhaps more accurately—there are everywhere present in the film traces of the desire to negate.

The narrative concerns a wealthy patroness of the arts, Helen Wright (Joan Crawford) and her love affair with the young violinist she supports, Paul Boray (John Garfield). Their desire is from the very beginning an impossible one, not only because Helen is already married but perhaps more importantly because

she is the hyperbolized figure of an excessive female sexuality which must ultimately be eliminated. Her presence makes manifest the male's impotence.
This excess, the threat posed by her sexuality, is constituted by the text in several
different ways. First, the very notion of a patroness of the arts indicates a perversion of the traditional male/female power relation in the realm of economics
since the male is, in effect, "kept" by the woman. Secondly and as previously
mentioned, Helen embodies a female sexuality which ignores or negates marital boundaries and which cannot, therefore, be contained within the family.
The film underlines her resistance to the family by providing two oppositional
female figures: Paul's mother, who provides him with the initial "gift" of the
violin and continually oversees, with disapproval, his sexual behavior/activities
with Helen; and Gina, the conventional and healthy girl-next-door, the one
whom Paul's mother has already chosen as his future wife. At one point in the
film, the mere presence of Helen, forcefully established through a series of
point-of-view shots attributed to Gina, is sufficient to drive Gina, who is unable
to sustain the gaze at Helen, out of the concert hall. Upon leaving the hall, she
is forced to walk by poster after poster displaying Paul holding a violin. But in
the final scene of the film, close-ups of Gina, once again seated comfortably in
the concert hall, and a shot of the mother, belatedly entering her private balcony
room (a space formerly occupied by Helen) have a direct syntactical connection
with Helen's suicide. The mother and the girl-next-door, allowable representations of femininity, combine forces to drive the figure of excessive female
sexuality into the ocean.

   A rather drastic punishment it would seem, but her transgression is enor-
mous and is signaled not only by her alcoholism—Helen drinks excessively and
is rarely shown without a glass in her hand (she drinks like a fish you might say).
More importantly, the danger she represents has to do with the fact that she up-
sets and reverses the opposition between spectator and spectacle in terms of its
alignment with sexual difference. Helen is the agent of scopophilia—she fixes
Paul Boray with her gaze. He performs, she watches. But her rather violent appropriation of the gaze does not remain unqualified. She is represented as my-
opic (the moments of her transformation from spectacle to spectator thus
captured and constrained through their visualization as the act of putting on
glasses) and eventually eliminated from the text, her death equated with that of
a point of view.[7] Her nearsightedness is a signifier of the perversity of her scopophiliac relation with the male. There is a difficulty in the gaze, particularly
in relation to that of the mother whose steady looks at her son—usually connoting a moral rebuke—are also singled out by the text. Paul's mother is the
phallic mother *par excellence*, her look is the look of knowledge. When she first
sees Helen at Paul's recital she knows immediately the danger this woman poses
for her son, and her look at Paul conveys this knowledge. The mother is repre-

sented as a collection of sayings which can only be characterized as clichés—social knots of meaning, knowledge in its most stagnant form, incapable of transformation: "I have eyes, I can see what's happening"; "I wasn't born yesterday"; "You have to get up pretty early in the morning to fool me." All these clichéd sayings have to do with seeing and knowing and insure for the mother a certain epistemological solidity. She sees, she knows. Helen's vision, in contrast, is distorted, unclear, disturbed.

The eyeglasses frame Helen's eyes in more ways than one. They demarcate her look as aberrant by visualizing it as a unique gesture—thus insuring that she can always be caught in the act of looking. Yet, this particular and quite literal framing of the gaze is only one of a series of incessant and elaborate framing procedures which are designed to contain an aberrant and excessive female sexuality. For framing is the film's preferred strategy when it wishes to simultaneously state and negate. At the moment Helen first sees Paul Boray she is standing in front of a mirror with a rather ornate frame (figure 1)—a mirror which reflects the object of her gaze, Paul. There is a cut to a shot of Paul playing the violin (figure 2) and the reverse shot of Helen once again as she puts on her glasses (figure 3). The placement of the mirror behind Helen guarantees that while she holds Paul in her gaze, we can hold her in ours—her status as subject is coincident with her status as object. The mirror functions to reduce the necessity of an extended reverse shot which would not only deflect the spectator's gaze from Helen but feminize the male as spectacle. Within the general frame of the film, Helen is framed even more precisely by the male gaze. Almost every time that Helen is positioned as a spectator and looks intensively, a male character looks at her in the act of looking—a strategy which is a negation of her gaze, of her subjectivity in relation to vision. The male gaze erases that of the woman. This is at times a function of the mise-en-scène (figures 4 and 5) and at times a function of the editing (figures 6, 7, 8).

In these instances, control is from the periphery of the image (and it might be added, the periphery of the narrative). The power of the gaze is exercised from the margins of the frame, and it is through this process that the female gaze is bracketed or quoted—hence, the oppressiveness of the mise-en-scène. The procedure mimics, within the diegesis of the film, the relation between film and spectator as encapsulated in Bazin's well known claim—"the object of the shot is not what she is looking at, not even her look; it is: *looking at her looking.*" Heath refers to this "looking at looking" as a "totalizing security," as the "bind of a coherence of vision."[8] This totalizing force and organization of vision works to efface, or at the very least contain, the female look.

The activation of frames here strains toward writing, hence the possibility of negation within an iconic system. The very strength of this containment and the striving after negation indicate a very precise moment of ideological dan-

1–4

5–8

ger—the woman's assumption of the gaze. The tendency, then, is to reproduce, rearticulate frames and framing processes everywhere. This framing activity becomes particularly obsessive in the climactic scene of the film—especially after the final moment of dialogue that introduces the extended "Tristan and Isolde" sequence (which, as mentioned previously, is constituted solely by the signifying materials of music and image). With no one else present, Helen turns directly toward the camera (although her gaze is slightly to the side of it) and proposes a toast (figure 9)—a toast which can only be directed toward the audience, or more precisely, the female spectator: "Here's to the time when we were little girls and no one asked us to marry." The first person plural nature of this address is almost immediately countered by quasi-hysterical procedures of framing. Helen walks over to the side of the room and opens an album with Paul's picture on it (figure 10). The representation of Helen (the painting on the wall) dominates the frame. It takes up and repeats in its own configuration the position of her head looking down at the picture of Paul. Her active look becomes the demure looking down of a woman who is being looked at—insured by the replication of a gesture naturalized within the mise-en-scène by a diegetic frame. But this narcissistic collapse of subject and object of vision becomes even more pronounced later in the scene when Helen is once again haunted by her own image. The shot (figure 11) is of a reflection of Helen in a glass door, the ocean vaguely perceptible in the background of the image. Her image is framed by the baroque grillwork of the door. Helen raises her glass (figure 12) and throws it through the door, freeing her reflection from its encasement (figure 13) but only momentarily. For there is immediately a cut to the opposite side of the door and Helen is doubly framed by the grillwork and the hole of her own making (figure 14). Helen succeeds in breaking her own mirror image, breaking the object of her point of view, only to produce *another* frame (the hole in the glass) through which she becomes visible, framed for the spectator. The insistent, obsessive framing indicates the inevitability of a continual transformation of the female subject of the gaze into the object of the gaze. And here, in this scene which precedes her suicide, the syntax of the film insures that the transformation of femininity into object—framed and fetishized —is synonymous with death.

The initial shot of this sequence which details Helen's reflection and reaction to that reflection and the shot discussed earlier whereby the need for a counter shot is obviated by placing a mirror behind Helen have similar projects. Both shots attempt to collapse divisions constituted by editing between seer and seen—to collapse the shot/reverse shot, in other words, into the single image. They effect a certain confusion of syntax or collapsing of difference which can only be righted, redressed through Helen's death. This disturbance of codification is repeated at the level of the soundtrack as well, where the diegetic tends

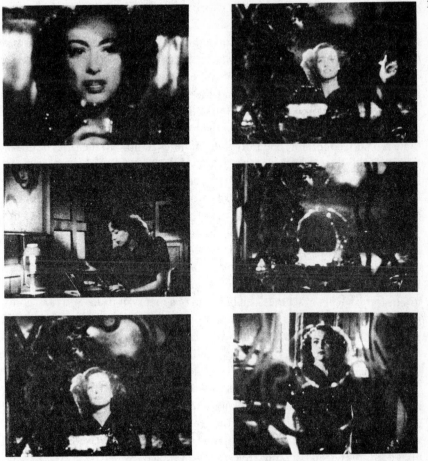

to merge with the extradiegetic. During the first part of the scene, Helen listens to Paul's violin rendition of "Tristan and Isolde" as it is broadcast over the radio. The source of the music is clearly diegetic—motivated and localized. Yet as she walks out to the beach, the music, rather than decreasing in volume with greater distance from the radio, appears to be amplified and to become, through a barely observable slippage, the extradiegetic music which accompanies her death scene. But this movement from the diegetic to the extradiegetic is reversed once again. With Helen's gesture of placing her hands over her ears to drown out the sound, the music becomes subjectivized, psychologically motivated, and diegetic once again. Music as the bad object, as the site of overindulgent or excessive affect is constrained by its confinement to female subjectivity.

The collapsing of the shot/reverse shot structure and the confusions between diegetic and extradiegetic are directly linked with female subjectivity. For excessive femininity is precisely that which does not respect boundaries or limits—frames, in effect. There is a persistent subtext in the film which appears to resist the epistemological implications of the frame: an emphasis on liquids and fluidity. Helen drinks excessively and is constantly pouring herself or others a drink. But the thematic of liquids is not contained or confined by her characterization as an alcoholic. Beyond the rather grandiose themes of water/sexuality/death invoked at the end of the film, there are traces of this obsession with fluids which extend throughout the text. Toward the middle of the film, there is a rather aberrant, certainly uneconomic fixation on the rings of liquid that a martini glass leaves on a table. Many of the transitions from one scene to another are constituted as transitions from one fluid to another—for example, a cut from Helen spraying soda into a glass to the breaking of waves in the ocean or from the dripping shower in the apartment Helen provides for Paul to the spray of a fountain. This emphasis on fluids seems to attach itself to Helen's excessive sexuality. Insofar as it signals that which exceeds set forms, boundaries, or limits, it is reminiscent of the construction of femininity described by Luce Irigaray in her essay, "The Mechanics of Fluids." In that essay, Irigaray points to a historical delay in science's elaboration of a theory of fluids and to a "complicity of long duration between rationality and a limited mechanics of solids."[9] Her association of femininity with what she refers to as the "real properties of fluids"—internal frictions, pressures, movement, a specific dynamics which makes a fluid nonidentical to itself—is, of course, merely an extension and a mimicking of a patriarchal construction of femininity. But it is surely one which is at work in *Humoresque*, which constantly formulates and reformulates female sexuality as an excessive relation to a boundary or a limit. In the shot in which Helen's reflection is superimposed over the ocean viewed through the glass door, the ocean becomes Helen's mirror image. And to have excessive female sexuality killed by its own image is to reveal the film's project—and that of the love story in general—as the tautological demonstration of the necessity of the failure of female desire.

And yet, there are leakages, as it were. The logic of continually undermining female subjectivity and desire seems to break down under the pressure of the insistent address to women in the love story. The very fact that Helen is granted a limited but nevertheless direct address to the female spectator—an address which invokes a time before the double bind of the marriage proposal, a time when the "little girl" does not yet have to bear the heaviest part of the burden of "femininity"—indicates that something is amiss. Helen is not subjected to a process of reformation. She must die because her excess is not recuperable.

The death of the female protagonist is not at all unusual in the subgenre of the love story (and it is a topic to which I will return later). But there are also other means of attaining closure which seem, on the surface at least, to be more benevolent, but are ultimately much more problematic. The most significant of these strategies is that of "allowing" the woman to *choose* one man over another (she invariably chooses the "right" man so that this group, unlike the other, is characterized by a "happy ending"). The act of making a choice is structurally determinant in films like *Daisy Kenyon* (1947), *Kitty Foyle* (1940), and *Lydia* (1941) (although in *Lydia* the woman chooses not to make a choice because the man she really loves does not even remember her).

In *Kitty Foyle*, whose subtitle is "The natural history of a woman," the choice Kitty (Ginger Rogers) must make between two men is clearly articulated along the lines of class difference. Her hometown suitor is from a wealthy family with a long aristocratic history (Kitty herself is from the "wrong side of the tracks"), while the suitor she ultimately chooses is a poor but honest and ideal-istic doctor. The temporal structure of the film dictates that it span the few hours she is given to make her choice—hours filled with flashback memories elabo-rating her relation to the two men. The film begins, however, with scenes which are, curiously, extraneous to the main narrative. Titles announce that this film is a "story of the white-collar girl—new to the American scene," and a scene in which men in a crowded cable car rise to give a woman a seat, evincing a nos-talgia for a time before "women's suffrage," is contrasted with a contemporary scene in a crowded subway car in which no one rises for the woman. The im-plication is that Kitty's dilemma, the necessity of making a very painful choice, is inextricably linked to the status of the "new woman" as an independent work-ing woman.

The Joan Crawford character in *Daisy Kenyon* is also a working woman—a clothes designer. But in this film, the two men struggle for her, while she in-vokes her work in order to flee both of them. The major difference between Dan O'Mara (Dana Andrews), a successful lawyer, and Peter Lapham (Henry Fonda), a suffering veteran and boat designer, is that Dan's violence toward Daisy is represented explicitly, while Peter's is only implicit, masked by an ap-parent benevolence and laissez-faire attitude. Each of the men maintains a dif-ferent relation to the law and the power it embodies. Dan, the lawyer, believes that a contract is a guarantee—he draws one up in order to effect a divorce be-tween Daisy and Peter. Peter, on the other hand, knows that silence and the gaze are more powerful laws. He offhandedly refers to their marriage contract as a formality and claims that he doesn't want a wife "on formalities." But Peter can afford to wait in the background because he *knows* what Daisy will ultimately do—it is almost as though he possessed narrational omniscience. Daisy herself becomes more and more isolated as the two men move closer together and begin to act in complicity with one another—meeting in a bar to discuss in a "civi-lized" manner which one of them Daisy wants and, later, playing cards while waiting for Daisy to come and announce her decision. In the end, any choice she is given is a fairly oppressive one, and although she attempts to send both of them away, Peter tells Dan, "That's *my* house and *my* wife," and returns to Daisy (who has already poured two drinks in anticipation of his return).

Hence, the central action of these films is that of coming to a decision, making a choice (often between two men who are ultimately quite similar). All filmic "events" or scenes revolve around and attach themselves to that choice. The films suggest that this is the one moment in a woman's life when she is allowed a positive action, when she must choose the man on whom the rest of the actions in her life will depend. In terms of the narrative structure as a whole, therefore, the choice is a privileged moment but it is also an endpoint. In his analysis of narrative in S/Z, Roland Barthes isolates a code of narrative actions and labels it the "proairetic" code. The proairetic code is made up of actions that "when subjected to a logico-temporal order . . . constitute the strongest armature of the readerly" and "can be assigned no logic other than that of the probable, of empirics, of the 'already-done' or 'already-written'. . . ."[10] The code of actions assumes a certain logic of human behavior and it is this code which "principally determines the readability of the text."[11] The "choice" films have a special affinity with the proairetic code. In fact, *proairesis*, as the *Oxford English Dictionary* informs us, is the Greek term for "choosing one thing before another." Barthes interprets the term very loosely and uses it to specify the minutest and most trivial of actions, but when it is read more literally as pertaining to the primary action of choosing, the logic of human behavior assumed by the proairetic code is revealed as a sexually differentiated logic. In the classical or readerly narrative as Barthes describes it, a series of choices made by the protagonist gives the narrative the structure of an intricately branching tree. Yet, in the love story, choice does not determine or control the narrative trajectory. Instead, the narrative culminates in a choice, indicating that the act of choosing is of monumental and climactic significance for the woman and, furthermore, that it is the endpoint of a long and arduous struggle. This tendency induces a sense of stagnancy and nonprogression which is evidenced in the temporal structure of the films—dominated by duration and repetition. Such a cyclical or repetitive relation to time is apparent even in films which do not fall into the "choice" category.

The "already-written" relation of women to time is the passive "activity" of waiting—waiting at windows, at train stations, in isolated apartments, or waiting for phone calls or letters. In contrast to the "thickening of time" which Pascal Bonitzer associates with the suspense film,[12] the love story would seem to depend on a thinning out of time, its expansion. The eventlessness and duration of such a temporality are at odds with what we think of as narrative temporality or with what Kristeva refers to as "obsessional time": "time as project, teleology, linear and prospective unfolding; time as departure, progression, and arrival—in other words, the time of history."[13] Women in the love story witness departures and arrivals, but there is little, if any, progression. They live in a state of expectation which is never fulfilled or fulfilled only in imagination, as in the final scene of the 1941 version of *Back Street*. *Back Street* is a particularly telling example of the ways in which pathos is produced around the figure of the waiting woman. Its protagonist, Ray Smith (Margaret Sullavan), gives up her job, reputation, friends, and the possibility of marriage so that she will have the time to wait for those precious moments when her lover can get away from his work or family. The pathos is perhaps most intense in a New Year's Eve scene in which her loneliness is magnified by the discrepancy between her patient waiting, the candles and champagne all ready, and the celebrations and merriment of her neighbors in the courtyard. *My Foolish Heart* (1949) constructs comic scenes around the phenomenon of women in a boarding school all waiting expectantly for phone calls from boyfriends. The most traumatic moment in Catherine Sloper's (Olivia de Havilland's) life in *The Heiress* (1949) is the moment when she realizes that she is waiting in vain for her lover, Morris Townsend (Montgomery Clift), to come and elope with her—forcing her to acknowledge that her father was right after all, that he really was "after her money." Waiting can even override the demand of a satisfactory closure: at the end of *When Tomorrow Comes* (1939), the female protagonist, whose lover is hopelessly married to a woman who is mentally ill, tells him "I'll be waiting" (presumably for the convenient death of the mad wife), and the film fades out on her close-up. Madame Bovary, in Vincente Minnelli's adaptation (1949), waits anxiously for the coach sent by her lover to free her from a suffocating life in a small town, but in a violent scene, the coach passes her by. Scenarios of waiting are crucial components of the love story and are offered as points of recognition and identification for the female spectator—"Yes, that's right, I've waited, too." "If you want a love story you must accept the waiting." If, by chance, it is the man who waits, he is, as Barthes points out, "feminized" by this relation to time and the other and suffering.[14]

This emphasis on duration and nonprogression is not only represented explicitly as waiting. At a more general level, the temporal structure of the films is often insistently repetitive or cyclical. The end of *The Letter* (1940) comes full circle and is a direct reply to the opening scene, even in its formal aspects. In the beginning of the film, after a shot of the moon and a shot of a sign locating the scene in a rubber plantation in Singapore, a languid camera movement traces a path down a tree to rubber dripping into a bucket, across a thatched open-sided hut where native workers rest on hammocks or play games, and, after a barely perceptible wipe, across a fence with the house in the background. A shot is heard, a bird is startled and flies off of the fence, and Leslie (Bette Davis) is introduced as a violent intrusion upon a peaceful scene, shooting a man repeatedly until the revolver is empty. Shots of the moon passing in and out of clouds, darkening and then exposing the scene, are motivated here by glance/object shots attributed first to the "head boy" and then to Leslie. Later in this scene, after Leslie has locked herself in her room, the head boy picks up a piece of lace, barely begun, and examines it. The density of the texture of the film is linked to a heightened significance attached to objects —her lace, the letter, the moon, the rubber, a dagger. At the end of the film, in line with the logic of transgression-punishment which informs it, Leslie is in her turn killed by the man's wife, represented as an enigmatic woman of mixed descent, a Eurasian. One death balances the other. Here an unmotivated shot of the moon emerging from clouds (or a shot motivated only by an anonymous narrational logic) precedes a shot in which Leslie's lifeless body is illuminated by its rays. In a shot reminiscent of the opening of the film, the camera tracks up from the body, past the fence, and toward the house as music from a party becomes audible. The image dissolves to a shot of the lace, much closer to completion here, and a track in to the lace then dissolves to a final shot of the moon. The narrative comes full circle and returns to mark the sites of significance of its originating scene, most prominently the obvious symbol of female sexuality.

Repetition and a cyclical structure are also crucial to the narrative construction in *Letter from an Unknown Woman*. Its doubling of significant scenes has frequently been noted.[15] There are two cafe scenes, two high-angle shots from the top of a staircase as Stefan brings a woman to his apartment, and two scenes of departure at a train station where Lisa says good-bye first to her lover, then to her son. A carriage arrives at the beginning of the film and departs at the end. At the microlevel of the love story's signifying process, repetition is associated with objects or phrases or songs. The majority of these films link a very specific musical theme with the couple's desire, and this theme is repeated every time they are together. As in *Humoresque*, the theme or song tends to slide almost imperceptibly from the extradiegetic realm to the diegetic (e.g., in *Intermezzo*, where the heroine even refers to herself at one point as the "intermezzo" of the man's life). In the love story, there is an exacerbation of repetition as a major mechanism of the classical text. But the love story also tends to transform repetition from a tool of cognition into an instrument of pure affect. This is the case not only with love themes but with objects and words as well, intensified through repetition to the point where their mere mention evokes an entire scenario of passion and desire. In *Now, Voyager*, the object of such a repetition is a ritual whereby Paul Henreid lights two cigarettes in his mouth and then hands one to Bette Davis. The phrase "poor Uncle Wiggly" is constantly repeated in *My Foolish Heart* to indicate the healing of pain by the love the phrase signifies. In this same film, Dana Andrews tells Susan Hayward she has aristocratic ears and gradually substitutes other parts of the body—mouth, hands, eyes—during the remainder of the narrative. The exchange of a good luck charm in the shape of a monkey serves the same function in *Waterloo Bridge*. The repetition of an object, a saying, or a song marks it as the signifier of love for this couple—a love which is theirs alone. The man and the woman must have some kind of entity which is demarcated as the signifier of their love solely through the mechanism of repetition in order to demonstrate that there is no repetition in love—each love is unique and unrepeatable. This is especially true for the woman. For while the man is frequently married to someone else with whom he is generally not quite in love (*Back Street; Now, Voyager; When Tomorrow Comes; Intermezzo*), the woman almost always gives up everything, including other marriage proposals, for the sake of her love. Even outside the boundaries of the institution of marriage, the idea that the woman must be faithful to one man prevails. Adultery is allowable insofar as it itself mimics the matrimonial bond.

Hence, the temporal modality necessitated by the discourse of the love story rests on the assumption that it is the woman who *has the time* to wait, the woman who *has the time* to invest in love. A feminine relation to time in this context is thus defined in terms—repetition, waiting, duration—which resist any notion of progression. As Barthes points out, this logic corresponds to a historical sexual differentiation in which the burden of absence is generally carried by the woman:

> Absence can exist only as a consequence of the other: it is the other who leaves, it is I who remain. The other is in a condition of perpetual departure, of journeying. . . . Historically, the discourse of absence is carried on by the Woman: Woman is sedentary, Man hunts, journeys; Woman is faithful (she waits), man is fickle (he sails away, he cruises). It is Woman who gives shape to absence, elaborates its fiction, for she has time to do so; she weaves and she sings; the Spinning Songs express both immobility (by the hum of the Wheel) and absence (far away, rhythms of travel, sea surges, cavalcades).[16]

Although waiting is not a "proper" subject *for* narrative, it can potentially be productive *of* narrative. It is interesting that Barthes' metonymic chain here moves from absence to waiting to weaving and spinning. For as we noted in the discussion of the medical discourse films, Freud and Breuer linked hysteria to the daydreams "to which needlework and similar occupations render women especially prone." What the theoretical discourses have in common is the association of the woman, the construction of "fictions of absence," and weaving or needlework. The processes of narration and weaving seem to have something in common insofar as various strands or themes must be intertwined in the telling of a story. And it may not be too farfetched to note that when women work in the love story they frequently have jobs relating to textiles, clothing, fabric. Daisy Kenyon is a clothes designer, Ray Smith in *Back Street* works in a dry goods store and buys fabrics from travelling salesmen, and Lisa in *Letter from an Unknown Woman* models gowns. But the two films which deal with this problematic most explicitly and in extremely "telling" ways are *The Letter* and *The Heiress* (1949).

In *The Letter*, Leslie Crosbie (Bette Davis) is accused of murdering a man but the "story" she tells—a story which everyone initially believes—is that the man sexually attacked her and she shot him in self-defense. In actuality, she was in love with the man and murdered him because he refused to give up his Eurasian wife for her. The new district officer of the area, a young man named Withers, is clearly smitten by her and is impressed by "the way she told that story." Leslie also has a hobby—lacemaking. Withers notices a piece of her lace in the beginning of the film and exclaims, "Oh, that's beautiful. Just the kind of thing you'd expect her to do." The lace is particularly important as a metaphor for the process of narration itself —both demand exactitude, precision, and a patience with detail. Her lawyer points out that in telling her story Leslie never deviates, never changes a single word. After the trial Withers announces that he "can't get over the way you gave your evidence—everything so exact down to the last detail." But the lawyer comes to learn the true story through the evidence of the letter and accuses Leslie of resorting to lacemaking in order not to think about what she is doing. Lace becomes a substitute for the real. And, indeed, lace is riddled with holes, with absences; it covers inexactly. Leslie wears the lace as a veil or disguise in her meeting with the Eurasian woman—a meeting in which the similarities of the two women are marked. The lace signifies Leslie's control—her control over her own image. In the beginning of the film, the piece of lace she works on, the one noticed by both the head boy and Withers, is quite small. At the end of the film it is almost completed. When the lace fails to divert her, to empty her of thought or desire, her story is over, and the Eurasian woman kills her in revenge. Lacemaking here clearly signals a form of narrational power for the woman. For lace figures the intricacy of the woman's story.

If women's sewing, weaving, lacemaking are indeed signifiers of a specific narrational desire, the vehemence with which they are culturally denigrated as lesser arts becomes more comprehensible. It is well known how Freud attempted to contain any threatening aspects of female production or initiative in this area by specifying the activity of weaving as a repetition of an originary desire to *mime the phallus* by braiding together the pubic hairs. [17] Barthes, in a passage which seems to uncannily evoke the logic of *The Letter*, compares the labor of narrative to that of lacemaking.

> The text, while it is being produced, is like a piece of Valenciennes Lace created before us under the lacemaker's fingers: each sequence undertaken hangs like the temporarily inactive bobbin waiting while its neighbor works; then, when its turn comes, the hand takes up the thread again, brings it back to the frame; and as the pattern is filled out, the progress of each thread is marked with a pin which holds it and is gradually moved for-

ward: thus the terms of the sequence: they are positions held and then left behind in the course of a gradual invasion of meaning. This process is valid for the entire text. The grouping of codes, as they enter into the work, into the movement of the reading, constitute a braid (*text*, *fabric*, *braid*: the same thing). . . .[18]

Any idea that narrative production is most closely analogous to what is considered a specifically feminine form of work is avoided later in the passage when Barthes resumes Freud's speculations and compares the text to a fetish—a phallic substitute. The phallus reasserts itself again. But Catherine Sloper, in *The Heiress*, manages to quite literally cut the thread of this type of reasoning. She fights back. What Barthes seems to unconsciously invoke, in the course of comparing narrative to lacemaking, is the vocabulary for yet another analogy, warfare: "positions held and then left behind in the course of a gradual invasion of meaning."

In *The Heiress*, an adaptation of Henry James' *Washington Square*, Catherine (Olivia de Havilland) is represented as a very plain young woman, socially awkward, who spends most of her time attending to her embroidery. Her father constantly compares her unfavorably to his beautiful and clever wife, whose image has gained in grandeur since her death. Catherine is, in his mind, a poor substitute for her mother. Catherine falls in love with a young man, Morris Townsend (Montgomery Clift), who is clearly a fortune hunter interested primarily in Catherine's rather large inheritance. Her father recognizes this aspect of Morris's character and threatens to cut off Catherine's inheritance if she marries him. He tells his daughter that she has nothing but money to attract a suitor—neither beauty nor brilliance, but "with one exception. You embroider neatly." As he speaks, Catherine lowers her head, in a shot where a large embroidery frame dominates the foreground. Catherine, who is determined from that moment to end all relations with her father, has arranged to meet Morris later that night in order to elope. But as she waits, her suitcase packed, she gradually realizes that Morris will not come. Years pass, her father dies, and Catherine becomes rich. Morris returns and, as she embroiders diligently, Catherine arranges once again to meet him later that night as originally planned. But after he leaves and despite her aunt's urging to pack quickly, Catherine returns to her embroidery, proclaiming, "I must finish it now for I shall never do another." When Morris arrives to meet her, she is at the end of the alphabet, carefully embroidering a Z. Catherine tells her maid not to answer the bell, and, as Morris pounds on the door with his fists, she commands the maid to bolt it. At the precise moment that the door is bolted against Morris, Catherine cuts the thread with a scissors and admires her completed work. The film ends with a shot of Morris still pounding his fists against the door. The narrative is finished, the threads finally tied together, and the man excluded from its discourse, waiting, infinitely, on the doorstep. While repetition as a textual mechanism dominates the subgenre of the love story, within each text and between texts, so that the spectator is constantly subjected to images of women waiting, enduring, here Catherine dominates the phenomenon of repetition. The woman *stages* a narrative repetition in her own interests, for her own pleasure (even if that pleasure is limited by its status as revenge). The love story must attribute desire to the woman and, in the process, something slips, escaping the classical text's operation of suturing contradictions, of dissolving the heterogeneous. Catherine climbs the stairs, site of the woman's specularization in the classical cinema, but she is held by no man's gaze.

Female desire is a necessary premise of the love story's structure. And even if it is a passive desire, signified most frequently by waiting, it nevertheless presupposes a desiring subjectivity and hence a figuration of absence and distance. Like the maternal melodrama, the love story activates an entire apparatus of waiting, near misses, separations, and accidental meetings (often at train stations—e.g., *Back Street* and *Waterloo Bridge*). But unlike the maternal melodrama, the distance between the subject and the object of desire is not always measured against an imaginary plenitude or originary unity (as between mother and child). It is interesting to note the large number of *unhappy* endings in this group of films, accompanied by a consistent stress on static in the lines of communication, blockages, breakdowns, and so forth. While the maternal melodrama insists that the gap between desire and its object is accidental rather than essential and hence reconfirms the possibility of a complete and transparent communication, the love story frequently interrogates that very possibility. One of the ways it does so is by representing the various technologies of communication as not merely deficient but malevolent and threatening. Trains or boats, for instance, seem to exist only to take lovers away or adhere so rigidly to their time schedule that a meeting with a lover is just missed, often with dire consequences. *Back Street*, a film which delineates the demeaning and demoralizing position of the woman who loves a man outside the context of marriage, begins with a parade celebrating the arrival of the "horseless carriage" and announcing "the machine age is here." Across the time span of the film, the automobile develops quite rapidly, but the woman's position remains the same. At the end of *Back Street*, Walter Saxel dies, and almost immediately afterwards Ray dies as well, since she clearly has no more reason to live. But a "happy ending" in the form of a dream scene in which Ray doesn't miss the boat is collapsed onto the unhappy ending which depicts their deaths. These images in effect negate the narrative, for their absence from the diegetic "real" (their very fictitiousness) is the condition of the narrative's possibility. A full union between the man and the woman—with no gap or distance—can only be represented at the cost of their deaths.

Telephones, like trains, signify the very separation and distance conducive to desire. But they are also the ground for numerous misunderstandings, representing first and foremost the difficulties of communication. In *Deception*, an overheard telephone conversation deepens the husband's suspicions about his new wife. Paul Boray's final phone conversation with Helen in *Humoresque* is defined by his inability to recognize her plight. In *Back Street*, Walter Saxel's attempt to set up a meeting with Ray in which he plans to propose to her is undermined by the background noise at the boat launch which makes a telephone discussion all but impossible. Furthermore, he makes a phone call to her from his deathbed, but a stroke has impaired his ability to speak to her. Telephones are the site of "noise" in a relationship. Daisy Kenyon waits impatiently for Peter to call and, when he does, berates him for not having called on time. Lucille, Dan's wife, intercepts a telephone call between Dan and Daisy which generates the events leading to their divorce. Toward the end of the film, there is a sequence in which the telephone becomes very explicitly an instrument of torture or menace to Daisy. Fleeing New York for her home on the Cape in order to be alone, Daisy is hounded by the ringing of the phone. Closer and closer shots of a huge telephone are intercut with close-ups of a suffering Daisy until she finally leaves the house, gets in her car, and drives away. But as she drives, the ringing of the phone continues on the soundtrack until the moment when she crashes the car. There is a slippage in these films whereby technology first seems to heighten the anguish but eventually becomes the cause of that anguish. Technology makes it possible to represent the absent presence so essential to the construction of a love story.

There is, however, a more "old-fashioned" means of articulating the effects of such a presence-in-absence: letters. The number of film titles which invoke this method of communication testifies to its significance: *Love Letters* (1945), *Letter from an Unknown Woman* (1948), *The Letter*, *A Letter to Three Wives* (1948). The letter is first and foremost evidence of a crime: the crime of one man assuming another's identity (*Love Letters*); the crime of a man's failure to recognize the woman who bore his son (*Letter from an Unknown Woman*); adultery and murder (*The Letter*); or just adultery (*A Letter to Three Wives*). Writing often conceals as much as it reveals and, like the telephone, is open to abuse or "noise." In *Love Letters*, it illustrates the woman's linguistic subordination to the man. Jennifer Jones, an amnesiac, and her adoptive mother, suffering from a stroke, cannot articulate or describe the most traumatic event of their lives. The problem of identity links this film to the paranoid group discussed in chapter five. Jennifer Jones falls in love with the man who wrote her love letters—in effect, she falls in love with the writing itself. But the letters are a fraud, and she finds that the man she married is not their true author. The identity of the husband, his true nature, is at stake, but since the woman's identity is a function of her reflection in the man, this is also a problem of self-identity for the woman. Hence, after the husband's acknowledgment that he never wrote the letters and his death, Jennifer Jones becomes an amnesiac, her past and her identity erased. Furthermore, she loses the ability to write and is terrified when she herself receives a letter. Joseph Cotten, the real author of the letters, marries her without being able to tell her his connection with the letters since this would, given the prognosis of the doctors who claim her memory must gradually return, drive her mad. When Jones finally does manage to write a letter to Cotten, she can only echo the words of his love letters and maintain, "The letter seemed to write itself." Later, as she poses for Cotten's gaze, she speaks the words from one of his letters—the sentence "speaks itself." Her discourse of love is simply a repetition of his. While the letters do constitute a kind of deception, the film does not relate this distortion to the possibility that "saying" and "meaning" may not coincide. On the contrary, it supports the idea of an immediacy of expression so that Cotten, by simply writing the letters, comes to believe them and to fall in love with the woman to whom they are sent.

However, this immediacy of expression or feeling is usually manifested in the love story through the medium of vision. The classical cinema believes in "love at first sight," perhaps because it so conveniently fits within its highly developed system of point-of-view and glance/object editing. The existence of love must be established quickly because, in fact, the body of the film is usually devoted to the delineation of the blockades to the fulfillment of that love. The woman is given the possibility of desiring, but the ways in which that desire is formulated or narrativized tend to suggest that it is an imaginary desire, particularly if it occurs outside the bounds of marriage. Female desire is nourished by an overactive imagination.

Vincente Minnelli's 1949 adaptation of *Madame Bovary* is particularly insistent on this point. The film utilizes a framing device in which the author Flaubert (James Mason) is on trial and defends his novel against charges that it is immoral in its representation of a "woman of insatiable passions," "a monstrous creation" who is "a disgrace to France and an insult to womanhood." Flaubert attributes Emma Bovary's aberrant behavior to her absorption of the excesses of fiction—to "ridiculous dreams of high romance" and "images of beauty that never existed" which are derived from love songs and, most importantly, forbidden novels.[19] Flaubert claims that it is "our world" that created her and hundreds of thousands of women like her, not he. Allowing women to read such novels sets their imaginations loose. Women read and imitate—they perceive no distance between fantasy and reality. In the film *Madame Bovary*, the camera consistently lingers on the pictures Emma pins to the wall of her room, pictures which dwell on the pleasures of romance and faraway places. Every time her desire leads her into trouble or difficulty, the camera returns to those pictures as if pinpointing them as the cause. Early in the film, the camera pans across the pictures and over to Emma, looking intently into a mirror, linking the romantic representations directly to Emma's narcissistic image of herself.

This theme recurs in other films of the genre. In *Kitty Foyle*, a young Kitty is warned by her father of the dangers of believing in fairy tales. He admonishes her for having her head "stuck in that Cinderella stuff" and claims that tales of Cinderellas and princes are "the ruination of more girls than forty actors." In *Now, Voyager*, Bette Davis describes her romantic feelings as a young girl to the doctor and maintains, "That's all I had to go by—novels." Laura, in *The Enchanted Cottage* (1945), is represented as very "homely," and she maintains, "Women like me find refuge in our dreams, in which we are as lovely and desirable as the most beautiful woman."[20]

The emphasis on the threatening aspects of an untethered female imagination and on the woman's excessive relation to fiction is not confined to the cinema and has a long history. It is an important aspect of Rousseauean thought picked up and expanded by Pierre Roussel, who in 1777 wrote of the woman and "her imagination, overly mobile and hardly capable of a steady seat."[21] While it is fairly easy for a patriarchal society to keep the woman's body "in its place," it is her mind which always threatens to wander—hence the dangers of needlework, daydreaming, and novels. Pam Cook maintains that the films themselves contain the evidence that female desire is always yoked to the register of the imaginary.

> I would argue that the marked ambiguities inherent in the narrative structure and ironic *mise-en-scène* of the women's picture are the cinematic equivalent of the discourses of fantasy and romance in women's romantic fiction, which, as Janet Batsleer has pointed out, relies on an overt and excessive use of cliché, superlatives and purple prose to create a utopian dream world. The women's picture is similarly marked as 'fiction,' or daydream, locating women's desires in the imaginary, where they have always traditionally been placed.[22]

This is one strategy of containing female desire. Its effect is to magnify the distance between that desire and the real.

The essentially fictive character of female desire is frequently demonstrated by the woman's demand for "all or nothing." Lydia, in the film of that name, presents the classic statement: "If I can't have all there is, I don't want any of it." This rationalization is frequently produced in order to explain why the heroine cannot accept the marriage proposal of a marginal male character who is represented as a potentially good husband but with whom the heroine is not in love. Early in *Back Street*, Ray tells the bicycle shop owner who wants to marry her, "If I fall in love it'll have to be all the way or not at all." In this manner, she legitimates all the suffering which is hers for the rest of the film. The ultimate consequence of this "all or nothing" attitude and of situating desire in the imaginary is illustrated by those films in which a woman spends almost her entire life loving a man who, when he meets her again, does not even recognize her (*Lydia, Letter from an Unknown Woman*). The work of these films consists of an elaboration of the tremendous gap between the woman's investment in affect and that of the man. For in the love story everything signifies—even the most apparently trivial event elicits violent emotions. The unimposing detail, the infinitesimal event reverberate and immediately become novelistic.[23] This, together with the cultural convention of associating the woman with the detail and the trivial, at least partially explains the positioning of the love story as a feminine genre.

As noted earlier, however, the genre does seem to require that the male character undergo a process of feminization by his mere presence within a love story. The male stars who tend to play the romantic leads in these films—Charles Boyer, John Boles, Louis Jourdan, Paul Henreid, Leslie Howard—were clearly not chosen for their overly "masculine" qualities. This feminization of the male lead has frequently been noted. Tania Modleski, for instance, claims that the feminized man is attractive "because of the freedom he seems to offer the woman: freedom to get in touch with and to act upon her own desire and freedom to reject patriarchal power."[24] To a certain extent this is certainly true—the male lead is rarely *explicitly* repressive in contradistinction to a patriarchal authority. But in a way this makes his frequently implicitly patronizing behavior and the myth of romance associated with him all the more repressive. Yet, the feminization of the male in the love story, I would argue, ultimately has a somewhat different function. Men in the love story frequently do "act like women" insofar as they are attentive to detail, minute incidents, and the complexities of intersubjective relations. They often attempt to read the woman's face for its hidden meanings in the same way that women are consistently taught to read faces, to decipher motives. What is fascinating about this process is the supposition that underlies it: that men in the love story are what women would want them to be, and what they want them to be is like themselves. The thematics of narcissism, the type of relation—or more accurately, nonrelation—to the other which Freud labelled specifically feminine, returns to haunt the love story. Women in the love story are always beautiful, and in the cases where they are not (e.g., *The Enchanted Cottage*) they are transformed through the magic of the imagination—the gaze of the other—into highly attractive women. Overhead shots of a woman looking beautiful as she lies on a bed—but not *looking* at anything, her gaze unfocused—are common (e.g., *Love Letters, The Enchanted Cottage*). The very figure of narcissism—the mirror—is omnipresent.

But, ideally, the mirror image does not reflect the woman alone. There is a scene in *Madame Bovary* which makes this explicit. Emma is at an aristocrat's ball, dancing with the most handsome and wealthiest men, fulfilling, in short, all her fantasies. At a certain point in the scene, Emma glimpses her reflection in a mirror and is captivated—held—by the image of herself in an exquisite gown surrounded by admirers. She will later remember this sight when she is reduced to the level of meeting Leon Dupuis in a dirty hotel room, their kiss reflected this time in a broken mirror. It is not the image of herself which constitutes the lure in this form of narcissism. It is, rather, the image of herself held in the gaze of a man. The logic is that of Alban Berg's *Lulu*: "When I looked at myself in the mirror I wished I were a man—a man married to me."[25] The feminization of the male in the love story facilitates the female spectator's divided identification with both the man and the woman—the man desiring the woman, the woman desired by the man. The narcissism which requires the relay of the male gaze also seems to require an identification with the subject of that gaze so that the female spectator identifies doubly—with the subject and the object of the gaze. Perhaps this is why, in the love story, it is frequently difficult to tell whether the man or the woman is the protagonist (e.g., in *Waterloo Bridge*, *Humoresque*, *Leave Her to Heaven*). The double identification of the female spectator enables a confusion whereby the woman's story is represented as the memory or vision of the man (in *Waterloo Bridge* and *Letter from an Unknown Woman*). Object choice becomes a concept correlative to narcissism. For the woman in the love story there are only departures from and returns to narcissism.

The love story, more than other subgroups of the woman's film, solicits an identification with the two major actants in the drama. The process is reminiscent of Freud's description of hysterical identification and, in fact, the notion of love as a kind of barely controlled hysteria is widespread. Freud links it directly to conventions of language use.

> Identification is most frequently used in hysteria to express a common *sexual* element. A hysterical woman identifies herself in her symptoms most readily—though not exclusively—with people with whom she has had sexual relations or with people who have had sexual relations with the same people as herself. Linguistic usage takes this into account, for two lovers are spoken of as being "one."[26]

The idea that two lovers are not two separate, integral individuals enables the representation of female desire as necessitating a divided subjectivity. The feminization of the male character has the effect of exacerbating the mirror effect of the cinema. What the spectator really loves is a scene and, from there, the cinema as a whole, in the confirmation of its imaginary hold.

Despite all this—despite the vast machinery designed to buttress the female spectator's narcissism, to represent her imagination as a dangerous force, and to lock her within a time schema which is dominated by repetition—I would still argue that the love story is one of the most vulnerable sites in a patriarchal discourse. Its flaw is to posit the very possibility of female desire. For this reason it often ends badly, frequently with the death of the female protagonist, its melodrama verging on tragedy (e.g., *Humoresque, Letter from an Unknown Woman, Leave Her to Heaven, Waterloo Bridge*, etc.). The inability of a large proportion of love stories in the '40s to produce the classical happy ending—or perhaps, more accurately, their tendency to equate satisfactory closure with the death of the woman who desires excessively—is a sign of the love story's vulnerability, the fragility of its project. In *The Letter, Madame Bovary*, and *Letter from an Unknown Woman*, the women quite literally love themselves to death. As Hélène Cixous points out, "Men say that there are two unrepresentable things: death and the feminine sex."[27] This curious and negatively defined compatibility is demonstrated by the preferred closure of many of these films. In *Madame Bovary*, Flaubert/James Mason claims that the Truth gleaned from Emma's story more than compensates for her death: "There is Truth in her story and a morality that has no Truth in it is no morality at all . . . . Truth lives forever, men [sic] do not." Emma's life becomes a lesson. The "unhappy ending" of her death is overshadowed by the "happy ending" of the film's framing narrative in which we are told that Flaubert's acquittal was "a triumph in the history of the free mind."

In a patriarchal society, the myth of romantic love is always there to act as an outlet for any excess energy the woman may possess, to, somewhat paradoxically, *domesticate* her. But, it is precisely because there is so much at stake here that the genre has the potential to interrogate the woman's position—to explode in the face of patriarchal strictures. For the myth of romantic love is at odds with the domestic routinized work expected of women and this is a structuring contradiction which generates others. It is also why the genre must contain films like *Kitty Foyle* which ostensibly work to deny the very premise of the love story—films in which the woman learns to accept the real man over the fantasized prince. As Flaubert/James Mason says of Emma Bovary, "We had taught her to find glamour and excitement in faraway places and only boredom in the here and now." Mason speaks here of novels, but the cinema, too, is a machine for the generation of glamour, fantasy, excitement; it acts as a travelogue taking the spectator to faraway places. If the female spectator is to invest energy in the love story, the films must also be able to count on her ability to differentiate between fiction and the real. They must insure that her desire is safely—and consciously—ensconced in the imaginary and that her knowledge of "real life" will compensate for the excesses of the love story. In short, they assume that the woman can move into the position of fetishist, carefully balancing knowledge and belief. But this, according to the filmic discourse, is precisely what the woman *cannot* do—she is too readily *taken in* by the image. Her excessive sympathy does not allow her an adequate distance.

These contradictions surface in various ways in the discourse of the love story but tend to hover around the theme of sexuality outside marriage. As mentioned previously, this type of sexuality is acceptable as long as it mimics exactly the marriage bond and the woman remains faithful to the man (as in *Back Street*). In the "choice" films the woman tends to ultimately choose the most marriageable man (e.g., *Kitty Foyle, Daisy Kenyon*). The unthinkability of certain kinds of female sexuality is evidenced by a difficulty in naming. What *is* a woman if she is not a wife? As she contemplates the possibility of moving to South America with a married man, Kitty Foyle's mirror image—the manifestation of her superego—asks her, "How will they describe you?" The answer is never made explicit either here or in *Waterloo Bridge*, where the characters constantly verge on the pronunciation of the word or words which would pinpoint Myra's (Vivien Leigh's) identity as a prostitute. Myra resorts to prostitution after she is mistakenly informed by a newspaper of her fiancé's death in battle and when she can find no other job. When her fiancé returns, alive and well, she accidentally meets him at the train station when she is looking for customers. The situation is an impossible one for the classical text. The word "prostitution" is never spoken in the film, the characters constantly producing statements like "I know what you mean," "I understand—you don't have to say it," and "What you're thinking, what you're telling yourself can't be true, is true." This empty space, the unsaid, anticipates her death. For prostitution is absolutely irrecuperable. Myra's fiancé, Roy, can cross class lines in order to become engaged to her, but once she slips into prostitution, she is lost, her death inevitable. The woman associated with excessive sexuality resides outside the boundaries of language; she is unrepresentable and must die because, as Claire Johnston points out, death is the "location of all impossible signs."[28]

Insofar as the woman evinces a desire which exceeds the boundaries of marriage, she is problematic. While the maternal is associated with certainty and the obvious, the woman's status as wife or lover is less sure, always subject to doubt. As Heath points out, with reference to the nineteenth-century novel, adultery is a kind of linguistic problem, a collapse of distinctions:

> To commit adultery is to adulterate, to render counterfeit, corrupt, to debase "by base admixture" (the definition given by the OED). Adultery, in fact, is "category-confusion," the slide from identity to indifference, a total indistinction of place. What guarantees identity is the woman who is then equally the weak point in its system: if she gives, everything gives; moving from *her* right place, the adulterous woman leaves *no* place intact (hence the legal bias: the English divorce laws of 1857, for example, make adultery grounds for divorce from the wife but not from the husband). . . . As mother the woman is sure, as wife always potentially unsure. . . .[29]

In most of the films of the love story group, identity is insured by the fact that it is the man who commits adultery, who steps outside the boundaries of marriage.

Only the man can survive this situation. If the woman does commit adultery (*Humoresque, The Letter*), she must die. A generic grouping which raises female sexuality as a central issue of its discourse must inevitably entangle itself in the web of this complexity. The problem of the maternal and its relation to female desire is rarely touched on, but when it is, it becomes the subject of a somewhat perverse discourse. In *My Foolish Heart*, Eloise (Susan Hayward) becomes pregnant outside the context of marriage. The father dies before he can marry her, and Eloise proceeds to "steal" her best friend's boyfriend and marry him. She maintains the pretense that the child is his, and the child, as a consequence of her deception, is represented as unbalanced, strange. In both *The Gay Sisters* (1942) and *The Strange Love of Martha Ivers* (1946), all difficulties can be traced to the attempt to maintain a rather aberrant matriarchy, and order is restored only with the return of a satisfactory patriarch. Even in an extremely conservative film such as *Kitty Foyle*, the maternal must be placed in abeyance because, when it appears in a woman's life, it is all encompassing, leaving little room for the man. Kitty in fact states explicitly that what women really want is babies, not men. Motherhood is usually foreign to the discourse of the love story because it always threatens to completely displace female desire.

Films such as *Leave Her to Heaven, The Strange Love of Martha Ivers, The Letter*, and *Deception* can perhaps best be described as the perverse underside of the love story. The love story in the 1940s is invaded by the conventions of film noir and the women often resemble the ominous femme fatale. An extensive use of shadows and a darker image characterize films like *The Letter* and *Deception*. The female protagonist is depicted as enigmatic, indecipherable, her representation fully consistent with the popular antifeminist psychology of a book like *Modern Woman: The Lost Sex*. In that book, Lundberg and Farnham attempt to demonstrate that the woman's psyche is much more complicated than that of the man.

> Women in general are a more complicated question than men, as a few of the poets have sensed, for they are more complicated organisms. They are endowed with a complicated reproductive system (with which the male genito-urinary system compares in complexity not at all), a more elaborate nervous system and an infinitely complex psychology revolving about the reproductive function. Women, therefore, cannot be regarded as any more similar to men than a spiral is to a straight line.
>
> Each sex represents an organic tracing of reality. But in one instance the tracing is simple (relatively), in the other complex and even devious. [30]

In *The Letter* and *Deception* the women weave fictions of increasing complexity. In *The Letter*, the setting in Singapore, the lighting, and the mise-en-scène underline the threat of deceptive femininity. Leslie, barely visible behind a white lace shawl, and the Eurasian wife of Hammond, weighted down by jewelry and makeup and dressed in black, have something in common insofar as they both represent enigmas; they are the inverted mirror images of each other. The film demonstrates that, for the woman, native justice is more accurate, more appropriate than Western justice, exemplified by a court system which finds itself baffled in the face of her femininity. In the Oriental store, Leslie is fascinated with and lured by the dagger, the instrument of her own death. And it is ultimately another woman, the Eurasian woman, representing an incomprehensible mixture of different categories—East and West—who kills her. Leslie's attraction to this woman is an attraction to her own death.

*Leave Her to Heaven* displaces and *misplaces* the femme fatale figure in a domestic setting where the excessiveness of the woman's desire is particularly visible and particularly dangerous because its only outlet is a family scene. Ellen's (Gene Tierney's) incestuous relation to her father is indicated early in the film and is used to at least partially explain the absolute evil which she embodies. She first "steals" Richard (Cornell Wilde) from her cousin and marries him. Her major defect is overpossessiveness; she is not content to be the object of desire, not content with either being or appearing, she must have, appropriate, possess. Unwilling to share Richard with anyone, she arranges the death by drowning of his crippled younger brother. In the same vein she later throws herself down the stairs in order to induce a miscarriage. And, finally, when she is convinced that she has lost Richard to her cousin Ruth, Ellen commits suicide, leaving evidence that Ruth murdered her so that the two will never be able to get together. Her dying words as she grasps Richard's arm are "I'll never let you go." *Leave Her to Heaven* takes the form of a flashback account narrated by a lawyer. The film is a legal discourse about a domestic drama which is transformed into a criminal drama. Ellen's relation to an excessive, *wild* desire is signaled from the very beginning of the film by her appropriation of the gaze, by the fact that she stares intently at Richard.

Women, when they love, are driven to atrocious acts. In *My Foolish Heart*, Eloise is obsessed by one question which the flashback narrative is designed to answer, "I was a nice girl, wasn't I?"—the term "nice" denoting asexuality. Eloise is ultimately not a "nice girl" but her best friend's comment at the end of the film—"After all, I could have been the girl in the brown and white dress, anybody could've"—indicates the status of the "bad girl" as a kind of placeholder in an oppressive system of sexual difference. More frequently, the woman not only goes *too far*, but goes astray. In *Deception*, the woman totally misreads the situation. Her purportedly specifically feminine skill in deciphering the intentions and motives of others has gone awry. Images of Bette Davis shooting Claude Rains on a shadowy staircase in *Deception* or emptying her revolver to kill an unfaithful lover in *The Letter*, images of Gene Tierney calmly watching as a young crippled boy drowns or planning the death of her own child—these images seem to condense all the fear and anxiety associated with an actively desiring female subjectivity.

The love story verges on the territory of film noir in the '40s because its own terms begin to lose their viability. When the sadism of narrative described by Mulvey becomes so intense that the woman must die over and over again, in film after film, something is clearly amiss, the love story gone bad. The films *exhibit* the relation between female sexuality and death; they *exhibit* the difficulties of female sexuality. This is never so manifest as in the films (*Humoresque*, *Waterloo Bridge*) which depict the death of the woman's point of view. In *Waterloo Bridge*, Myra commits suicide by throwing herself in front of a lorry. But this death is represented not in long or medium shot but as a series of shots of the heavy lorries rolling by crosscut with closer and closer shots of Myra, the light from the trucks sliding over her face until her eyes totally fill the frame. Before she dies she becomes pure gaze, pure point of view, and it is this which is eliminated from the text. She is reduced to the man's memory of her voice.

The attraction of these films does have something to do with processes of fascination and identification. And a necessary by-product of such processes seems to be the recognition of the impossible position of women in relation to desire in a patriarchal society. Lacan speaks of the *cause* of desire rather than its object because he does not conceive of desire as so strictly directed or oriented; it is not of the order of a transitive sentence. Desire is always in excess—even if it is simply the desire to desire, the striving for an access to a desiring subjectivity. The desiring woman and her excessive sexuality may be theoretically unrepresentable (according to the logic of a masculine theory, in any event); she may be doomed to die in order to insure closure for the narrative, but for a moment of cinematic time she is at least present, flaunting her excess. And one sometimes gets the sense, from the love story, that "anybody could've been her."

# 5

## Paranoia and the Specular

Both Freud and Hollywood have occasion to link female paranoia insistently with the misuse of a visual representation (whether mimetic or abstract). In *The Two Mrs. Carrolls* (1947), Humphrey Bogart plays an artist whose psychosis is signified by a tendency toward an abstraction which can only be understood, within the confines of the classical Hollywood text, as *mis*representation. His models are always women, women he is eventually compelled to marry, and as long as his painting remains within the realm of mimesis, of purported adequation to its referent, the marriages remain healthy. But abstraction in his art is the index of sexual dissatisfaction and signals the actual murder of his first wife and the attempted murder of the second (Barbara Stanwyck). The fear the woman feels is thus allied with a transformation into a visual representation connoting violence. Similarly, it is no accident that in a case of female paranoia treated by Freud (as described in "A Case of Paranoia Running Counter to the Psychoanalytical Theory of the Disease"), the woman's delusion involves *having her picture taken*—that is, being photographed by two men who intend to use the compromising photograph against her. Paranoia and the specular regime appear to be intimately welded in both the filmic and the psychoanalytic delineation of a female phobia.

*The Two Mrs. Carrolls* belongs to a cycle of films[1] initiated by Alfred Hitchcock's adaptation of Daphne Du Maurier's 1938 novel, *Rebecca*, in 1940. This cycle might be labeled the "paranoid woman's films," the paranoia evinced in the formulaic repetition of a scenario in which the wife invariably fears that her husband is planning to kill her—the institution of marriage is haunted by murder.[2] Frequently, the violence is rationalized as the effect of an overly hasty marriage; the husband is unknown or only incompletely known by the woman. A

scene in *Secret Beyond the Door* (1948) exemplifies this tendency: a long flashback which details the meeting of Joan Bennett and the man she is to marry culminates with the image of her future husband, emerging from the deep shadows
of the church on their wedding day, accompanied by her surprised voice-over,
"I'm marrying a stranger." The conjunction of sexuality and murder, the conflation of the two verbs, "to marry" and "to kill," is even more explicit in *Suspicion* (1941), in a windy scene on a hill in which Joan Fontaine's resistance to
Cary Grant's attempts to kiss her is met with his question, "What did you think
I was going to do—kill you?" As Thomas Elsaesser points out in reference to
*Rebecca*,

> Hitchcock infused his film, and several others, with an oblique intimation of female
> frigidity producing strange fantasies of persecution, rape, and death—masochistic rev-
> eries and nightmares, which cast the husband into the role of the sadistic murderer.
> This projection of sexual anxiety and its mechanisms of displacement and transfer is
> translated into a whole string of movies often involving hypnosis and playing on the
> ambiguity and suspense of whether the wife is merely imagining it or whether her hus-
> band really does have murderous designs on her. . . .[3]

A crucial premise of the films is thus aligned with the very signifying material
of the cinema and manifests itself as a crisis of vision in relation to sexuality: Is
the husband really what he appears to be?

Gothic.

    These films appropriate many of the elements of the gothic novel in its
numerous variations from Horace Walpole and Ann Radcliffe to Daphne du
Maurier and beyond: the large and forbidding house, mansion, or castle; a secret, often related to a family history, which the heroine must work to disclose;
storms incarnating psychical torment; portraits; and locked doors. Norman Holland and Leona Sherman refer, rather succinctly, to the gothic formula as "the
image of woman-plus-habitation."[4] The female gothic narrative is incarnated
in cinematic texts in a relatively strictly delineated historical period—from *Rebecca* in 1940 to the late 1940s (*Caught*, the only example cited in this chapter
which dates as late as 1949, is a weak, or perhaps more accurately, naturalized
version of the gothic). Gothic narratives do not, however, die out at the end of
their very short-lived cinematic career, but are displaced to another medium.

    The 1950s witness the beginning of a flourishing trade in gothic paperbacks
which continues to this day, and, as Holland and Sherman demonstrate, marketing strategies reveal quite clearly that the novels are aimed specifically at a
female audience.

> The *New York Times* of 18 June 1973 headed a feature article, "Gothic Novels for
> Women Prove Bonanza for Publishers." One publisher complained that his "stable of
> writers" could not satisfy the female market's demand for "gothics." Another, Simon

and Schuster, had doubled its sales of such "women's fiction." In all, gothics accounted for more than five percent of total paperback sales in the U.S.A.—$1.4 million profit.[5]

Despite the fact that, unlike in the case of the films, the authors are primarily women and the paperbacks are sold in supermarkets, the very strong link between contemporary gothic paperbacks and the films of the 1940s can be observed in the repetition of a fixed iconography on the covers of these books. As commentators on the gothic novel inevitably point out, often with a dismay over obsessive repetition which signals an automatic denigration of popular culture, the covers are always the same: "the color scheme is predominantly blue or green, there is a frightened young woman in the foreground, in the background is a mansion, castle, or large house with one window lit, there is usually a moon, a storm, or both, and whatever is occurring is occurring at night."[6] With the exception of the use of color, this image, broken down, its elements dispersed in a syntagmatic chain, accurately describes the most significant aspects of the iconography of the films (in both *Rebecca* and *Jane Eyre* [1944], for instance, a light in a window—in this context, moving from window to window—signifies a fairly localizable danger which threatens to exceed its spatial limits). The image exhibits in condensed form the specificity of the gothic narrative in its activation of a dialectic of internal and external and the effects of a transgression of the barrier between them, manifested most explicitly in the paranoid mechanism of projection.

However, although the paperbacks are recognized immediately as commodities for the (hopefully avid) consumption of female readers, the paranoid gothic films of the 1940s have not been consistently allied with the label, the  "woman's film."[7] For the woman's film is usually associated with excessive emotionality but not fear, love and sacrifice but not violence or aggression. And, in fact, the paranoid films are themselves instances of a kind of generic miscegenation—a transgression of generic boundaries. They are infiltrated by the conventions of the film noir and the horror film. Nevertheless, I would argue that, in their articulation of the uncanniness of the domestic, and more especially in their sustained investigation of the woman's relation to the gaze, the gothic films not only reside within the "genre" of the woman's film, but offer a  metacommentary on it as well. In their hyperbolization of certain signifying strategies of the woman's film, they test the very limits of the filmic representation of female subjectivity for a female spectator.

Despite the fact that the plots or narrative structures of the gothic films and paperbacks are similar if not identical, there are critical differences between the two which can be aligned with the specificity of their respective signifying materials. What the films are particularly suited to exploit is the problematic wherein male violence is delineated as an effect of the voyeuristic gaze. This axis of aggression is not, however, absent from the novels, as can be seen in the recurrence of certain descriptive passages: "Again I had that uneasy sense of a deeper meaning and knew that he watched me intently with his pale, luminous, eyes."; "It was curious how the pupils of his eyes expanded as she watched. Like a startled cat's, like a tiger's. Why should Katharine think his eyes were like a tiger's when the rest of his face was so bland and genial?"; "I felt the smile break on my face, and then I saw his eyes watching me, narrowed and fiercely intent."[8] While the female protagonist is constantly described in the act of seeing herself being seen (and desperately attempting to interpret the meaning of that look), the semiotic status of such an aggressive gaze is entirely different from its counterpart in the cinema. The literary representation of the visual register relegates it to the level of content while, in film, the organization of seeing, the relay of looks exemplified by such systems as the point-of-view and shot/reverse shot, exists as a structural feature of the classical cinematic text.

There is, therefore, something about the filmic representation of paranoia, female paranoia in particular, which foregrounds and even, at points, interrogates a fundamental semiotic mechanism of the cinema. This is what lends to the films their quality of metatextuality in relation to other women's films of the 1940s. The novels, unlike the films, have only a mediated access to the auditory and the visual—the two most significant registers of paranoia. The novelistic mode of narration, on the other hand, provides an access to interiority which is lacking in the classical cinema. The device of the interior monologue as well as the ability to construct a clear distinction between the first person and the third person make it possible for novelistic narration to establish relatively unambiguous binary oppositions between subjectivity and objectivity, the internal and the external. Because, in the most classical of cinematic texts, these oppositions are necessarily blurred or even collapsed from the beginning, the norm against which one could measure the extent of paranoia is lacking and must be forcefully constructed and maintained. This situation causes difficulties in the cinematic representation of paranoia which will be discussed in more detail later in this chapter.

Freud refers to the conviction of being watched or delusions of observation as the most striking symptom of paranoia. The ever-present sense of being on display for the gaze of a judgmental other is symptomatic of another condition within our culture as well—that of femininity. There is a sense then in which paranoia is only a hyperbolization of the "normal" female function of exhibitionism and its attachment to the affect of fear. In the home movie scene in *Rebecca*, which is analyzed in the next chapter, the Joan Fontaine character, by dressing to match the image of beauty provided by a fashion magazine, initiates the scene with an invitation to the masculine gaze. That look is turned against her, however, when her husband's aggressive disapproval later in the scene is represented in a threatening stare. Her only defense—the plea "Don't look at me like that"—is simply the verbalization of a violence already clearly signalled by the shot/reverse shot between Fontaine, cowering in fear and fragmented by the shadow of her husband interrupting the projection beam, and Laurence Olivier, framed by blackness, intense and unyielding in his exercise of the gaze.

In *Gaslight* (1944), the encroaching madness of Ingrid Bergman is evidenced by an almost total disintegration of narcissism, of a secure relation to her own body. Slowly walking down the stairs, she apprehensively checks every detail of her clothing. Ultimately, terrorized by the possibility that there is something wrong with the way she looks, she refuses to leave the house. Many of these films situate themselves within the terms of a dialectic between the heroine's active assumption of the position of subject of the gaze and her intense fear of being subjected to the gaze. The graphics of a poster for *Secret Beyond the Door* make this relationship quite explicit: "I looked in his eyes . . . and knew I was seeing *Death* staring back!"[9]

Perhaps the most intricate and elaborate example of the films' obsession with the aggressive nature of the process of looking and being looked at is a scene in *The Spiral Staircase* (1946) in which the eye in close-up acts as a metonymy for a murderous intention. Helen (Dorothy McGuire) is a mute servant in a very strange household. The film has already established the existence of a murderer in the neighborhood who is inclined to kill young women who are disabled or physically deficient in some way. The scene in question begins with a shot of Helen climbing the stairs—a shot which is only retrospectively readable as a reflection in a mirror. Helen stops in front of the mirror and, with her hands on her neck, mimics the ability to speak, intently watching her own image. After a cut to a point of view from the top of the stairs the camera, assuming an almost subjective autonomy, tracks to the right connecting Helen's fascination with the mirror to an unidentifiable figure hiding in darkness behind a statue. The camera then tracks slowly in to an extreme close-up of the wide and psychotic eye of this figure—an eye which, acting in its own way as a mirror, reflects the mirror image of Helen. The eye reflects a different image, however—in it, Helen's mouth is effaced.

To the extent that the female spectator identifies with Helen as victim, she is put in a position where she sees herself reflected in the mirror of a murderous gaze. But the scenario is actually more complex since what the eye captures and contains is the narcissism of the woman—her relation to the mirror, a dual relation broken here only by the third term of a markedly violent look. Furthermore, the eye not only appropriates her own point of view, but revises or rewrites it, introducing a deficiency, a lack which metaphorically indicates through excess the lack generally attributed to femininity. The effacement of the mouth is a mark of castration, but a quite specific castration of the woman in relation to the symbolic order of language—a signifying system to which she has no access. Helen relates only to the image and the film specifies a significant divergence between two readings of that image, one male, the other female. Helen's own vision of her mirror image is realist and mimetic—the sign maintains a one-to-one correspondence with its object. The reading of the unidentified eye, on the other hand, is symbolic. It introduces a form of stylization which denaturalizes the image without forcing it to lose its truth. Rather, the masculine gaze constructs another order of truth in which absence is fully significant. When associated with the woman, that absence is a motive for murder. The eye as mirror of femininity precedes and somehow induces violence.

Yet, there is another, more fundamental, sense in which aggressivity is the mirror of narcissism in the cinema. Film theory has insistently linked the cinema with the register of the imaginary as described by Jacques Lacan. Metz's description of the cinematic signifier as imaginary embraces the metaphor of the screen as mirror—reflecting everything but the spectator, yet nevertheless corroborating "his" unity, coherence, and identity just as the mirror does in its tracing of the bodily form.[10] The relationship between the spectator and the image, grounded in an absence, is characterized by the lure and fascination of presence. The narcissism of the imaginary relation consists in its dyadic nature and hence its resistance to the intrusion of the triangular (or Oedipal) structure of the symbolic. Lacan has consistently associated aggressivity with narcissism, primary identification, and the imaginary: "Aggressivity is the correlative tendency of a mode of identification that we call narcissistic, and which determines the formal structure of man's ego and of the register of entities characteristic of his world."[11] The aggressivity stems from the alienation via an image specific to the mirror phase which constitutes itself as "a primary identification that structures the subject as a rival with himself."[12] The imaginary has a social dimension as well in which identification is tantamount to an equation, and desire of the subject is defined as the desire of the other. As Anika Lemaire points out, the imaginary order dictates "the constitutional aggressivity of the human being who must always win his place at the expense of the other, and either impose himself on the other or be annihilated himself."[13] The imaginary component of the cinematic signifier would seem to entail that the supposedly placid or pacifying effect of movie spectatorship is actually haunted by a veiled aggressivity. As Jacqueline Rose argues, aggressivity and paranoia are latent to the cinematic system, becoming manifest only when the stability of that system is threatened.[14]

The woman's film frequently does constitute a threat to this system in a very important sense. While the mainstream Hollywood cinema organizes vision in relation to both spectacle and truth, and hence pleasure and fascination, the woman's film evinces a certain impoverishment of this mechanism. It is quite appropriate that Laura Mulvey, in her influential essay on visual pleasure, limits her discussion to a Hollywood cinema populated by male protagonists acting as relays in a complex process designed to insure the ego fortification of the male spectator.[15] Yet, there is a sense in which the woman's film attempts to constitute itself as the mirror image of this dominant cinema, obsessively centering and recentering a female protagonist, placing her in a position of agency. It thus offers some resistance to an analysis which stresses the "to-be-looked-at-ness" of the woman, her objectification as spectacle according to the masculine structure of the gaze. Hence, within the woman's film, the process of specularization undergoes a number of vicissitudes which can be mapped. One assumption behind the positing of a female spectator (that is, one who does not assume a masculine position with respect to the reflected image of her own body) is that it is no longer necessary to invest the look with desire in quite the same way. A certain despecularization takes place in these films, a deflection of scopophiliac energy in other directions, away from the female body. In this particular cycle of gothic films, the very process of seeing is now invested with fear, anxiety, horror, precisely because it is objectless, free-floating. The aggressivity which, as Rose has demonstrated, is contained in the cinematic structuration of the look is released or, more accurately, transformed into a narrativized paranoia. This subclass of the woman's film clearly activates the latent paranoia of the film system described by Rose.

Paranoia, in Freudian psychoanalysis, is technically defined as a defense against homosexuality and the concomitant "fixation at the stage of 'narcissism' "[16] (in which the object of desire is chosen on the basis of resemblance, likeness, *mimesis*). Because Freud defines a passive homosexual current as feminine, paranoia, whether male or female, involves the adoption of a feminine position. Speaking of the case which was most decisive in the formulation of his theory of paranoia—the case of Senatspräsident Schreber—Freud claims that "the exciting cause of the illness was the appearance in him of a feminine (that is, a passive homosexual) wishful phantasy."[17] And indeed, Schreber's body is slowly and painfully transformed, in the course of his delusion, into that of a woman. The relationship he maintains with God in his delirium necessitates that he cultivate a continual state of "voluptuousness." Sensual pleasure is spread out over every part of his body so that the entire body, in effect, becomes a kind of erotogenic zone.[18] The "feminine" component of paranoia thus consists of a passivity which is the product of the active construction of a systematic delusion of persecution and the dispersion of sexuality across the whole of the body.

Yet, there is a contradiction in Freud's formulation of the relationship between paranoia and homosexuality, because homosexuality presupposes a well-established and unquestionable subject/object relation. There is a sense in which the very idea of an object of desire is foreign to paranoia. For paranoia is constituted by a disturbance of subject/object relations, at points the total breakdown of a division between them. This destabilization of the opposition between subject and object is evidenced most strongly by the compensatory mechanism which is specific to paranoia—projection. Projection is instrumental to the establishment of the opposition between internal and external, subject and object. In Freudian theory, the infant expels and projects into the external world what it finds in itself of the unpleasurable, and incorporates or retains what is pleasurable (projection and introjection both being conceived on the model of the oral drives). In this way, the subject constructs for itself—even before it attains the status of subjecthood—the territories and spaces, both internal and external, which will constitute its world.

When the paranoiac has recourse to projection, therefore, it is in a desperate attempt to reassert, reconstitute the opposition between subject and object which the patient lacks. As Freud points out, projection is evidence of a process of reconstruction and recovery.[19] But projection has a multiple valence, for it is also a witness to the fragility of the very distinction between subjectivity and objectivity. By constantly transforming an internal representation into an exterior perception, projection destabilizes the opposition between internal and external, subject and object, so that the boundary between the two is continually in flux. As Laplanche and Pontalis explain, "The paranoiac projects his intolerable ideas outwards, whence they return in the shape of reproaches: '. . . *the subject matter remains unaffected*; what is altered is something in the *placing* of the whole thing.' "[20] In a movement which is peculiarly Freudian, the symptom which indicates a movement toward cure at the same time partakes of the disease.

Projection is thus bound up very intimately not only with the constitution of a space for the subject (along the lines of the division internal/external), but with the very concept of subjectivity, which is dependent on the differentiation between an interiority and an exteriority, an ego and an object. The delirium associated with paranoia is characterized by nondifferentiation. As Julia Kristeva points out,

> The discourse of desire becomes a discourse of delirium when it forecloses its object . . . when it establishes itself as the complete locus of *jouissance* (full and without exteriority). In other words, no other exists, no object survives in its irreducible alterity. On the contrary, he who speaks, Daniel Schreber, for example, identifies himself with the very place of alterity, he merges with the Other, experiencing *jouissance* in and through the place of otherness.[21]

At the extreme end of paranoia as psychosis, we witness the annihilation of both the object of desire and subjectivity itself, manifested most explicitly in the paranoiac's delusion of the "end of the world." Here, the mechanism of projection breaks down altogether.

Hence, the paranoid activation of projection is only an intensification and perversion of what Freud describes as a normal, nonpathogenic mechanism, fundamental to the establishment of an opposition between ego and external world and hence crucial to any epistemology which posits a subject and an object of knowledge.[22] From this perspective, the excessive systematicity characteristic of paranoid delusions is evidence of a kind of epistemology gone awry, and the abuse of projection is symptomatic of a regression to a stage before the constitution of a subject/object division—a stage which is barely thinkable because it partakes so fully of the nondifferentiation characteristic of the imaginary. In "Negation," Freud points to the originary nature of this nondifferentiation: "The antithesis between subjective and objective does not exist from the first. It only comes into being from the fact that thinking possesses the capacity to bring before the mind once more something that has once been perceived, by reproducing it as a presentation without the external object having still to be there."[23] The subject/object distinction, and hence access to the symbolic order, is predicated on absence. This is why Lacan defines paranoia as the foreclosure of the paternal signifier, that is, the phallus, *the* signifier of difference itself. Paranoia, in its repudiation of the Father, allies itself with the dyadic structure of narcissism, the imaginary, the pre-Oedipal.

This regressive character, as well as an affiliation with epistemology and its obsession with causes and origins, evidences strong links between paranoia and the primal scene. Nowhere is this more apparent than in Freud's interpretation of the delusion of a female paranoiac in "A Case of Paranoia Running Counter to the Psychoanalytical Theory of the Disease."[24] The case concerns a young single woman, living with her mother, who after a great deal of persuasion consents to visit the apartment of a man who works in the same office. During lovemaking she hears a noise coming from the direction of a desk in front of a window which is covered by a heavy curtain. Her friend attempts to convince her that the noise is that of a clock. But on leaving his apartment, the woman sees two men standing on the staircase, one of whom holds an object which looks like a wrapped box. This meeting is the instigation for the patient's paranoid delusion. She imagines that the box was really a camera and that the noise she heard during lovemaking was actually the click of that camera. The man, hiding behind the heavy curtain, photographed her in order to compromise her, and the patient violently reproaches her friend. During the course of a second consultation, Freud learns that this was in reality the second visit to her friend's apartment. After the first, the woman saw her friend talking to an office superintendent, an elderly woman who is described as having white hair like the patient's mother. Basing her argument on looks, whispers, and the way in which the elderly superintendent behaves toward her after this conversation, the analysand becomes convinced that not only did her friend tell the superintendent about their lovemaking, but that the two of them are lovers as well. The friend mollifies her and ultimately persuades her to come to his apartment a second time, after which she forms the delusion concerning the compromising photograph.

Freud's interest in this case is dictated by the fact that it seems to contradict the psychoanalytic description of paranoia as a defense against homosexuality. For the woman's delusion of persecution appears instead to be a defense against a heterosexual relationship, and the persecutor is consequently of the opposite, not the same, sex. But the patient's second story reconfirms, for Freud, his own theory of paranoia, guaranteeing that the originary persecutor is female (the elderly superintendent, as mother figure). This analysis of the situation is buttressed by Freud's concentration on the "accidental" noise, the click, which forms the basis of the patient's second delusion. Freud claims that the noise "is merely a stimulus which activates the typical phantasy of eavesdropping, itself a component of the parental complex,"[25] thus linking the scene of lovemaking to that originary fantasy of the primal scene. Indeed, Freud reallocates the parts in this scenario: the lover is the father, the patient has taken the mother's place, and the place of listener is assigned to a third person.

> We can see by what means the girl has freed herself from her homosexual dependence on the mother. A partial regression has taken place; instead of choosing her mother as a love-object, she has identified herself with her, she herself has become the mother. The possibility of this regression points to the narcissistic origin of her homosexual object-choice and with that to the paranoiac disposition in her.[26]

Here, paranoia attests to a total assimilation to the place of the mother.

The delusory scenario of this patient, as Guy Rosolato demonstrates in an excellent analysis of Freud's essay, is richly suggestive of the complexity of the figures of paranoia.[27] The fixation to the primal scene elucidates the paranoiac's activation of sound and image as the material supports of the symptom (the obsessions with "hearing voices" and "being watched"). For the young child watching and listening to its parents in the primal scene must itself remain unseen, unheard. As Rosolato points out, sound has a double polarity at the level of this originary fantasy. For it can potentially "betray" not only the parents but the little voyeur as well: sound would expose the parents for their act and the child for its desire to see that act.[28] Sound exists, in this context, as a betrayal of the desire to see.

A dialectic of concealing and revealing is hence already at work in the primal scene, bringing into play the figure of the surface which separates and has the power to veil or expose. Rosolato delineates the variety of surfaces at work in that remake of the primal scene, the delusion of the female paranoiac described above: the heavy curtain which is behind the first "obstacle" of the writing desk and in front of the window, the photographic apparatus concealed within the package, and the photographic negative itself, as a surface which "fixes" the situation.[29] The paranoid fascination with the surface is overdetermined. The surface is first of all constitutive of the scene to which the paranoiac is fixated—its screen (in the sense of the dream-screen of Lewin for example).[30] Furthermore, the fact that the image of the body in paranoia is not mediated by the phallus, as the mark of potential rupture and differentiation of a unified and continuous surface, leads to what Rosolato refers to as a "fantasmatic reduction to the surface and the projections upon it."[31] The paranoid body is all sexuality, a diffuse and nonlocalizable sexuality which, because it is nondifferentiated, is of course unsymbolizable. This indistinction of the body is echoed in the paranoiac's fantasy scenario, by the also indistinct and vague sound—the click of the alleged camera—which in its turn must be captured and contained as an indicator of the exposed surface of a photographic image. But the most crucial determinant of the fascination with the surface is its function of articulating the poles of the opposition which most concerns the paranoiac: internal/external.

The primal scene must, however, always remain incomplete for the paranoiac. Referring to the structure of the delusion belonging to Freud's female patient, Rosolato explains:

> The Oedipal situation here does not sustain its triangular development. It is reduced to a double dual relation: a relation with a man which is not completed and a relation with the mother which is crushed in a narcissistic identification. An empty space signals as point of appeal what remains outside, rejected, foreclosed: the phallus and the Father. . . . With the paranoiac, a dissymmetry is established which blocks primary identification in favor of the maternal axis and involves an appeal directed toward this lack concerning the father. . . .[32]

The lack is "filled" by a supplementary metaphor—the systematic delusion itself—which replaces the signifier of the father. Thus the delusion is a desperate attempt on the part of the paranoiac to compensate for the absence of the paternal signifier. By the same token, paranoia is characterized by a narcissistic over-identification with the mother. As Kristeva points out, only the triadic structure of the Oedipal scenario can guarantee the formulation of a working distinction between subject and object and the corresponding defeat of a narcissism which threatens all identity: "The paternal agency alone, to the extent that it introduces the symbolic dimension between 'subject' (child) and 'object' (mother), can generate . . . a strict object relation."[33]

This rather long digression into the psychoanalytic theorization of paranoia was necessitated by the complexity of the issues raised by the condition and the elaborate nature of the figures of paranoia, many of which are activated by the textual work of the paranoid gothic films. The aspects of paranoia delineated above which seem most relevant to the paranoid structure of the films are: (1) the foregrounding of epistemology in relation to paranoid speculation and the systematicity of the delusion; (2) a destabilization of the oppositions between internal and external, subject and object; (3) the foreclosure of the paternal signifier and corresponding fusion with the maternal; (4) the mobilization of the auditory and the visual as the two most important material registers of the paranoid delusion.

The obsession with epistemology in these films is, not surprisingly, linked to the fact that they all reside well within the boundaries of the suspense film, structuring their narratives by playing off the known against the unknown, fetishizing the secret. But, there is a crucial displacement of the problematic of knowledge in these films. In the films of the medical discourse, the woman is quite clearly the *object* of knowledge, her body the site of a continual examination of symptoms. But here, in the paranoid gothic films, there is a concerted effort to locate her as the subject of knowledge. The narrative structure produces an insistence on situating the woman as agent of the gaze, as investigator in charge of the epistemological trajectory of the text, as the one for whom the "secret beyond the door" is really at stake.

In this cycle, dramas of seeing become invested with horror within the context of the home, and sexual anxiety is projected onto the axis of suspense. The paradigmatic woman's space—the home—is yoked to dread, and to a crisis of vision. For violence is precisely what is hidden from sight. Hence, one could formulate a veritable topography of spaces within the home along the axis of this perverted specularization. The home is not a homogeneous space—it asserts divisions, gaps, and fields within its very structure. There are places which elude the eye; paranoia demands a split between the known and the unknown, the seen and the unseen.

Thus, many of these films are marked by the existence of a room to which the woman is barred access. In *Gaslight* it is the attic where the husband searches for the dead aunt's jewels; in *Dragonwyck* (1946) it is the upstairs tower room where the husband exercises his drug addiction; in *Rebecca* it is both the boathouse-cottage detached from the house and Rebecca's bedroom, ultimately approached by the female protagonist with a characteristically Hitchcockian insistence on the moving point-of-view shot toward the closed door. In *Jane Eyre*, the secret locked in the tower room, actively concealed from Jane, is excessive femininity ("Her excesses drove her into madness," Rochester tells Jane). *Secret Beyond the Door* bases itself on the hyperbolization of this mechanism, a proliferation of rooms which the husband collects. In accordance with his architectural determinism (which, in a perverse reversal of German Expressionism, stipulates that a room does not reflect but determines what happens within it), the husband constructs exact replicas of rooms in which famous murders have taken place, concealing the final room—the wife's bedroom—from the eyes of both the public and his wife.

The suspense generated by such strategies is no different in its dictation of subject positions from the more generalized cinematic suspense grounded by what Pascal Bonitzer refers to as the "rule of the look and nothing else":

> In this system, each shot engages the spectators as subjects (as potential victims) of another shot, and the "image of the worst" governs the progression; each shot, in its difference of intensity, portends and defers "the screen of the worst" for the spectators, subjects of the fiction: this is the principle of suspense. . . . Suspense is not just a genre. . . . It is, from the point of view I have just expounded, essential to cinema. . . . But only insofar as this system is one for ordering the depth of field, which constitutes the take not only as a passive recording of the scene, but as a productive force in its own right expressing, producing the *fading* of a point of view (and of a point of view that is . . . rather paranoiac). [34]

The cinematic generality of this system of suspense is specified by the woman's film in only two ways: (1) through the localization of suspense in the familiarized female space of the home in relation to a close relative, almost always the husband; (2) in the violent attribution of the investigating gaze to the female protagonist (who is also its victim). This second specification effects a major disturbance in the cinematic relay of the look, resulting in so much narrative stress that the potential danger of a female look is often reduced or avoided entirely by means of the delegation of the detecting gaze to another male figure who is on the side of the law. *Gaslight* is a particularly good example of this strategy. Quite often the female protagonist is endowed with the necessary curiosity and a desire to know but is revealed as impotent in terms of the actual ability to uncover the secret or attain the knowledge which she desires. In *Undercurrent* (1946), Katherine Hepburn is obsessed with the traces of her husband's absent brother but does not even recognize him when she first confronts him in person. In *Jane Eyre*, Orson Welles actively demands a dissociation of seeing and understanding from Joan Fontaine when he tells her, "What you see may shock you. Don't try to understand." The trajectories of the films consistently trace the passivation of the female subject of the desire to know. As Joanna Russ points out with reference to the modern gothic novels, *"They are adventure stories with passive protagonists."* [35]

Nevertheless, in many of the films, and in the best tradition of the horror film, affect is condensed onto the image of a woman investigating, penetrating space alone. And it is the staircase, a signifier which possesses a certain semantic privilege in relation to the woman as object of the gaze, which articulates the connection between the familiar and the unfamiliar, or between neurosis and psychosis. An icon of crucial and repetitive insistence in the classical representations of the cinema, the staircase is traditionally the locus of specularization of the woman. It is *on the stairway* that she is displayed as spectacle for the male gaze (and often the icon is repeated, as though it were nonproblematic, within the same films—think of Hazel Brooks, the "other woman" in *Sleep My Love* (1948), descending the stairs in her scanty lingerie or the woman in *Dragonwyck*, dressed in her best clothes, who poses on the staircase when her future husband comes to call).

But the staircase in the paranoid woman's films also (and sometimes simultaneously) becomes the passageway to the "image of the worst" or "screen of the worst," in Bonitzer's terms. In *Dragonwyck*, film noir lighting intensifies the sense of foreboding attached to Gene Tierney's slow climb up the stairs in the attempt to ascertain what her suspicious husband does in the tower room prohibited to her. Both the title and the mise-en-scène of *The Spiral Staircase* depend on an amplification of the affect attached to this central icon of the genre. In *Sleep My Love*, the space of the house is dominated by three tiers of stairs on or near which the female protagonist is attacked by distorted voices, faints, and is finally hypnotized in her husband's attempt to induce her to murder. What Barbara Stanwyck finally discovers in the room at the top of the stairs in *The Two Mrs. Carrolls* is her own distorted and grotesque portrait, painted by her husband and evidence of his psychotic plan to kill her. The woman's exercise of an active investigating gaze can only be simultaneous with her own victimization. The place of her specularization (the stairway) is transformed into the locus of a process of seeing designed to unveil an aggression against itself.

The deployment of space in the woman's film is motivated rather directly by a fairly strict mapping of gender-differentiated societal spaces onto the films—the woman's place is in the home. Although this is quite clearly the case in the family melodrama (where the space of the house frequently dictates the weight of the mise-en-scène), the house in the paranoid subgroup, as described above, is foregrounded in relation to mechanisms of suspense which organize the gaze. An advertising poster for *Dark Waters* (1944) asks, "Have you ever really been afraid? . . . of a man? . . . of a house? . . . of yourself?[36] Horror, which should by rights be external to domesticity, infiltrates the home.[37] The house does not simply externalize internal feelings, as in melodrama; rather, it represents the division internal/external and its very instability, a configuration whose social and psychical ramifications are crucial to an understanding of the cultural construction of femininity. And the fixation on and destabilization of the opposition internal/external is also, as we have seen, central to paranoia and its chief mechanism, projection. Insofar as the inside/outside dichotomy of paranoia is articulated with that of interiority/exteriority and hence subject/object, the paranoid woman's films explore the putting into crisis of the female subject. The ontological problem—that is, the problem of feminine identity—is thus transformed into a spatial problem. The "properly feminine" space of the home is haunted by an insistent exteriority.

The work of the films thus consists of a defamiliarization, a denaturalization of what is seemingly most familiar and most natural—the spaces and components of the home. This process involves not only the rooms and the stairways previously discussed, but also elements which more clearly involve the articulation of an interior and an exterior—doors and windows. Doors, as Thierry Kuntzel points out, constitute one of the "most privileged hermeneutic figures" of the classical cinema.[38] The paranoid gothic films simply exacerbate a generalized tendency of the suspense film—the tendency to organize dramas of seeing around the phenomenon of the closed or locked door and the temptation it offers, thus bringing into play what Bonitzer refers to as the "obsessional mechanisms of the forbidden and of transgression."[39] Most importantly, for the paranoiac, the door is yet another surface which separates one space from another, activating the dialectic of concealing and revealing. In *Jane Eyre*, Rochester's domestic secret is hidden behind a heavy door which he warns Jane not to open on any account. Tracking point-of-view shots toward the closed door of Rebecca's bedroom emphasize the transgressive nature of the Joan Fontaine character's entrance into that space. In *Secret Beyond the Door*, which structures its entire narrative around the relation to a locked door, Celia waits until the middle of the night when the household is asleep to venture into the long hall lit only by the small circle from her flashlight and open the door labeled with the number 7. In each of these instances, what the woman confronts on the other side of the door is an aspect of herself: in *Jane Eyre* it is excessive femininity in the figure of the woman who occupies the place Jane herself desires—that of Rochester's wife; in *Rebecca* it is the room belonging to the woman that the protagonist envies and takes as her ego ideal—again the first wife; in *Secret Beyond the Door* it is Celia's own bedroom (formerly the space of the first wife). The door in these films opens onto a mirror, and the process is one of doubling or repetition, locking the woman within a narcissistic construct.

There is also a sense in which the door, as Kuntzel maintains, is very strongly linked with certain technical devices of the filmic enunciation—the fade-out or the dissolve—because both "(dis)join two different places, two different scenes."[40] The suspense film's concentration on the door as a focal point of the spectator's scopophilia is thus a strategy of internalizing or diegeticizing an element of the enunciation. Bazin deplored the semiotic implications of this tendency in what he called "doorknob cinema," referring to the inevitable close-up of the doorknob as "less a fact than a sign brought into arbitrary relief by the camera, and no more independent semantically than a preposition in a sentence."[41] For Bazin, this usage of the door is proof of the unbearability of a sign or a symbol in a discourse which is asymptotic to the real. This type of "hypersignification" and its disturbance of the iconic or indexical quality of the filmic discourse is evident in a scene from *Secret Beyond the Door*. Celia, standing at a window and watching her husband Mark benevolently caring for a dog's injured paw, continues to wonder what he is really like. In a voice-over which conveys her thoughts she asks herself, "What goes on in his mind? He keeps it locked like this door." There follows, on the image track, a cut to a shot of the door labeled number 7, a direct literalization of her phrase "this door." The shot ruptures the spatial continuity of the scene and seems to appear from nowhere. For the markers of subjectivity or interiority (a dissolve, extreme close-up concentrating on the eyes, loss of focus) are absent. And yet the door is extradiegetic to the scene (although not to the film). Because it is not present in the space occupied by Celia, it could not be the object of a point-of-view structure.

This type of rupture of the diegesis in order to illustrate a single thought is highly unusual in the classical text and demonstrates the excessiveness of the meaning attached to doors in these films. The hypersignification of elements which are given psychological import is peculiar to films of the '40s which attempt to incorporate psychoanalysis. The opening and closing of a door (the ruling rhetorical figure of a film like *Spellbound* [1945], which deals directly with psychoanalysis) is quite frequently a metaphorical representation of the opening and closing of the mind, repression and disclosure. And psychoanalysis is often presented as the key. This forcing of the discourse is symptomatic of difficulties in the classical film's representation of interiority. In *Shock* (1946), a woman who is about to witness an event which leaves her in a state of catatonia dreams of a huge doorknob, represented in expressionistic form, which she finds impossible to turn.

The last site in this topography of spaces within the home with a pronounced semantic valence in relation to processes of specularization is the window. Within the women's films as a whole, images of women looking through windows or waiting at windows abound. The window has special import in terms of the social and symbolic positioning of the woman—the window is the interface between inside and outside, the feminine space of the family and reproduction and the masculine space of production. It facilitates a communication by means of the look between the two sexually differentiated spaces. That interface becomes a potential point of violence, intrusion, and aggression in the paranoid woman's films. In *The Two Mrs. Carrolls* the traces of the poisoned milk which Barbara Stanwyck throws out the window are discovered on the sill by her psychotic artist husband Humphrey Bogart, who later penetrates her locked bedroom in a vampirelike entrance through the window. In *Rebecca*, Mrs. Danvers attempts to seduce the Joan Fontaine character into committing suicide at the window. In these films the house becomes the analogue of the hu-

man body, its parts fetishized by textual operations, its erotogenic zones meta-
morphosized by a morbid anxiety attached to sexuality. It is the male character
who fetishizes the house as a whole, attempting to unify and homogenize it
through an insistent process of naming—Manderley, Dragonwyck, Blaise
Creek, Thornfield.

When the outside threatens and invades the inside, the boundaries and
identity of the home begin to be questioned, and another psychoanalytic category, one that has close affinities with paranoia, is brought into play—the uncanny. Within the cinema, it is hardly surprising that the uncanny should be
activated by means of dramas of seeing, of concealing and revealing. Freud
himself, in his article "The Uncanny," repetitively and obsessively returns to
the relations of vision to the uncanny effect: the "evil eye," the sight of himself
in a mirror misrecognized, the fear of losing one's eyes embodied in Hoffmann's
story "The Sandman." Even his etymological investigation of the word *unheimlich* ("uncanny") revolves around the possibilities of seeing and hiding. Freud's
rather long tracing of the linguistic deviations of the word serve finally to demonstrate that *heimlich* ("belonging or pertaining to the the home, familiar") is
eventually equated with its opposite *unheimlich* ("strange, unfamiliar, uncanny"): "Thus *heimlich* is a word the meaning of which develops in the direction of ambivalence, until it finally coincides with its opposite, *unheimlich*."[42]
This sliding of signification is possible only because the word for "home" is semantically overdetermined and can be situated in relation to the gaze. For the
home or house connotes not only the familiar but also what is secret, concealed,
hidden from sight. When what is "of or like the home" is synonymous with its
opposite, we are quite close to the signifying field of the gothic narrative. The
house, in these films, is certainly uncanny.

But for Freud, the paradigmatic process through which the familiar becomes strange is situated as the male's relation to the female body: "It often happens that neurotic men declare that they feel there is something uncanny about
the female genital organs. This *unheimlich* place, however, is the entrance to
the former *Heim* [home] of all human beings, to the place where each one of us
lived once upon a time and in the beginning . . . the prefix '*un*' is the token of
repression."[43] The female genitals are uncanny because they represent, for the
male, the possibility of castration and the concommitant rupture of the unified
body image which supports a narcissistic identity. As Samuel Weber points out
in a reinterpretation of the essay on the uncanny, Freud had good reason for his
somewhat intuitive linking of an obsession with the eyes or vision to the uncanny and hence to castration anxiety. The subject's understanding of feminine
castration is indeed based on a visual perception, but it is a kind of "negative perception," a perception of the absence of the maternal phallus.[44] The only object
of the gaze is difference itself. The image of feminine castration threatens the

primacy of the system that Freud called "Perception-Consciousness" and "confronts the subject with the fact that it will never again be able to believe its eyes, since what they have seen is neither simply visible nor wholly invisible. . . . It robs the eyes of the desired phenomena and thus alters the structure of perception. . . ."[45] Castration anxiety thus puts into crisis the relation of visual perception to such notions as certainty and immediacy.

The uncanny, in Weber's analysis, is consequently a form of defense against castration anxiety and its assault on the unity and integrity of perception. But it is an ambivalent defense—it protects the subject against the image of castration, but it does so by continually reenacting, for the subject, the process of seeing which unveils the horrifying picture of lack. The uncanny is a defense

> which is ambivalent and which expresses itself in the compulsive curiosity . . . the craving to penetrate the flimsy appearances to the essence beneath. . . . This desire to penetrate, discover and ultimately to conserve the integrity of perception: perceiver and perceived, the wholeness of the body, the power of vision—all this implies a *denial* (*Verneinung* is the Freudian term) of that almost-nothing which can hardly be seen, a denial that in turn involves a certain structure of narration, in which this denial repeats and articulates itself.[46]

Thus for both Freud and Weber, the uncanny is the return of the repressed, and what is repressed is a certain vision of the female body as the signifier of castration and hence disunity. The uncanny defense against castration consists, paradoxically, not simply of blinding itself to the image of the castrated female body but of looking and looking again, as if replaying the original trauma would in some way ameliorate it. The foregrounding of the very process of seeing in the suspense film, and its simultaneous association with both pleasure and unpleasure, desire for and fear of the image of the monstrous or horrible, allies it with the uncanny as a mode of defense. Suspense in the cinema—for Bonitzer the "rule of the look and nothing else"—therefore involves a kind of fetishization of vision itself, a reassertion of the integrity of perception along the lines of sexual difference.

Yet this interpretation, as it stands, begs the question. For the house is uncanny to the woman, not the man. Not only is it a woman who is given the status of subject of the gaze in the paranoid subgroup, but the films as a whole purportedly formulate their textual address in anticipation of a female audience. And one can easily ask: what does the above analysis have to do with the female spectator for whom castration cannot pose a threat since she has nothing to lose? The different relation of the woman to the look must necessarily pose problems for a class of films which depends so heavily on the mechanisms of suspense and the very possibility of attributing the gaze and subjectivity to the woman.

The paranoid gothic films exhibit a special kinship with the suspense film but also, and perhaps even more importantly in this context, with the genre of the horror film. The horror film intensifies and structures its affect of fear by positioning a female character as the one who looks and who ultimately unveils the terror-inciting monster.[47] The question arises as to why the horror film, historically and in its contemporary form, consistently chooses to subject a woman rather than a man to this image of horror. Of course, the representation of the woman traditionally provides an image of passivity and vulnerability which heightens the potential of a dangerous violence. But a physical restraint such as weakness or vulnerability cannot be a sufficient explanation for the insistence of the convention. Rather, the positioning of a woman as the recipient of visual terror is determined by the psychical construction of sexually differentiated processes of seeing.

Male scopophilia has a well-defined and quite specific object—the female body. The male gaze is fixed to the image of the castrated maternal body and obsessed with its implications for the coherence of male identity. The concepts of beauty, attractiveness, or visual pleasure as applied to the female body act as compensations for her lack. The visual pleasure that body gives to the male thus has its basis in ontological security. The woman, on the other hand, cannot *look* at that body (except in the mirror of her own narcissism) because she *is* it. Female scopophilia is a drive without an object, an undirected and free-floating drive which is conducive to the operation of the phobia. For true horror is fear without a definable or specifiable object. Because female vision is objectless, free-floating, it is more proper to what Kristeva, in *Powers of Horror*, calls the "abject" (and abjection, according to Kristeva, is stronger than the uncanny). The abject, which is anterior to the opposition between subject and object, is the "not yet object"; it is the nonobject of the search for "something to be scared of."[48]

> If the object, however, through its opposition, settles me within the fragile texture of a desire for meaning, which, as a matter of fact, makes me ceaselessly and infinitely homologous to it, what is *abject*, on the contrary, the jettisoned object, is radically excluded and draws me toward the place where meaning collapses.[49]

The "place where meaning collapses" is, in our culture, the place allotted to a femininity which is excluded from language and the symbolic order. Elsewhere Kristeva refers to the abject as "the horrible and fascinating abomination which is connoted in all cultures by the feminine."[50] In *Jane Eyre* the place where meaning collapses is the space assigned to the madwoman, a point-of-view shot from a room in blackness. The madwoman is never shown—she is unrepresentable.

So when the woman in filmic narrative confronts the nonobject of her own fear, what she confronts is herself. As Linda Williams has very lucidly demonstrated in the case of the horror film, the monster acts as a kind of mirror, its deformities reflecting back to the woman an image of her own lack, her castration.[51] The monster's position of exhibitionism is equivalent to that of the woman. Thus, in the horror film, what the woman actually sees, after a sustained and fearful process of looking, is a sign or representation of herself displaced to the level of the nonhuman. In the paranoid woman's film, on the other hand, the female character does not encounter a mutilated signifier of herself but, instead, the traces of another woman who once occupied her position as wife (in *Jane Eyre*, *Rebecca*, *Secret Beyond the Door*), or even her own iconic image (as in *The Two Mrs. Carrolls* when Barbara Stanwyck sees the grotesque portrait of herself painted by her husband, which, in its turn, echoes the abstract portrait of his first wife—"The Angel of Death"). In both instances of self-confrontation, a narcissistic structure is produced by the collapse of the subject/object distinction.

There is a crucial and repetitive insistence, in these films, on the existence in the past of a woman who once occupied the place of the female protagonist and whose fate—often a violent or unexplained death—the protagonist seems destined to share. The woman sees herself slowly becoming another, duplicating an earlier identity as though history, particularly in the case of women, were bound to repeat itself. Often the first wife is never visually represented (this is the case in *Rebecca*, *Jane Eyre*, and *The Two Mrs. Carrolls*), but the process of repetition is nevertheless evident, the visual void of the original woman filled by hints, traces of her presence (the omnipresent initial "R" in *Rebecca*), and verbal references. Frequently, the doubling manifests itself most clearly when the second woman assumes the position of the first as a bedridden invalid, an inevitable signal of the husband's attempt to murder her in the same way as he did the first wife (e.g., in *Dragonwyck* or *The Two Mrs. Carrolls*).

*Dragonwyck* multiplies its female predecessors of the protagonist, providing not only a first wife but a female ancestor, a great-grandmother, whose portrait hangs over the harpsichord in the parlor. All three of the women are clearly linked by the function of motherhood—the husbands' only desire involves their ability to produce a son, an heir who will carry on a markedly patriarchal tradition (Van Ryn, the character played by Vincent Price, is a patroon who controls a feudalistic system of farming in the Hudson Valley). The first wife, when she fails to bear a son, is poisoned by her husband. According to a maid, the great-grandmother was forced to commit suicide when her husband separated her from their son, the real object of his desire. The portrait of the great-grandmother is a witness to the legend of her continuing presence. In the maid's account of the story, the great-grandmother returns to play the harpsichord and sing whenever an impending disaster (usually a death) threatens the Van Ryn family.

Portraits are consistently present in the films as significant items of the genre's iconography.[52] The portrait becomes the signifier of repetition itself, formulating an insistent relation between mimetic representation and the feminine. In *Gaslight*, the female protagonist's murdered aunt is represented by a huge portrait which bears a striking resemblance to Ingrid Bergman. *The Two Mrs. Carrolls* establishes the portrait and disturbances in the mimetic process as the dominant and structuring figure of its narrative. What is at stake is the play of identity and difference, the breakdown of that dialectic, and the resultant fusion, which is presented as specifically feminine. The force of the pull toward the initial (historically prior) female figure is demonstrated explicitly by the structure of a syntagm from *Rebecca*. Joan Fontaine, who plays a character who remains nameless, is represented throughout the first part of the film as passive and incompetent, incapable of assuming the position of mistress of Manderley, overshadowed by the ghost of the absent first wife, Rebecca. Finally, in a scene in which she orders the housekeeper, Mrs. Danvers, to remove every trace of Rebecca's possessions, the Fontaine character appears to assert her identity by forcefully claiming, "I am Mrs. de Winter now." Because the character is nameless, however, her assertion of identity can only be the same as a reassumption of the place of Rebecca (who was also "Mrs. de Winter"). Within the field of language the woman is allowed no access to difference and is consigned to an inevitable repetition of the same. Furthermore, the scene of her precarious assertion of identity is immediately followed by a montage sequence of the protagonist's preparations for a masquerade ball, her search for a costume, a different identity to surprise and please her husband. Ultimately she takes Mrs. Danvers's suggestion and chooses for her costume a *copy* of the dress worn by a female ancestor (Caroline de Winter) whose portrait hangs in the hallway—without realizing that this was the costume worn by Rebecca at a previous masquerade ball. Her repetition or doubling of Rebecca thus takes place via a portrait, another instance of doubling. When the Joan Fontaine character descends the stairway (the traditional locus of female specularization discussed earlier), preparing herself as spectacle for the eyes of her husband, she is unexpectedly confronted with the look of horror which greets her unintended mimesis of Rebecca. Her efforts to masquerade, to become someone else in order to please her husband, are thwarted by the spectre of a return to Rebecca, an inescapable mimesis.

This insistent recall to the origin is, of course, an insistent recall to the mother. In *Dragonwyck* it is explicit: the function of motherhood underlies the repetition. In other instances, the appeal to the maternal referent is less literal and depends on the projection onto history of a triangular structure. The husband is often a rather strong father figure to the second wife, and the first wife, due to her historical position, takes on retrospectively the aspect of the mother.

Thus, the protagonist, like the female paranoiac in "A Case of Paranoia Running Counter to the Psychoanalytic Theory of the Disease," takes the place of the mother in the primal scene. In this mimesis of the mother, the corresponding death of subjectivity which accompanies the fusion and nondifferentiation this mimesis implies is literalized by means of the husband's murderous tendencies. The female protagonist's phobia must, therefore, involve a fear of assuming the place of the preceding female (the mother).

Paranoia, as we have seen, is characterized by the foreclosure of the paternal signifier (which would enable the constitution of an opposition between subject and object) and a concomitant fusion with the mother. Although neither Freud nor Lacan points this out, the etiology of paranoia suggests that it corresponds not to a pathological but to a "normal" psychical condition in the case of the female. For separation from the mother and the acknowledgment of difference as represented by the paternal signifier are, in any event, more difficult for the female subject than for the male.[53] In other words, the female never fully resolves her Oedipal complex and is thus linked more strongly to the realm of the pre-Oedipal than the male. From an initial state of autoeroticism, both sexes locate the mother as their first object. Hence, the externalization or, more accurately, the very constitution of the object for the male subject is synonymous with sexual differentiation. Externalization for the female is merely an encounter with the same, and the girl-child experiences very early the failure and collapse of the oppositions internal/external, subject/object. The male subject must relinquish the mother as the object of desire and find another object through displacement. But the female subject must make a much more radical displacement of her object of desire—from mother to father to father replacement—and the very radicality of the change precludes its successful accomplishment. In the Freudian formulation, the female subject does not institute a search to "refind" the object; she becomes that object.

The paranoid gothic films evince a terror of the annihilation of subjectivity which is attendant upon that psychical trajectory. In the literary gothic narrative, the way in which the novels exploit "separation anxiety" and the overcloseness of the relation between mother and daughter has frequently been noted. As Tania Modleski points out, with reference to the modern gothic novel,

> it is not only that women fear being *like* their mothers, sharing the same fate, but also that, in an important sense, they fear *being* their mothers—hence the emphasis on identity in physical appearance, the sensation of actually being possessed, the feeling that past and present are not merely similar but are "intertwined," etc. In each case, the heroine feels suffocated—as well as desperate and panic stricken in her inability to break free of the past. . . . Gothics, then, serve in part to convince women that they are not their mothers.[54]

This "convincing" is certainly possible at the level of character typology and plot, but it is more problematic when one takes into account the structural features of the narrative and, even more importantly, the relations between subjects (reading or viewing) and texts. This is particularly true in the cinema, where the elaboration of distinctions between subjectivity and objectivity, internal and external, has historically been more difficult than in literature. For what is involved is more than the question of whether a woman can be something other than her mother (although this is clearly an important question). Rather, at stake is a fundamental relation to processes of signification which takes as its conflicting poles the space of the maternal and the space of the paternal.

It is, therefore, not so much a question of the difficulty of feminine identity (although the identity proffered by the mirror in the Lacanian schema, illusory as it may be, is clearly more problematic for the female for whom boundaries must remain less well defined). The crucial consideration, instead, is that of access to subjectivity with all this entails of an access to language. What we are dealing with, then, is not really a loss of identity but a return to the locus of its unthinkability—psychosis—the preverbal, the space outside language, a space which in psychoanalysis is, properly speaking, maternal.

Paranoia evinces a lack in relation to the paternal function. The delusion of paranoia is built up to fill that lack—to take the place of the missing paternal signifier, the Name of the Father, hence the Law. There is a sense, then, in which the paranoid delusion is a simulacrum of law. In the gothic films, this simulacrum of legality is constituted by a hyperbolization of the image of the aggressive, punishing, castrating Father—an image which compensates for a precise lack of castration anxiety on the part of the paranoid subject. The obsession with a potentially murderous fatherlike husband is thus a cover for a more intense fear concerning the maternal figure and the annihilation of subjectivity. Indeed, in some of the films, the defensive cover takes over, and, at the manifest level, the films appear to be organized almost completely in relation to the father as the figure of law. In Suspicion and The Spiral Staircase, the paternal influence affects even the iconography: the father assumes the space consistently assigned to the maternal figure in other films of the group—the portrait.[55] Yet what the films actually explore is not the anxiety and ultimate security of the castration complex but the underside of the Oedipal trajectory—the maternal space it assumes as a point of departure, a scenario to be rejected.

For Freud the uncanny is effected by the return of the repressed, and what is repressed, above all, is castration anxiety. But there is another side to repression which involves a fear of the maternal body as signifying something quite different from castration. Kristeva refers to this phobia attached to the maternal as the ignored aspect of the two-sided formation Freud described in mythical terms as a phylogenetic primal scene in Totem and Taboo. The two aspects of the formation are the taboo against murder, which founds society, the exchange of women, and the signifying order; and the taboo against incest, which is consigned to the realm of the inexplicable. Freud suggests very strongly that "incest dread" is originary, a bedrock of culture which has no determinant but itself and which will, perhaps, never be explained. Kristeva attempts to explain it as a phobia of nondifferentiation, of uncertain and unstable identity, of "the non-separation of subject/object on which language has no hold but one woven of fright and repulsion."[56]

The taboo against murder, which also embodies a proper fear of the father and of castration, is, as Kristeva points out, both defensive and socializing. Incest dread, on the other hand, raises the spectre of all that is excluded from society but haunts it at the margins—in short, what is condensed onto the concept of femininity insofar as it drifts toward the realm of psychosis, a realm which is above all outside language and thus anterior to the distinctions between pleasure and pain, inside and outside. What is in process here is that stage between auto-eroticism and object-choice which Freud labeled narcissism, a very strange phase since it precedes the constitution of an external object but nevertheless strives for an object relation: ". . . we are faced with the strange correlation between an entity (the ego) and its converse (the object), which is nevertheless not yet constituted; with an 'ego' in relation to a non-object."[57]

The consequences of such an ambiguous narcissistic relation go very far toward explaining the phobia attached to the maternal.

> On the one hand, the non-constitution of the (outside) object as such renders unstable the ego's identity, which could not be precisely established without having been differentiated from an other, from its object. The ego of primary narcissism is thus uncertain, fragile, threatened, subjected just as much as its non-object to spatial ambivalence (inside/outside uncertainty) and to ambiguity of perception (pleasure/pain). On the other hand, one has to admit that such a narcissistic topology has no other underpinning in psychosomatic reality than the mother-child dyad. . . . Incest prohibition throws a veil over primary narcissism and the always ambivalent threats with which it menaces subjective identity. . . . the other threat to the subject [is] that of being swamped by the dual relationship, thereby risking the loss not of a part (castration) but of the totality of his living being.[58]

The mother/child dyad, exemplary of the narcissistic relation, does not therefore connote solace or a soothing idyllic relation, but instead annihilation, nothingness, the disappearance of the subject's being. Kristeva, however, relegates the "feminine" to what is confronted in the phobia and fails to sexually differentiate the subject/presubject of the process of confrontation (although incest generally connotes heterosexuality and the implication is, therefore, that this subject is male). Yet, it is clear that the female subject has more difficulty in freeing herself from the narcissistic dyad. It is thus more strongly true in the case of the woman that she never quite attains the status of subject, never quite leaves the shadow of nondifferentiation associated with the maternal space.

In the paranoid gothic films, the woman's gaze, free-floating, objectless, and conducive to the phobia, is subjected to a return to its like, a narcissistic folding over upon itself. The women's films as a whole precipitate a narcissism of looking (woman at woman) which is the dilemma of the genre and must be mitigated or concealed. Even here, in the most explicitly phobic of the films, the narcissism is overlaid, deflected by the stress on a violence inhabiting the institutionalized heterosexual relation of marriage. Just as exogamy, which institutes a "man/woman strangeness" at the level of matrimony,[59] seeks to allay the dread of incest, the concentration in the films on that very strangeness in the marriage relation—the risk of not knowing one's husband well enough—conceals the more fundamental terror of nondifferentiation and the eclipsing of subjectivity within the maternal space. Exogamy is, after all, a reinforcement of the opposition internal/external at the level of social relations.

As we have seen, the women's films in general evince a consistent inability to sustain a coherent representation of female subjectivity in the context of phallocentric discursive mechanisms. It is perhaps symptomatic of the paranoid films' metatextuality that the difficulty is most acute in this subgroup which puts into crisis the very opposition subjectivity/objectivity, narrativizing the specifically feminine predicament of an obliteration of the precise boundaries of identity within the maternal space.

But it is also the case that the cinema itself, harboring a latent paranoia, consistently confuses subjectivity and objectivity, failing to elaborate a solid boundary between them. The novel, as mentioned earlier, has conventionalized methods for making such distinctions and for confining and constraining its "vision" to a single character (the interior monologue, the use of the first person pronoun). It is therefore capable of constructing a norm of objectivity against which the extent of paranoia can be measured. In the cinema, on the other hand, for reasons having to do with the classical organization of the material of the signifier, the representation of subjectivity tends to exceed its own boundaries and constraints, bleeding over into a purportedly "neutral" diegesis. It is extremely difficult to *localize* subjectivity. This has to do, at least partially, with the multiplicity and diversity of strategies activated to signify the subjective—a multiplicity necessary precisely because subjectivity is reduced to interiority, and interiority, by definition, is invisible, inaccessible to the camera. Its numerous signifiers include, among others, facial expression (the eyes, in particular, as "window to the soul"), the voice-over, mise-en-scène as an externalization of the internal, the point-of-view shot, music, and optical devices used to introduce a dream or daydream.

Among the elements of this list, only the point-of-view shot, the voice-over, and the optical devices are specific to the cinematic apparatus. The optical devices which introduce the thoughts or dreams of a particular character constitute the greatest disruption of spatial and temporal continuity in the representation of subjectivity. The diegesis of the film must literally be brought to a halt, its spatio-temporal coordinates displaced in favor of those of a subjectivized scenario which is initiated by means of a stylized violence against a unitary image. This type of disruption is illustrated, specifically in relation to female subjectivity, by a scene from *The Spiral Staircase* in which Helen imagines a wedding ceremony in which she and the doctor are married. Her point-of-view image of the hallway breaks up, through a kaleidoscopelike optical effect, to reveal this wedding scenario. Helen's daydream of happiness turns into a nightmare when she is unable to say "I do." This is one of two moments in the film, linked by this very parallelism, in which Helen's inability to speak becomes most terrifying to her. The other moment is when she realizes that there is a murderer in the house, attempts to telephone for help, and finds that she cannot. Marriage and violence are both associated with an intensification of anxieties linked to the muteness of the woman, her exclusion from language.

But this rather insistently metaphorical sequence can only exist at the expense of the forward trajectory of the narrative. Furthermore, and somewhat paradoxically, there is a sense in which its level of reality cannot differ from that of the rest of the film. Through the force of the realism usually attached to the image in the classical cinema, Helen's subjectivity unwittingly becomes an objectivity. Although optical devices bracket the sequence, they cannot completely undermine the status of the image as *the* support of the film's truth, its ground of knowledge. This aspect of the image—its nearly automatic guarantee of knowledge—explains certain difficulties in the relation of the point-of-view shot to subjectivity as well. While the placement or positioning of the image is subjective in the point-of-view structure, its content is not and cannot be unless it is "distorted" through blurring, wavering, loss of focus, etc. (typical signifiers of drunkenness or being drugged). As Stephen Heath points out,

> what is "subjective" in the point-of-view shot is its spatial positioning (its place), not the image or the camera. . . . a true subjective image would effectively need to mark its subjectivity *in the image itself.* . . . The implication of this, of course, is then the strength of the unmarked image as a constant third person. . . . Point of view, that is, depends on an overlaying of first and third person modes. There is no radical dichotomy between subjective point-of-view shots and objective non-point-of-view shots; the latter mode is the continual basis over which the former can run in its particular organization of space, its disposition of the images.[60]

It is the "strength of the unmarked image as a constant third person" which contributes to the dispersal of subjectivity in the classical film—its constant transgression of its own limits.

This fundamental condition of filmic representation goes very far toward explaining the unsatisfactory closure of a film like *Suspicion*, whose ending belies an ability to localize subjectivity in the point-of-view shot and signals the consequent collapse of the opposition between subjectivity and objectivity. The revelation, very suddenly, at the end of the film that Johnnie (Cary Grant) is really not a murderer, that Lina's (Joan Fontaine's) suspicions are entirely unjustified, lacks credibility. Whether or not the effect of a sudden turnaround in the ending can be traced to an extratextual determinant (the demand made on Hitchcock to recognize Cary Grant's star status and free him of all culpability[61]), the "flaw"—within the terms set by the classical text—is instructive. For, while Johnnie manages to justify all his actions and answer all of Lina's questions, this "knowledge" of his character is presented through dialogue. And dialogue is far too weak to counter the weight of the imagery which supports Lina's suspicions throughout the film.

On the one hand, there is a concerted effort to localize this fear, to specify that the vision of Johnnie's murderous impulses belongs solely to Lina. During a game of anagrams, for instance, Lina inadvertently spells out the word "murder." Hitchcock cuts from the word "murder" to a point-of-view series linking Lina's gaze first to the word then to her husband Johnnie. Lina next looks at the photograph of a cliff by the sea (the location of Johnnie and Beaky's planned housing development). That photograph and the scenario situated within it wherein Johnnie pushes Beaky off the cliff are superimposed over a close-up of Lina, in this case clearly signaling a privileged access to Lina's subjectivity. On the other hand, the image of Johnnie which follows the word "murder" is subjective only by virtue of its placement within a syntagm—the image itself in no way differs from that of numerous close-ups of Johnnie elsewhere in the film which are not ascribed to Lina's subjectivity. But even more importantly, Lina's fear of Johnnie's murderous impulses is not confined to the point-of-view shot or the subjective sequence. Rather, it exceeds those limits and permeates the mise-en-scène. Her phobia contaminates the "third-person mode" of the image in numerous ways: through the spiderweb effect of the shadows which appear to engulf her in the large hallway of the house; by means of Johnnie's sudden presence in the first plane of the image as she clips hedges, his broad and ominous back to the camera, blocking the spectator's visual access to Lina; in the organization of the scene in which Johnnie brings her warm milk which she fears is poisoned—the light under the door, the overhead shot down on Johnnie at the foot of the stairs, the light in the milk drawing attention to its presence. Because Lina's subjectivity is allowed to infuse the entire film, because *Suspicion* fails to maintain a legible division between subjectivity and objectivity, its belated attempt to construct a norm of objectivity for purposes of closure cannot succeed.

The point-of-view structure in itself, because it depends so heavily on the image as its pivotal element—an image which can be divorced only with great difficulty from the third person mode—would appear to be an inappropriate or at least insufficient vehicle of subjectivity. More suitable, perhaps, is the voice-over, particularly insofar as it lends itself readily to a usage which parallels that of the interior monologue in literature. The voice-over has a privileged relation to interiority—it can make accessible that which is not and cannot be visible. Its independence from the image allows it to signify delusion or misrecognition—as is often the case in film noir—and, hence, to more fully represent subjectivity. The deviation from the truth attributable to this voice-over nevertheless guarantees the unity and integrity of a subjectivity which is capable of being either right or wrong. In the woman's film, however, the voice-over undergoes a number of vicissitudes, and the female character is ultimately dispossessed of this signifier of subjectivity as well. When the voice-over is introduced in the beginning of a film as the possession of the female protagonist who purportedly controls the narration of her own past, it is rarely sustained (e.g., in *Rebecca* or *Secret Beyond the Door*, or the voice-over reading the journal of a secondary female character in *Experiment Perilous* [1944], which moves from one narrational source to another). Instead, voices-over are more frequently detached from the female protagonist and mobilized as moments of aggression or attack exercised against her.

*Secret Beyond the Door* is a particularly telling example of the narrative fate of female subjectivity as represented in the voice-over. The film begins with Celia's (Joan Bennett's) voice-over on her wedding day: "I remember long ago I read a book that told the meaning of dreams. If a girl dreams of a boat or ship she will reach a safe harbor. But if she dreams of daffodils she will be in great danger." In the beginning of the film, the representation of her subjectivity is insistent and forcefully links together death or violence and desire. Her voice-over accompanies a flashback which details her first meeting with Mark (Michael Redgrave)—in a Mexican street during a fight between two men over a woman ("Death was in that street," the voice-over tells us). Immediately after a knife is thrown and barely misses Celia's hand, her voice-over links this violence with the violence of the gaze: "Suddenly I felt eyes touch me like fingers. He saw behind my makeup something that no one had ever seen, something I didn't know."

Celia's voice-over is sporadically but consistently present for the first two-thirds of the film and reinforces her position as the subject of an investigation which necessitates at points her assumption of the position of subject of the gaze. Although the central concern of her investigation is the discovery of what her husband Mark keeps behind the locked door labeled 7, her voice-over is also often obsessed with analyzing her relation with Mark. When he leaves her on their honeymoon after finding himself temporarily locked out of her bedroom, she asks herself over and over again why he has ceased to love her. As she drives a car later in the film, the voice-over is the medium for her thoughts about leaving her husband.

But Celia's voice-over, insistent and aggressive as it is in the first part of the film, disappears in the last section and is displaced by Mark's. After Celia finds out that room number 7 is an exact duplicate of her own room and thus signals that it will become the scene of her own murder, she runs away from the house into the fog. An unidentifiable figure emerges out of the fog and walks toward her. There is a fade to black on the image track, accompanied by a woman's scream. The film cuts from blackness to a shot of Mark in his room, and for the first time he is given a voice-over—one which proves to be very misleading, for it implies that he has indeed murdered Celia ("It will be a curious trial . . . charged with the murder of his wife. . . ."). Celia later comes back to the house unharmed (the figure in the fog, it turns out, was another male friend). Yet the blackness together with the scream signify an extraordinary violence—a discursive rather than a physical violence, for this scene marks the end of Celia's voice-over. Not only is there a forceful and disruptive transfer of the discourse from Celia to Mark via a void in the image track, but the narrative also displaces its hermeneutic question from her relation to a locked door (number 7) to his (the locked door of his childhood, when his mother left him alone to go out with "another man"). The remainder of the narrative is devoted to the psychoanalysis of Mark, to the attempt to open the "locked door" of his mind. What the void on the image track gives witness to is the death of female subjectivity. As Stephen Jenkins points out in an analysis of the film, "Any notion of the possibility of female discourse within the text is always undercut, (dis)placed, qualified."[62]

Although the voice-over in the woman's film is not always dealt with in such a violent manner, it is not infrequently subjected to a loss of unity, coherence, and consistency. Quite often, as mentioned earlier, it is completely separated from any notion of the authority of the female protagonist and, in fact, turned aggressively against her. For the voice is also the material support of the symptom—"hearing voices"—in paranoia. In *Undercurrent*, Ann (Katherine Hepburn), lying in a sleeper compartment on a train, is subjected to a mixture of voices which torment her: Alan, her husband, saying "I love you," closely followed by Sylvia, a friend, repeating, "It isn't such a shocking idea when you've lived with it for awhile. . . ." The "shocking idea" refers to the notion that Ann's husband is a murderer. The voices which keep Ann from sleeping are immediately succeeded by the shriek of the train's whistle and a cut to a close-up of its wheels. As Sally (Barbara Stanwyck) paces in her bedroom in *The Two Mrs. Carrolls*, her own voice-over addresses her in the second person: "It's all very clear now, he's poisoning you." In *Rebecca*, the Joan Fontaine character tosses and turns in bed as the voice-over of Mrs. Van Hopper describes Maxim's

*[handwritten margin note: Voice over Adds to 'hearing things' paranoid state.]*

late wife: "She was the beautiful Rebecca Hendrik, you know—they say he simply adored her." As Paula (Ingrid Bergman) reads and clutches a glass of milk in her bedroom in *Gaslight*, the voice-over of her husband repetitively insists, "Your mother was mad; she died in an asylum." The bedroom or a bed is almost always the space of this assault by voices—effecting a further conflation of sexual anxiety and violence. What is usually a privileged vehicle of subjectivity—the voice-over—takes on the form of an aggressive attack. The disembodied voice returns to haunt the woman. Although this strategy is not limited to the representation of *female* subjectivity within the classical cinema as a whole, its very predictability in the paranoid gothic films underlines the significance of its effects here.

In a more general sense, female subjectivity undergoes a reversal and transformation into a self-directed aggressivity through the depiction of the vicissitudes of female desire. In the beginning of *Dragonwyck*, Miranda (Gene Tierney) complains that she has "tried to be like everyone else and want what I'm supposed to want." She is ultimately punished for her desire and her mother knowingly proclaims, "Maybe Dragonwyck should have remained something you read or dream about." A poster for *Caught* includes a warning about the realization of female desire: "Dazzling Romance, Dream of Every Girl, Turned Into Nightmare of Terror!" The construction of female desire in close relation to danger and violence, the tendency of subjectivity to exceed the limits of the point-of-view shot and dream sequence, the detachment of the voice-over and its transformation into a mode of attack—all testify to an instability in the cinematic representation of subjectivity which is not confined or specific to the woman's film, but nevertheless appears to be exacerbated within the genre. Doubtless this phenomenon is at least partially determined by the constant association of women with madness or paranoia—an association which necessitates a disintegration of the unity of the cinematic sign, a dissociation of its two major components, sound and image. Unanchored and disembodied sounds, images which strive but often fail to disengage themselves from a diegesis weighted down by objectivity—the privileged form of aggressivity here is clearly that of the look and the voice.

This undoing of the stability of the cinematic sign is fully compatible with the paranoid foreclosure of the paternal signifier, the third term which is alone capable of stabilizing and regularizing signification by enforcing the unity of the sign. The image and voice in these films act as the "third persons" of the paranoid delusion (the agents of persecution), and ultimately it is the cinema itself, through its organization of image and sound, which attacks the woman, becoming the machine of her torment. This operation is literalized in a significant number of the films which explicitly activate the materials of the cinematic signifier, or even the cinema itself, in an assault on the female protagonist. In *Dark Waters* the villains, in their attempt to drive the woman insane, first take her to the movie theater to see a documentary they know will disturb her. They next manufacture sounds (a phonograph record incessantly calling her out into the Louisiana bayou). Their work could be characterized as a kind of audiovisual terrorism whose effects are ultimately apparent in her statement of insecurity later in the film: "I always see or hear things that aren't there."

The transformation of absence into signification, in effect the work of the cinema, is given aggressive implications in *The Spiral Staircase* as well. The film begins in a makeshift movie theater, the lobby of the village hotel, where a silent film, *The Kiss*, is accompanied by piano music. Helen, the protagonist, is introduced as a spectator, deeply engrossed in the melodrama as it unfolds on the screen. The voyeurism of the movie theater is redoubled by a focus on the hotel manager and two children peeking at the film, illicitly, from behind a heavy black curtain. *The Kiss* becomes a "kill," when the camera tilts upward from a shot of Helen sitting directly in front of the projector to the chandelier on the ceiling, the image subsequently dissolving to a scene in the hotel room above, which becomes the scene of a murder. The movie music bleeds over into the murder scene and is only gradually merged with and replaced by the soundtrack of the film proper. The murderer in the closet is represented as a huge eye in close-up—an eye which (as in the scene discussed earlier in this chapter) reflects its victim. The murder itself is invisible, however, taking place in off-screen space, signaled only by the victim's clenched hands—an image which is obliterated by the return to the movie screen below, where the heroine's dead body has just been retrieved from the ocean. The murder scene and movie are further sutured by the synchronization of the end of the film with the sound of the victim falling to the floor. The parallel between the eye in the closet and the hotel manager behind the curtain constitutes the cinema spectator as a murderer, the woman as the screen. As much as Helen might wish to retain the status of spectator, her absorption in the film, her identification with the heroine, become an overabsorption and an overidentification as the narrative trajectory assigns her to the role of victim.

In the primal scene, the pre-text of the paranoid scenario, sound is dissociated from image and functions in part as a betrayal of spectatorship, a betrayal of the desire to see. The paranoid films, in their appropriation of the woman's look, problematize the very possibility of a female gaze. In its collapsing of the opposition between subject and object, its foreshortening of the distance necessary for the voyeur, what the maternal space activated in these films disallows is the concept of spectatorship. *Caught* and *Rebecca*, analyzed in detail in the next chapter, are particularly explicit elaborations of this contradictory relation of the woman to the screen. The difficulty, if not impossibility, of representing the woman in the position the films forcefully ascribe to her—that of subject of the gaze—is most succinctly articulated in a line from *Rebecca*: "Most girls would give their eyes for a chance to see Monte."

# 6

## Female Spectatorship and Machines of Projection: *Caught* and *Rebecca*

*Caught* and *Rebecca* are especially interesting, even exemplary, instances of the woman's film because each of them directly confronts the issues of female spectatorship and the woman's relation to processes of imaging. Both films explore the contradictions which emerge when the attempt to position the woman as subject of the gaze is accompanied by an acknowledgment of her status as the privileged content of the image. Her desires are strongly circumscribed by her relation to spectacle. Each of these films contains a scene in which the camera almost literally enacts this repression of the feminine—the woman's relegation to the status of a signifier within the male discourse. The camera movements in these scenes can be described as hysterical—frantically searching for, retracing the path of, the lost object, attempting to articulate what is, precisely, not there. As such, the camera movements have the status of symptoms.

*Caught* and *Rebecca* also exemplify the process, described in the last chapter, whereby female desire is transformed into fear in relation to the apparatus of the cinema. The two films belong to the subgenre of the gothic-influenced woman's film and thus activate paranoia as a primary psychical mechanism. Although *Caught*, a later instance of the subgenre, tends to modernize and naturalize the gothic aspects of the paranoid films and hence to suppress much of the iconography or gothic machinery, it nevertheless maintains the centrality of the axis of seeing and its relation to aggressivity. *Caught* and *Rebecca* both present scenarios which mobilize the elements of the theatrical situation in the cinema. The female protagonist is herself transformed into a movie spectator within the diegesis, and the films demonstrate that, even as she spectates, the force of the tendency to reduce the woman to an image is inexorable. The sense of surveillance, of constantly being watched—even as she herself watches—is overwhelming.

Thus, as argued in the previous chapter, the metaphor of paranoia may prove even more appropriate for a delineation of this subgroup of the woman's film than that of hysteria. As Freud points out in his analysis of Dr. Schreber, whose most striking symptom is his assumption of the position/body of the woman, paranoia is systematically disintegrative.[1] Hysteria condenses, paranoia decomposes. In this respect, both *Caught* and *Rebecca*, by privileging moments in which the cinematic apparatus itself undergoes a process of decomposition, situate themselves as paranoid texts. Both films contain scenes of projection in which the image as lure and trap is externalized in relation to the woman. The films disarticulate the components of the apparatus which construct the woman as "imaged"—camera, projector, and screen—and incorporate them within the diegesis as props. In this mise-en-scène of cinematic elements, camera, projector, and screen are explicitly activated as agents of narrativity, as operators of the image.

Yet, this gesture of disarticulation does not preclude an elaboration of the woman's relation to spectacle. In fact, the desire of the woman in both films is to duplicate a given image, to engage with and capture the male gaze. In *Caught*, the image is that of a woman in a mink coat; in *Rebecca*, that of "a woman of thirty-six dressed in black satin with a string of pearls." And in both films, movie projection scenes act to negate each of these appropriations of an image, to effect a separation on both literal and figurative levels between the woman and the image of her desire (always situated as a desire to be desired or desirable, hence as subordinate).

The background of the credit sequence in *Caught* is constituted by a series of pages in a fashion magazine, slowly flipped over in synchronization with credit changes to reveal women posing in front of monuments and art works, women posing in the latest fashions (figures 1 and 2). Merging with the body proper of the film, this background becomes the first shot, its incorporation within the diegesis signaled by the addition of voices-over and pointing fingers, metonymic signifiers of female desire (figures 3, 4, 5, and 6). The voices-over— "I'll take this one," "That one," "This one's for me"—are the indexical actualizations of the female appetite for the image, an appetite sustained by the commodity fetishism which supports capitalism. And the ultimate commodity, as here, is the body adorned for the gaze. The logic of this economics of desire culminates in the final magazine image of the scene, a sketch of a woman modeling a fur coat, the unmediated signifier of wealth (figure 7). The camera marks its significance by tracking back at this moment (accompanied by the voice-over, "I'd rather have mink") to incorporate within its image the two women whose fantasies are complicit with the fashion industry (figure 8). Signifier of economic success, the fur coat (which becomes mink, aligning itself with Leonora's desire) is the site of a certain semantic wealth in the text, resurfacing again and again to mark the oscillations of female subjectivity. In the image, significantly, it is a sketch which replaces the human model as support of the coat. The fur coat overpowers the body, given only as trace.

This first scene initiates the narrative trajectory along the line of an investigation of the contradictions and convolutions of female spectatorship. Owners of the look in this instance, the women can only exercise it within a narcissistic framework which collapses the opposition between the subject and the object of the gaze—"This one's for me." The woman's sexuality, as spectator, must undergo a constant process of transformation. She must look, as if she were a man with the phallic power of the gaze, at a woman who would attract that gaze, in order to be that woman. There is a necessary movement or oscillation between the periphery of the image to its center and back again. The convolutions involved here are analogous to those described by Julia Kristeva as "the double or triple twists of what we commonly call female homosexuality": " 'I am looking, as a man would, for a woman'; or else, 'I submit myself, as if I were a man who thought he was a woman, to a woman who thinks she is a man.' "[2] For the female spectator exemplified by Maxine and Leonora in this scene, to possess the image through the gaze is to become it. The gap which strictly separates identification and desire for the male spectator (whose possession of the cinematic woman at least partially depends on an identification with the male protagonist) is abolished in the case of the woman. Binding identification to desire (the basic strategy of narcissism), the teleological aim of the female look demands a becoming and, hence, a dispossession. She must give up the image in order to become it—the image is *too* present for her.

And this is precisely the specular movement traced by *Caught*. Within the space of two scenes, the look is reversed—Leonora (Barbara Bel Geddes) dons the mink coat and adopts the pose of the model, soliciting the gaze of both male and female spectators (figures 9, 10, 11). She now participates in the image, while her dispossession is signaled by the rhythmic chants which punctuate her turns, "$49.95 plus tax." The economics of sexual exchange are on display, for it is not only the coat which is on the market. Leonora receives an invitation to the yacht party at which she will later meet millionaire Smith Ohlrig (Robert Ryan), and, as her friend Maxine points out in the face of Leonora's resistance to the invitation, "How else do girls like us get to meet guys like Smith Ohlrig?"

When Leonora actually marries Ohlrig, her transformation into the image is completed by the newspaper montage sequence announcing the wedding, framing and immobilizing her in the photograph (figures 12, 13, 14).

These three moments of the narrative trajectory—defining the woman as, successively, agent, object, and text of the look—would seem to be self-contained, to exhaust the potential variations of Leonora's relation to the image. Yet, the film recovers and rewrites its own beginning in the projection scene, situating Leonora once more in the place of the spectator. But this time she is explicitly located as a spectator who refuses to see, in a cinema delimited as male. By the time of the projection scene, Leonora is fully in place; she owns the mink coat and no longer has to model it. Her alienation from the cinematic apparatus is manifested by the fact of her exclusion, her positioning on the margins of the process of imaging. The cinema which Ohlrig forces her to attend is described only as the "movies for my new project," and all its spectators, except Leonora, are male (a situation which Leonora attempts to resist with the excuse she weakly presents to Ohlrig immediately preceding the screening: ". . . so many men.").

The first shot of the sequence, with a marked keystone effect, presents the first image of Ohlrig's documentary, which appears to be a kind of testament to the technological power of industrial enterprise (figure 15). Ohlrig positions himself as the most prominent spectator, his gaze held by the image, the projector's beam of light emanating from behind his head (figures 16 and 17). The images celebrating machinery and its products are, however, only a prelude to the image which really fascinates Ohlrig—his own (his excitement contained in the anticipatory voice-over which assumes the language of the cinéphile, "Wait 'til the next shot.") (figure 18). The relation between the image and himself is articulated at this moment by a pan rather than a cut, the camera movement apparently motivated by the shadow of a figure[3] crossing in front of the screen to sit next to Ohlrig (figures 19 and 20).

It is at this point—the moment of Ohlrig's most intensely narcissistic fascination—that Leonora's offscreen laugh breaks the mirror relation between Ohlrig and his image. Within this shot, Ohlrig turns to face Leonora, acting as a pivot for the displacement of the spectator's attention from the movie screen to the woman as screen. Assuming his quasi-directorial power, Ohlrig stops the projector and lights Leonora, transforming her from voice into image (figures 21 and 22). This shot initiates a shot/reverse shot series which dominates the sequence, the deployment of space inscribing a hyperbolized distance between Ohlrig and Leonora (figure 23). The reverse shot here, with Leonora in the foreground on the left and Ohlrig in the background on the right, is a crucial condensation of sexual and cinematic positions and invites a number of comments. (1) The keystone effect characterizing the projected documentary image shown

12–16

17–21

previously together with Leonora's placement in this shot retrospectively situate the point of view on the screen as coincident with hers. Nevertheless, both her laugh and the fact that she faces *away* from the screen indicate her refusal of this position as spectator, the marked absence of that diegetic spectatorial gaze which would double and repeat that of *Caught*'s own spectator. Leonora's glance is averted from Ohlrig and his cinema. (2) The mise-en-scène situates the screen directly behind Leonora's head (lending it the beatific power of a halo), just as, in the previous and following shots, the projector is situated directly behind Ohlrig's head. There is a kind of sexual/cinematographic symmetry which the shot/reverse shot sequence rigorously respects. Leonora's face emerges from the confines of the screen as though the medium had suddenly gained a three-dimensional relief. In a perverse movement, the close-up of the woman is simultaneously disengaged from the diegetic screen and returned to it. (3) The eye-lines attributed to the two characters are staggered in relation to one another. The directions of their looks are correct, but the planes of the image are not (i.e., in an image with no illusion of depth, they could be, would be, looking at each other). As it is, however, Ohlrig stares at the empty screen while Leonora looks in the direction of the projector. Ohlrig becomes the displaced and dislocated spectator of Leonora's image, the mise-en-scène articulating a difficulty in the gaze.

The remaining shots of the shot/reverse shot sequence frame a dialogue in which Ohlrig attempts to ascertain Leonora's guilt (figures 24 and 25). He immediately assumes, in paranoid fashion, that her laugh is a response to his own image—the last image of his film presented in the scene. But Leonora's guilt lies rather in not watching, in dissociating her entertainment from the screen and laughing instead at something said by the man sitting next to her. Ohlrig eliminates the competition, which is both sexual and cinematic (figures 26 and 27), and resumes his cinema at the expense of Leonora—blackening her image in order to start the show. Leonora, however, leaves, asserting her final alienation from his spectacle despite his orders that she stay (figure 29). Invisible support of a cinema which excludes her, Leonora demonstrates by means of her exit the force of that silent complicity. For without her presence, Ohlrig cannot continue the show. After emptying the theater, he paces back and forth, his rage punctuated by the beam of the projector (figures 30, 31, 32).

The projection sequence as a whole marks an important turning point in the narrative. The interruption of the filmic flow of images within the diegesis, here as in *Rebecca*, is the metaphor for the disintegration of a short-lived family romance. Spectator of a cinema whose parameters are defined as masculine, Leonora is dispossessed of both look and voice. Yet, the trajectory which traces her dispossession in relation to the image is not completed until the end of the film. For, when Leonora leaves Ohlrig as a result of this scene, she takes a piece of the image with her—the mink coat, signifier of her continuing complicity in the process of imaging.

Hitchcock's *Rebecca* also contains a crucial scene in which the film effects a decomposition of the elements which collaborate in making the position of female spectatorship an impossible one. The home movie sequence depicts a process of projection constituted as an assault on the diegetic female spectator. This scene as well is preceded by the delineation of female desire in relation to the fixed image of the fashion magazine. A preface to the projection scene, the shot of the fashion magazine whose pages are slowly turned is here unlocalized (figures 33 and 34). Unlike *Caught*, *Rebecca* elides the establishing shot which would identify the woman as viewer and, instead, dissolves immediately to her transformation into the image, an image she had previously promised Maxim (Laurence Olivier) she would never appropriate for herself—that of a woman "dressed in black satin with a string of pearls" (figure 35). The character played by Joan Fontaine (who is never given a proper name) enters the cinema in the hope of becoming a spectacle for Maxim (figures 36, 37, 38), but is relegated to the position of spectator—spectator of the images Maxim prefers to retain of her, those taken on their honeymoon.

Space here precludes the possibility of an in-depth analysis of this sequence,[4] but it is necessary to make several points relating it to the sequence from *Caught*. (1) Maxim, like Ohlrig, is in control of both lighting and projection (figures 39 and 40), while the mise-en-scène frequently positions the projector itself *between* Fontaine and Maxim as a kind of barrier or limit to their interaction (figure 41). (2) The movie projected is a proper "home movie," unlike that of *Caught*, the logic of its syntax hence supposedly more arbitrary, linking disparate shots designed to capture pregnant moments for a private family history. (Maxim says at one point, "Won't our grandchildren be delighted when they see how lovely you were?") The images of Fontaine feeding geese constitute a denial of the image she has constructed for herself by means of the black evening dress, while Maxim's binoculars give him a mastery over the gaze even within the confines of the filmic image (figures 42 and 43). (3) Like *Caught*, the projected movie is interrupted twice, displacing spectatorial investment from the screen to the woman. The first interruption is caused by a film break (figures 44 and 45) which coincides with and appears to negate Fontaine's remark, "I wish our honeymoon could have lasted forever." When Maxim attempts to fix the film the interruption is prolonged by the entry of a servant who reveals the discovery that a china cupid is missing—a cupid Fontaine had broken and hidden earlier in the film. This forced pause in the home movies serves to emphasize Fontaine's inability to deal with the servants, to fully assume her position as mistress of Manderley, in short, to effectively replace Rebecca. The home movies are resumed but this deficiency in her image, her discomfort in the eve-

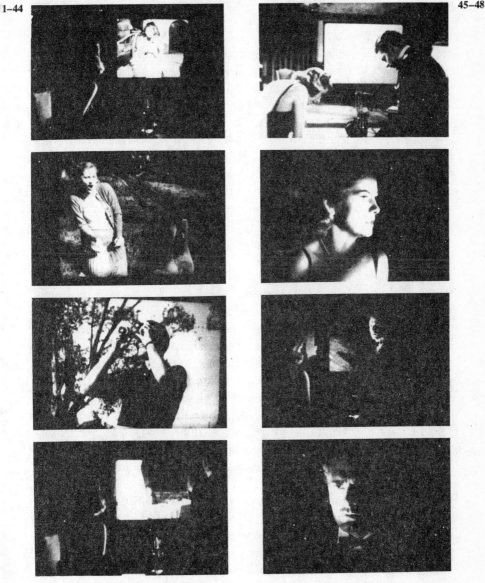

ning gown chosen to imitate Rebecca, leads to the second interruption of the screening. When Fontaine suggests that Maxim must have married her so that there would be no gossip, he abruptly walks between Fontaine and the screen, blocking the image with his body and effectively castrating her look (figures 46, 47, 48). Substituting himself for the screen, he activates an aggressive look back at the spectator, turning Fontaine's gaze against itself. The absolute terror incited by this violent reorganization of the cinematic relay of the look is evident in her eyes, the only part of her face lit by the reflected beam of the projector (figures 49, 50, 51). Furthermore, the image Maxim blocks with his body is her own while the image revealed as he finally moves out of the projection beam to turn on the light is that of himself, once again holding the binoculars (figures 52 and 53). (4) All these aggressions and threats are condensed in the penultimate shot of the sequence which constitutes the most explicit delineation of projection as an assault against the woman. The projection light reflected from the screen fragments and obscures Fontaine's face (figures 54 and 55), contrasting it with the clarity, coherence, and homogeneity proffered by the home movie image of the next shot. The camera positions itself so as to coincide with the diegetic projector and slowly tracks forward toward the final image of the couple together, taken, as Maxim points out, by an autonomous camera mounted on a tripod (figures 56 and 57). At this point, the rule dictating that the home movie conform to an arbitrary and contingent syntax is broken by the insertion of a cut to a closer shot of the couple (a cut, furthermore, interrupting a shot still supposedly taken by an autonomous camera [figures 58 and 59]). The cut guarantees a certain rhetorical finesse, a satisfying closure which demonstrates the stability of the couple and simultaneously sutures the diegetic film to the larger film. For the camera continues to track forward until the edges of the screen disappear and the home movie coincides with *Rebecca* itself.

It is as though in both *Caught* and *Rebecca*, the diegetic film's continuous unfolding guaranteed a rather fragile binding of the drives in the heterosexual unit of the harmonious couple. Its interruption, in each instance, signals the release of aggressive tendencies. In this way, the films play out the problematic of paranoia in its relation to the process of imaging and, simultaneously, the institution of marriage. As Rose points out, paranoia is "the aggressive corollary of the narcissistic structure of the ego-function."[5] The women's films as a group appear to make a detour around or deflect the issue of spectacle and the woman's position (an obsession of the dominant cinema addressed to the male spectator), and hence avoid the problem of feminine narcissism. Yet, this narcissism returns and infiltrates the two texts by means of a paranoia which is linked to an obsession with the specular. The projection scenes in both films are preceded by the delineation of a narcissistic female desire—the desire to become the image which captures the male gaze. Nevertheless, it is as though the aggressivity

which should be attendent on that structure were detached, in the projection scenes, and transferred to the specular system which insures and perpetuates female narcissism—the cinematic apparatus. Thus, the aggressivity attached to her own narcissism is stolen and used against the woman; she becomes the object rather than the subject of that aggression.

The desire to be looked at is thus transformed into a fear of being looked at, or a fear of the apparatus which systematizes or governs that process of looking. From this perspective, it is interesting to note, as mentioned earlier in chapter 5, that in the only case of female paranoia Freud treats, described in "A Case of Paranoia Running Counter to the Psychoanalytical Theory of the Disease," the woman's delusion concerns being photographed. Recall that this case involves a young woman who, during lovemaking with a male friend, hears a noise—a knock or tick—which she interprets as the sound of a camera, photographing her in order to compromise her. In his analysis, Freud doubts the very existence of the noise: "I do not believe that the clock ever ticked or that any noise was to be heard at all. The woman's situation justified a sensation of throbbing in the clitoris. This was what she subsequently projected as a perception of an external object."[6] Female paranoia thus finds its psychoanalytic explanation in the projection of a bodily sensation from inside to outside, in a relocation in external reality.

Projection is a mechanism which Freud consistently associates with paranoia. Yet, he is reluctant to make it specific to paranoia, since it is present in more "normal" provinces such as those of superstition, mythology, and, finally, the activity of theorizing. For Freud, projection is instrumental in formulating the very condition of the opposition between internal and external reality, between subject and object. For projection enables flight (from the "bad object") and the possibility of a refusal to recognize something in or about oneself.[7] The invocation of the opposition between subject and object in connection with the paranoid mechanism of projection indicates a precise difficulty in any conceptualization of female paranoia—one which Freud does not mention. For in his short case history, what the woman projects, what she throws away, is her sexual pleasure, a part of her bodily image. The sound of her own body throbbing becomes the click of the camera, the capture of her image. For the female spectator in the cinema, on the other hand, the spectator so carefully delineated in *Caught* and *Rebecca*, the problem is even more complex. In the cinematic situation, in the realm of the image, the distinction between subject and object effected by projection is not accessible to the female spectator in the same way as to the male. For Leonora and Maxine in *Caught* and the Joan Fontaine character in *Rebecca*, the pictures in fashion magazines demonstrate that to possess the image through the gaze is to become it. And becoming the image, the woman can no longer have it. For the female spectator, the image is *too* close—

it cannot be projected far enough. The alternatives she is given are quite literally figured in the two films: she can accept the image—full acceptance indicated by the attempts to duplicate it (by means of the mink coat or the black satin dress); or she can repudiate the image (voluntarily in *Caught*, unwillingly in *Rebecca*). The absoluteness of the dilemma is manifested in the mutual exclusivity of its terms—a condition which does not mirror that of the male spectator, who, like Sean Connery in *Marnie* (as described by Mulvey), can "have his cake and eat it too." As a card-carrying fetishist, the male spectator does not have to choose between acceptance or rejection of the image; he can balance his belief and knowledge. Deprived of castration anxiety, the female spectator is also deprived of the possibility of fetishism—of the reassuring "I know, but even so. . . ."

To the extent that the projection scenes in *Caught* and *Rebecca* mobilize the elements of a specular system which has historically served the interests of male spectatorship, they are limit-texts, exposing the contradictions which inhabit the logic of their own terms of address as women's films. The relation between the female body and the female look articulated by the two films (a relation which always threatens to collapse into the sameness of equivalence), together with the overpresence of the image, indicate a difficulty in the woman's relation to symbolization. Sexuality, disseminated in the classical representation across the body of the woman, is for her nonlocalizable. This is why psychoanalytic theory tells us she must *be* the phallus rather than *have* it. As Parveen Adams points out, the woman does not represent lack; she lacks the means to represent lack.[8] According to the problematic elaborated by *Caught* and *Rebecca*, what the female viewer lacks is the very distance or gap which separates, must separate, the spectator from the image. What she lacks, in other words, is a "good throw."

Although the projection scenes in *Caught* and *Rebecca* do deconstruct, in some sense, the woman's position relative to the process of imaging, there is a missing piece in this mise-en-scène of cinematic elements—projector and screen are there, but the camera is absent. In *Rebecca* the home movie camera is briefly mentioned to justify the final shot, but in neither film is the camera visualized. The camera is, of course, an element whose acknowledgment would pose a more radical threat to the classicism which ultimately these texts fully embrace, particularly if the camera whose presence was acknowledged were nondiegetic. Yet, while it is true that indications of the presence of a camera are missing in the projection scenes, it is possible to argue that inscriptions of the camera are displaced, inserted later in the films to buttress a specifically male discourse about the woman. Paradoxically, in each of the films the camera demonstrates its own presence and potency through the very absence of an image of the woman. In a frantic, almost psychotic search for that image, the camera contributes its power to the hallucination of a woman.

In *Rebecca,* there is a scene late in the film which exemplifies the very felt presence of the woman who is absent throughout the movie, the woman whose initials continually surround and subdue the Joan Fontaine character—Rebecca. It is the scene in which Maxim narrates the story of Rebecca, despite his own claim that it is unnarratable ("She told me all about herself—everything—things I wouldn't tell a living soul."). The camera's very literal inscription of the absent woman's movements is preceded by a transfer of the look from narrator to narratee. Maxim, standing by the door, looks first at the sofa, then at Fontaine, then back at the sofa. Fontaine turns her glance from Maxim to the sofa, appropriating his gaze. From this point on, the camera's movements are precisely synchronized with Maxim's words: when he tells Fontaine that Rebecca sat next to an ashtray brimming with cigarette stubs, there is a cut to the sofa, empty but for the ashtray; as he describes Rebecca rising from the sofa, the camera duplicates that movement and then pans to the left—purportedly following a woman who is not visible. In tracing Rebecca's path as Maxim narrates, the camera pans more than 180 degrees. In effect, what was marked very clearly as Maxim's point of view, simply transferred to Fontaine as narratee, comes to include him. The story of the woman culminates as the image of the man.

*Caught* makes appeal to a remarkably similar signifying strategy in a scene in which Leonora's very absence from the image becomes the strongest signified—the scene in which her empty desk is used as a pivot as the camera swings back and forth between Dr. Hoffman (Frank Ferguson) and Dr. Quinada (James Mason) discussing her fate. The sequence begins with a high angle shot down on Leonora's desk, the camera moving down and to the left to frame Dr. Hoffman, already framed in his doorway. Moving from Hoffman across the empty desk, the camera constructs a perfect symmetry by framing Dr. Quinada in his doorway as well. The middle portion of the sequence is constituted by a sustained crosscutting between Hoffman and Quinada, alternating both medium shots and close-ups. The end of the sequence echoes and repeats the beginning, the camera again pivoting around the absent woman's desk from Quinada to Hoffman and, as Hoffman suggests that Quinada "forget" Leonora, back to the empty desk, closing the sequence with a kind of formal tautology. The sequence is a performance of one of the overdetermined meanings of the film's title—Leonora is "caught," spatially, between an obstetrician and a pediatrician (other potential readings include the theme of "catching" a rich husband which initiates the film, the fact that Leonora is "caught" in her marriage by her husband who wants to keep her child or that she is "caught" between Smith Ohlrig and Larry Quinada).

In tracing the absence of the woman, the camera inscribes its own presence in the film as phallic substitute—the pen which writes the feminine body. The two scenes demonstrate the technical fluency of the camera in narrating the woman's story, extended to the point of ejecting her from the image. In its fore-closure of a signifier—here, the woman's body—from the symbolic universe, the camera enacts its paranoia as a psychosis. It is as though, in a pseudogenre marked as the possession of the woman, the camera had to desperately reassert itself by means of its technical prowess—a prowess here embodied in the attribute of movement. The projection scenes discussed earlier effect a cleavage, a split between the image of the woman's desire (linked to stills—photographs or sketches without movement) and what is projected on the screen (in *Caught*, the machinery of industry, capitalist enterprise; in *Rebecca*, the images of Maxim's memory of her before the black satin dress). In each case, it is the man who has control of the projector and hence the moving image. Thus, the films construct an opposition between different processes of imaging along the lines of sexual difference: female desire is linked to the fixation and stability of a spectacle refusing the temporal dimension, while male desire is more fully implicated with the defining characteristic of the cinematic image—movement. The two scenes in which the camera inscribes the absence of the woman thus accomplish a double negation of the feminine—through her absence and the camera's movement, its continual displacement of the fixed image of her desire. Invoking the specific attributes of the cinematic signifier (movement and absence of the object) around the figure of the woman, the films succeed in constructing a story about the woman which no longer requires even her physical presence.

Nevertheless, each of the films recovers the image of the woman, writing her back into the narrative. At the end of *Caught*, in a scene which echoes the earlier one pivoting on Leonora's empty desk, her image is returned to the diegesis. Inserted, almost accidentally it seems, between two shots of Dr. Hoffman and Dr. Quinada, who are once more discussing her, is an image of Leonora in which the camera stares straight down at her lying in a hospital bed. In *Rebecca*, Joan Fontaine's full appropriation of Rebecca's position toward the end of the film coincides with the abolition of even the traces of Rebecca's absent presence. In the final shot of the film, the initial R which decorates the pillow of her bed is consumed by flames. This denial of the absent woman and the resultant recuperation of presence form the basis for the reunification and harmony of the couple which closes the film.

The closure in *Caught*, however, is less sure, the recuperation more problematic.[9] The oppressiveness of the mise-en-scène toward the end of the film is marked. This is particularly true in the scene inside an ambulance, in which sirens wail as Dr. Quinada tells Leonora how free she can be if her child dies. The claustrophobic effect of the scene issues from the fact that there are two simultaneous movements toward Leonora—as the camera moves gradually closer and closer, framing her more tightly, Dr. Quinada repeats its movement from another direction. By the end of the shot he appears to have nearly smothered her with his body. Lenora is caught in the pincers of this double movement as Quinada tells her, "He [Smith Ohlrig] won't be able to hold you. . . . Now you can be free." The camera's movement explicitly repeats that of Dr. Quinada in its domination, enclosure, and framing of the woman. In the next scene, in which the image of Leonora in a hospital bed is inserted between two shots of the doctors, the camera literally assumes Dr. Quinada's position in the ambulance, aiming itself directly down at Leonora. Dr. Quinada has just been informed by Dr. Hoffman in the hallway that the baby has died and his reply, the same words he used in the ambulance ("He can't hold her now—she's free"), constitutes the voice over Leonora's image.

But Leonora's ultimate "freedom" in the last scene is granted to her by Dr. Hoffman when he tells the nurse to take her mink coat away with the statement, "If my diagnosis is correct, she won't want that anyway." With the rejection of the mink coat comes the denial of the last trace of the image in its relation to Leonora. By means of the doctor's diagnosis, she becomes, instead of an image, an element in the discourse of medicine (as discussed in chapter 2), a manuscript to be read for the symptoms which betray her story, her identity. It is appropriate that the final scene in *Caught* takes place in a hospital. For the doctor, as reader or interpreter of that manuscript, accomplishes the final despecularization proposed by the text's own trajectory and the terms of its address. The final image of the film consists of the nurse slinging the mink coat over her shoulder and taking it away down the hospital corridor.

The movement of the narrative is thus from the representation of the mink coat which sparks desire to the rejection of the "real thing" (a rejection really made "on behalf" of the woman by the doctor). One could chart the elaboration of female subjectivity in the film according to the presence or absence of the mink coat. At the beginning of the film, Leonora's only desire is to meet a man rich enough to allow her to return to her home town with two mink coats—"One for my mother and one for me." A cut from Leonora at Dorothy Dale's School of Charm pretending that a cloth coat is mink to a tilt upward along the mink coat she models in a department store in the next scene establishes her rise on the social scale. When she leaves Smith Ohlrig after the projection scene discussed earlier, she takes her mink coat with her, and the coat immediately signals to Quinada her alliance with an upper class. Yet, when she briefly returns to Ohlrig after quitting her job as Quinada's receptionist, she realizes that he has not changed, and, as she calls Dr. Quinada on the phone, Leonora tells Franzi, "I'm through with that coat." Dr. Quinada subsequently buys Leonora a cloth coat, an action which initiates their romance. The opposition cloth/mink governs the economic thematics of the text.

The mink coat is thus the means by which the specular is welded to the economic—it functions both as an economic landmark of Leonora's social position and as the articulation of the woman's relation to spectacle and the male gaze. The texual mediations on the sexed subject and the class subject merge imperceptibly. Leonora's desire to own the mink coat is both narcissistic and so-cially/economically ambitious. Yet, the text attempts to prove the desire itself to be "wrong" or misguided since the man she marries in order to obtain the coat is dangerously psychotic. Dr. Quinada, unlike Smith Ohlrig, is a member of her own class; hence, Leonora's understanding of her own sexuality is simul-taneous with her understanding and acceptance of her class position. A poster for the film which situates Barbara Bel Geddes's face within the middle of the huge C of Caught, claims in bold letters: "You were a pretty waitress! You mar-ried a millionaire! You thought you were lucky! But, Oh! how you wish you were a waitress again!"

In Rebecca, the situation is somewhat similar, with important deviations. Generic considerations are here much stronger since Rebecca belongs more clearly to that group of films (discussed in chapter 7) which are infused by the gothic and defined by a plot in which the wife fears her husband is a murderer. In films like Rebecca, Dragonwyck, and Undercurrent, the woman marries, often hastily, into the upper class; her husband has money and a social position which she cannot match. The marriage thus constitutes a type of transgression (of class barriers) which does not remain unpunished. The woman often feels dwarfed or threatened by the house itself (Rebecca, Dragonwyck). A frequent reversal of the hierarchy of mistress and servant is symptomatic of the fact that the woman is "out of place" in her rich surroundings. Nevertheless, in films of the same genre, such as Suspicion, Secret Beyond the Door, and Gaslight, the economic/sexual relationship is reversed. In each of these, there is at least a hint that the man marries the woman in order to obtain her money. Hence, it is not always the case that a woman from a lower class is punished for attempting to change her social and economic standing. Rather, the mixture effected by a marriage between two different classes produces horror and paranoia.

By making sexuality extremely difficult in a rich environment, both films—Caught and Rebecca—promote the illusion of separating the issue of sexuality from that of economics. What is really repressed in this scenario is the economics of sexual exchange. This repression is most evident in Caught, whose explicit moral—"Don't marry for money"—constitutes a negation of the economic factor in marriage. But negation, as Freud points out, is also affir-mation; in Caught there is an unconscious acknowledgment of the economics of marriage as an institution. In the course of the film, the woman becomes the object of exchange, from Smith Ohlrig to Dr. Quinada.[10] A by-product of this exchange is the relinquishing of the posited object of her desire—the expensive mink coat.

There is a sense, then, in which both films begin with a hypothesis of female subjectivity which is subsequently disproven by the textual project. The narrative of *Caught* is introduced by the attribution of the look at the image (the "I" of seeing) to Leonora and her friend. The film ends by positioning Leonora as the helpless, bedridden object of the medical gaze. In the beginning of *Rebecca*, the presence of a female subjectivity as the source of the enunciation is marked. A female voice-over (belonging to the Fontaine character) accompanies a hazy, dreamlike image: "Last night I dreamed I went to Manderley again. It seems to me I stood by the iron gate leading to the drive. For a while I could not enter." The voice goes on to relate how, like all dreamers, she was suddenly possessed by a supernatural power and passed through the gate. This statement is accompanied by a shot in which the camera assumes the position of the "I" and, in a sustained subjective movement, tracks forward through the gate and along the path. Yet the voice-over subsequently disappears entirely—it is not even resuscitated at the end of the film in order to provide closure through a symmetrical frame. Nevertheless, there *is* an extremely disconcerting reemergence of a feminine "I" later in the film. In the cottage scene in which Maxim narrates the "unnarratable" story of the absent Rebecca to Joan Fontaine, he insists on a continual use of direct quotes and hence the first person pronoun referring to Rebecca. His narrative is laced with these quotes from Rebecca which parallel on the soundtrack the moving image, itself adhering to the traces of an absent Rebecca. Maxim is therefore the one who pronounces the following statements: "I'll play the part of a devoted wife." "When I have a child, Max, no one will be able to say that it's not yours." "I'll be the perfect mother just as I've been the perfect wife." "Well, Max, what are you going to do about it? Aren't you going to kill me?" Just as the tracking subjective shot guarantees that the story of the woman literally culminates as the image of the man, the construction of the dialogue allows Maxim to appropriate Rebecca's "I."[11]

The films thus chronicle the emergence and disappearance of female subjectivity, the articulation of an "I" which is subsequently negated. The pressure of the demand in the woman's film for the depiction of female subjectivity is so strong, and often so contradictory, that it is not at all surprising that sections such as the projection scenes in *Caught* and *Rebecca* should dwell on the problem of female spectatorship. These scenes internalize the difficulties of the genre and, in their concentration on the issue of the woman's relation to the gaze, occupy an important place in the narrative. Paranoia is here the appropriate and logical obsession. For it effects a confusion between subjectivity and objectivity, between the internal and the external, thus disallowing the gap which separates the spectator from the image of his/her desire.

In many respects, the most disturbing images of the two films are those which evoke the absence of the woman. In both films these images follow projection scenes which delineate the impossibility of female spectatorship. It is as though each film adhered to the logic which characterizes dreamwork—establishing the image of an absent woman as the delayed mirror image of a female spectator who is herself only virtual.

# 7

## The Shadow of Her Gaze

> And her eye has become accustomed to obvious 'truths' that actually hide what she is seeking. It is *the very shadow of her gaze* that must be explored.
>
> Luce Irigaray[1]

The preceding chapters constitute an attempt to expose those "obvious truths" of femininity as they are inscribed within the woman's film and to defamiliarize them, to break down and subject to analysis their very obviousness. For this reason, the project may seem too fully to embrace the stereotypes and given images of the "feminine," to accept those psychical conditions associated with the woman—masochism, narcissism, hysteria, intensification of affect or "emotionalism," an entire pathology of the feminine—far too readily. And in a sense this is true. These are the culturally constructed positions of femininity which the films represent and re-represent in particularly moving and intense forms. It is a mistake to believe that women have the option of simply accepting or rejecting these positions, a mistake buttressed by a misunderstanding of subjectivity and its relation to discourse. What is far more important than a declared rejection of such familiar tropes is the activity of analyzing them in relation to processes of representation and meaning, delineating the positions from which texts become readable and meaningful to female spectators.

The major breakthrough in feminist film theory has been the displacement of its critical focus from the issue of the positive or negative representations or images of women to the question of the very organization of vision and its effects. This has the decided advantage of demonstrating that processes of imaging women and of specifying the gaze in relation to sexual difference, like most forms of sexism, are far more deeply ingrained than one might initially suspect. From this point of view, it can never be enough simply to reverse sexual roles or to produce positive or empowered images of the woman. It is the constitution of vision as a process both within the filmic text (the representation of the woman seeing) and between text and spectator which most warrants attention. Part of my attempt here has been to demonstrate that the feminine does not exist in a patriarchal society merely as the negation or "Other" of the male. We are not always dealing with the binary opposition male/nonmale, and the phenomenon of spectatorship is a case in point. As Foucault maintains, the analysis of power through its negative means, censorship and repression, does not exhaust its effects. Power also works positively to construct the positions which subjects inhabit.[2] Western culture has a quite specific notion of what it is to be a woman and what it is to be a woman looking. When a woman looks, the verb "looks" is generally intransitive (she *looks* beautiful)—generally, but not always. When the woman looks in order to see, the trajectory of that gaze, and its relation to the otherwise nonproblematic opposition between subject and object, are highly regulated. Her positioning as a very specific kind of spectator lays the groundwork for and dovetails with her activity as a consumer.

The premise of the woman's film as it solicits the female gaze is that this gaze abolishes the distance conducive to voyeurism. The oppositions between "having" and "being" and between "being" and "appearing" are collapsed in order to produce a desire for the image/commodity which is all the more insistent as it fails to differentiate between the image/commodity as object and the spectator as desiring subject. The association of the woman with sympathy, empathy, and a type of overidentification with the image contributes to the commodification of the body which is so pervasive even, or especially, today. The discourse of psychoanalysis provides the theoretical rationalization of such a positioning of the woman in its conceptualization of hysteria. For, as Freud points out, hysterical imitation (which is only the surface manifestation of hysterical identification) is "sympathy, as it were, intensified to the point of reproduction."[3] The woman's film tends to rely heavily on pathos as the means of activating this type of relation to the screen. Pathos always connotes a loss or fading of individual subjectivity in the process of signification. As Bakhtin demonstrates, "A discourse of pathos is fully sufficient to itself and to its object. Indeed, the speaker completely immerses himself [sic] in such a discourse, there is no distance, there are no reservations."[4] One might add that the situation of the receiver of the discourse mimics that of the speaker—immersion and loss of a well-defined subjectivity. There is also a sense in which the discourse of pathos purports to be the most mimetic of discourses, presenting itself as an "unmediated impression deriving from the object itself . . . one unencumbered by any ideological presuppositions."[5] This is the mechanism by means of which the woman's film claims that it is only a text which speaks no more than the obvious, the already familiar truths of everyday life, the details of intersubjective relations.

Pathos is thus one way of containing the potentially disruptive effects of attributing the gaze to the woman, of delineating a specifically female subjectivity. The decade of the 1940s, with its reorganization of sexual roles due to the war and the intensity of its very felt need to sustain a consumer perception despite the shortage of commodities, marks a crisis point in the elaboration of female subjectivity. The films align themselves with an entire array of extracinematic discourses; they feel the effect of the introduction of psychoanalysis in the Hollywood cinema as a means of institutionalizing and directing the woman's discourse about herself, together with the necessity for new theories of the mother/child relation which constrain and limit maternal activity to a site which is neither too far from nor too close to the child. In the late '40s, the paranoia associated with relations between the sexes is evinced in the pervasive influence of the gothic form.

These pressures on filmic representation make it extremely productive to trace and analyze the trajectory of the female gaze, its vicissitudes across the four subgroups of the woman's film. In the films of the medical discourse, more than in any other group, the woman is most nearly the pure object of the gaze. She is deprived of subjectivity through the displacement of the sympathy one might have expected to characterize the relation between spectator and film to the diseased body of the female protagonist. This body is fully in sympathy with the psyche, hence the disease is not accidental or contingent, but essential to her being. The female body is above all symptomatic, and it is the doctor who is therefore endowed with a gaze—a gaze which demonstrates, for the male subject, the compatibility of rationality and desire. The logical outcome of this suppression of female subjectivity is the blindness of Bette Davis in *Dark Victory*. In the maternal melodrama, separation between mother and child is thematized, inducing distance and even voyeurism (as when Stella Dallas watches her daughter from afar). The window is the figure of this separation and of this distance manufactured in the service of the symbolic. But the pathos which plays a dominant role in the maternal melodrama works to close the gap between spectator and text. In the love story the attempted eroticization of the gaze is turned back on itself to produce the narcissism traditionally associated with the woman, the mirror constituting its most exemplary figure. The narcissistic relation of spectator to screen is transformed into a divided identification with the male character loving the woman and with the woman in the process of being loved. Yet the desire attributed to the female subject in this group of films is often so excessive that the only satisfactory closure consists in her death. When this becomes literally the death of a point of view, as in *Humoresque* and *Waterloo Bridge*, the mechanics of the love story and its failed attempt to contain and constrain female desire are exposed. Finally, it is in the paranoid gothic films that the attempt to attribute the epistemological gaze to the woman results in the greatest degree of violence. Due to the difficulty in localizing, confining, and restraining the representation of paranoid subjectivity in the cinema, the cinematic apparatus itself is activated against the woman, its aggressivity an aggressivity of the look and the voice, directed against her.

Despite the many differences between the various subgroups of the woman's film, one can trace a consistency in certain recurrent themes as well as in the dependence on a limited number of spatial and temporal categories. In terms of the representation of time, the woman's film shows a marked preference for a mistiming which facilitates the production of pathos (particularly in the maternal melodrama and the love story) and an expansion of time which simulates the type of time most fully associated with women—the time of waiting and duration. A time which is intensified through suspense and expectation is foreign to most of the films, found only in those of the gothic group and those strongly influenced by film noir such as *Mildred Pierce*. Similarly, space is constricted in the woman's film, usually to the space of the home. The opposition between inside and outside in relation to the house attains a significance which it rarely reaches in other genres. In *Reckless Moment*, the difficulties begin when the outside, in the guise of a figure from the underworld, invades the inside of the family home. The house often becomes uncanny or claustrophobic. In this narrowing of space the most humble of objects signifies, but for that very reason it is often difficult to tell that signification is taking place, that these films witness the transformation of the "natural" fact or domestic entity (which one usually takes for granted) into the sign. In a patriarchal society, women's genres are characterized by a kind of signifying glut, an overabundance of signification attached to the trivial. In the woman's film there is a hypersignification of elements of the domestic—doors, windows, kitchens, bedrooms. The staircase functions multiply as the site of the woman's specularization, her pathway from curiosity to terror, and as a symbolic prison (at the end of *Reckless Moment* and in *Beyond the Forest*). In watching a woman's film, one actively senses the contraction of the world attributed to the woman, the reduction of meaning and its subordination to affect.

Such an account of the spatial and temporal coordinates of the woman's film can be depressing insofar as it suggests that even in its deep structure this type of film is ideologically complicit. In feminist film criticism, it often seems that politics and pleasure are absolutely incompatible. This is due to the fact that feminist criticism manifests itself primarily as a work of negation of the given images, the given desires. And what often gets lost in the process is the issue of women's pleasure. This partially explains, I think, the temptation to return to genres specifically demarcated as feminine in order to retrieve something *for* the woman, something which belongs to her alone and escapes the patriarchal stranglehold. This is the logic behind studies such as that of Janice Radway on the paperback romance and its reception.[6] Such studies tend to emphasize the ways in which individual readers or spectators use the texts of mass culture for their own purposes and therefore produce more positive and empowering meanings than critics give them credit for. Another strategy for dealing with women's genres is that of reevaluation, taking the characteristics attributed to women in these texts and designating them as hierarchically superior to male values and attributes. This is, of course, to implicitly accept these characteristics or attributes as fully adequate definitions of femininity.

The question of pleasure is a difficult one, and it is tempting to advocate the usurpation of pleasure from patriarchal representations wherever that is possible. But it is crucial to remember that textual pleasure is produced primarily through processes of recognition and misrecognition. The texts of mass culture represent to the female spectator those gestures and desires which are purportedly "feminine," purportedly her own. And what is "recognized" by the spectator is something quite different from what is stolen—the gestures and desires become the basic elements of a complex signifying structure which reinforces a fairly rigid understanding of sexual difference. In short, we are dealing with a process of *mis*recognition. It is not that women's genres have nothing to do with a marginalized female culture which organizes certain experiences and specifies them as the property of women, but that something gets lost in the transition. As John Brenkman points out, mass culture involves a process of "respeaking."

> The mass-mediated discourse respeaks and so silences its socially rooted subtexts. . . . On the one hand, the mass communication is effective only insofar as we hear in it some echo of our actual or virtual collective speaking—which is why even the most manipulative examples of mass culture contain a residual utopian or critical dimension. On the other hand, the mass-mediated public sphere establishes a schism between what I hear and what I speak, such that I receive a message I would not speak and am forced to read in it the figure of my needs, my desires, and my identity—which is why effective resistance does not emerge from the reception situation itself.[7]

Femininity is *stylized* through the work of the woman's film. The genre returns to us the familiar scenarios of waiting, giving, sacrificing, and mourning ennobled and made acceptable by the very fact of their narrativization. What is needed is a means of making these gestures and poses *fantastic*, literally *incredible*.

And it is true that the credibility of these representations is sometimes undermined, in isolated images or scenes. In the process of "respeaking" the woman's desire something slips through. Or more accurately, perhaps, a "respoken" femininity is subjected to a respeaking in its turn. Double mimesis renders void the initial mime or, at the very least, deprives it of its currency. There is a slippage between the two representations. This type of doubling is described by Silvia Bovenschen when she claims, with respect to a recent performance by Marlene Dietrich, ". . . we are watching a woman demonstrate the representation of a woman's body."[8] Or, as Roland Barthes maintains, ". . . the best weapon against myth is perhaps to mythify it in its turn, and to produce an *artificial* myth."[9] In the woman's film, the process of remirroring reduces the mirror effect of the cinema, it demonstrates that these are poses, postures, tropes—in short, that we are being subjected to a discourse on femininity.

This "double mimesis" occurs in the woman's film at moments in the text where the woman appears to produce a reenactment of femininity, where her gestures are disengaged from their immediate context, made strange. In *Stella Dallas* this moment is a scene in which Stella effectively parodies herself, pretending to be an even more exaggeratedly embarrassing mother than she is in the rest of the film. She *exhibits* her garishness and lack of taste through her dress, her manners, her choices in men, music, and language—all in order to convince her daughter Laurel that she should forsake Stella for her father. It is this notion of maternal sacrifice which ultimately recuperates the scene, but for the duration of the pretense, at any rate, the excessiveness of her role is clearly visible. In *Gaslight*, this kind of doubling occurs at the end of the film when Ingrid Bergman acts out the part of the mad wife—a role which her husband had laboriously prepared for her by intensifying her self-consciousness about her looks and her memory. In *Dark Victory*, Bette Davis mimes sight; she pretends to be able to see in order to be the good housewife, packing for her husband, even finding a hole in his sock through the sense of touch. In another Bette Davis film, *Beyond the Forest*, she reenacts in exaggerated form her own narcissism, misapplying makeup and dressing up in a grotesque parody of herself that underlines the absurdity of the woman's status as spectacle.

But the most striking instance of this "double mimesis" is a scene in *The Gay Sisters* (Irving Rapper, 1942). Toward the middle of the film the eldest sister, Fiona (Barbara Stanwyck), tells her two sisters what she refers to as a "bedtime story." It is basically a story about how she tricked a man into marrying her so that she could obtain her inheritance. The man, Charles Barclay (George Brent), turns out to be the person who, in the present tense of the film, is attempting to claim for himself the property belonging to the Gaylord sisters. Her flashback account presents, in a distanced form, all the clichés of the love story. It consists of images which bear all the signs of a romance accompanied by Fiona's voice-over, which works to undermine the credibility of the images. In the images, Fiona plays the silent role of a shy and demure young woman. But her voice-over narration is clearly sarcastic, activating the prose of a cheap romance. That narration consists of phrases such as: "He got that spaniel look in his eyes," "His manly heart pounding," "I walked over and sat demurely," "I threw him a soft and pleading look," "I expected at any minute an orchestra to start up," and "I'll never forget the stink of those apple blossoms." The sequence forces a divergence between voice and body in the representation of the woman. Her voice is mocking, distanced, while her body assumes the poses of idealized romance—looking shyly down and away, not allowing the man to hold her hand. In a contradiction of the classical hierarchy of image over sound, the voice is clearly given more truth value here than the image. The image is false, and the woman's voice directs our reading of it. For her own purposes, the woman mimes the gestures and language of the romance. The disruptive effect of the sequence is, however, canceled by its rather violent ending, in which Barclay essentially rapes Fiona, claiming that it is his right as her husband. Furthermore, Fiona's sisters laugh at the ending of the story, implying that she deserved what she got. And ultimately the image reasserts its claim to truth at the end of the film, when Barclay and Fiona make up and "really" kiss. Nevertheless, the sequence does posit, if only for a short time, the possibility of a radical distance between the woman and her "own," fully feminized gestures.

The "doubling" in these films is particularly crucial in a discourse which is addressed specifically to women, since the prevailing filmic assumption is that female spectatorship is characterized by a closeness to, an affinity with, the image. Fiona's ability to hold the image at arm's length and to analyze it, as well as her ability to enact a defamiliarized version of femininity, bring to mind the strategy of *mimicry* advocated by Luce Irigaray.

> One must assume the feminine role deliberately. Which means already to convert a form of subordination into an affirmation, and thus to begin to thwart it. . . . To play with mimesis is thus, for a woman, to try to recover the place of her exploitation by discourse, without allowing herself to be simply reduced to it. It means to resubmit herself—inasmuch as she is on the side of the "perceptible," of "matter"—to "ideas," in particular to ideas about herself, that are elaborated in/by a masculine logic, but so as to make "visible," by an effect of playful repetition, what was supposed to remain invisible: the cover-up of a possible operation of the feminine in language. [10]

One does not necessarily have to believe in a specifically feminine relation to language in order to agree that it is only through a disengagement of women from the roles and gestures of a naturalized femininity that traditional ways of conceptualizing sexual difference can be overthrown. Mimicry as a political textual strategy makes it possible for the female spectator to understand that recognition is buttressed by misrecognition. From this perspective, fantasy becomes the site of a crucial intervention, and what is at issue is the woman's ability to map herself in the terrain of fantasy. The feminist demand of the cinema cannot be to return our gestures to us, nor to make them more adequate to the real (this type of mimesis is always a trap), but to allow for an active differentiation between gesture and "essence," a play with the signs previously anchored by a set notion of sexual difference. The fascination which the women's films still exert on us can be taken up and activated in the realm of fantasy rather than melodrama—particularly if fantasy is perceived as a space for work on and against the familiar tropes of femininity. Because everything depends, of course, on how one sees oneself. And it is now possible to *look elsewhere*.

# NOTES

## 1. The Desire to Desire

1. See, for example, Ian Watt, *The Rise of the Novel* (Berkeley and Los Angeles: University of California Press, 1957), pp. 43–47.

2. Pam Cook, "Melodrama and the Women's Picture," *Gainsborough Melodrama*, ed. Sue Aspinall and Sue Harper, British Film Institute Dossier 18 (London: British Film Institute, 1983), p. 17.

3. There is also a group of British "women's pictures" (see Pam Cook), and Christian Viviani refers to French and Italian instances of the maternal melodrama. ("Who is Without Sin? The Maternal Melodrama in American Film, 1930–39," *Wide Angle*, vol. 4, no. 2 [1980], pp. 4–17.) However, I have confined this study to the extensive field of American women's films.

4. Roland Barthes, *Camera Lucida: Reflections on Photography*, trans. Richard Howard (New York: Hill and Wang, 1981), p. 65.

5. Some of the most compelling examples of this type of analysis include: Tania Modleski, " 'Never to be thirty-six years old': *Rebecca* as Female Oedipal Drama," *Wide Angle*, vol. 5, no. 1 (1982), pp. 34–41; Linda Williams, " 'Something Else Besides a Mother': *Stella Dallas* and the Maternal Melodrama," *Cinema Journal*, vol. 24, no. 1 (fall 1984), pp. 2–27; Maria La Place, "Bette Davis and the Ideal of Consumption," *Wide Angle*, vol. 6, no. 4 (1985), pp. 34–43. La Place's article is an analysis of the star as a potential site of the assertion of female control over representation.

6. Leo A. Handel, *Hollywood Looks at Its Audience: A Report of Film Audience Research* (Urbana: The University of Illinois Press, 1950), p. 99.

7. The major texts in the area of feminist film criticism (along with important articles too numerous to detail) include: *Camera Obscura: A Journal of Feminism and Film Theory*; Teresa de Lauretis, *Alice Doesn't: Feminism, Semiotics, Cinema* (Bloomington: Indiana University Press, 1984); E. Ann Kaplan, *Women and Film: Both Sides of the Camera* (New York: Methuen, 1983); Annette Kuhn, *Women's Pictures: Feminism and Cinema* (London: Routledge and Kegan Paul, 1982); and Mary Ann Doane, Patricia Mellencamp, and Linda Williams, eds. *Re-vision: Essays in Feminist Film Criticism* (Frederick, Md.: University Publications of America and the American Film Institute, 1984). Kaja Silverman's *The Subject of Semiotics* (New York: Oxford University Press, 1983) is primarily intended as an introduction to semiotic theory but uses films extensively to illustrate that theory and to reflect on the condition of the female subject. Special issues of journals such as *Screen*, *Wide Angle*, and *Film Reader* have also contributed strongly to the elaboration of feminist film criticism.

8. This is the title of the first chapter of Kaplan's book *Women and Film*.

9. Laura Mulvey, "Visual Pleasure and Narrative Cinema," *Screen*, vol. 16, no. 3 (autumn 1975), pp. 6–18.

10. Linda Williams, "Film Body: An Implantation of Perversions," *Ciné-tracts*, vol. 3, no. 4 (winter 1981), pp. 19–35.

11. de Lauretis, *Alice Doesn't*, p. 119.

12. Ibid., p. 121.

13. The relevant texts here are Laura Mulvey, "Afterthoughts on 'Visual Pleasure and Narrative Cinema' Inspired by *Duel in the Sun*," *Framework*, nos. 15, 16, 17 (1981), pp. 12–

15; de Lauretis, *Alice Doesn't*, especially the chapter "Desire in Narrative"; E. Ann Kaplan, *Women and Film*, chapter one, "Is the Gaze Male?"; and my article, "Film and the Masquerade: Theorising the Female Spectator," *Screen*, vol. 23, nos. 3, 4 (September, October 1982), pp. 74–88.

14. Mulvey, "Afterthoughts," p. 15.

15. de Lauretis, *Alice Doesn't*, pp. 143–44.

16. Ibid., p. 151.

17. de Lauretis, "Oedipus Interruptus," *Wide Angle*, vol. 7, nos. 1, 2 (1985), p. 36.

18. Ibid., p. 38.

19. See Roland Barthes, "The Death of the Author," in *Image/Music/Text*, trans. Stephen Heath (New York: Hill and Wang, 1977), pp. 142–48; and Michel Foucault, "What is an Author?" in *Language, Counter-memory, Practice*, trans. Donald F. Bouchard and Sherry Simon (Ithaca: Cornell University Press, 1977), pp. 113–38.

20. See the dialogue in *Diacritics* (summer 1982) on this issue: Peggy Kamuf, "Replacing Feminist Criticism," pp. 42–47 and Nancy K. Miller, "The Text's Heroine: A Feminist Critic and Her Fictions," pp. 48–53.

21. Émile Benveniste, *Problems in General Linguistics*, trans. Mary Elizabeth Meek (Coral Gables: University of Miami Press, 1971), p. 224.

22. See Christian Metz, "History/Discourse: Note on Two Voyeurisms," trans. Susan Bennett, *Edinburgh '76 Magazine*, no. 1 (1976), pp. 21–25.

23. For a fuller discussion of these issues, see my article "Woman's Stake: Filming the Female Body," *October*, no. 17 (summer 1981), pp. 23–36.

24. See Luce Irigaray, *This Sex Which Is Not One*, trans. Catherine Porter (Ithaca: Cornell University Press, 1985); Hélène Cixous, "The Laugh of the Medusa," *New French Feminisms*, ed. Elaine Marks and Isabelle de Courtivron (Amherst: The University of Massachusetts Press, 1980), pp. 245–64; Sarah Kofman, "Ex: The Woman's Enigma," *Enclitic*, vol. 4, no. 2 (fall 1980), pp. 17–28; and Michèle Montrelay, "Inquiry into Femininity," *m/f*, no. 1 (1978), pp. 83–102.

25. Irigaray, *Speculum of the Other Woman*, trans. Gillian C. Gill (Ithaca: Cornell University Press, 1985), p. 133.

26. Ibid., p. 165.

27. Silverman, *Subject of Semiotics*, p. 173.

28. *Feminine Sexuality: Jacques Lacan and the École Freudienne*, ed. Juliet Mitchell and Jacqueline Rose (New York: W.W. Norton, 1982), p. 29.

29. Jean Laplanche, *Life and Death in Psychoanalysis*, trans. Jeffrey Mehlman (Baltimore: The Johns Hopkins University Press, 1976), p. 66.

30. Julia Kristeva, *Powers of Horror: An Essay on Abjection*, trans. Leon S. Roudiez (New York: Columbia University Press, 1982), pp. 62–63.

31. Christian Metz, "The Imaginary Signifier," *Screen*, vol. 16, no. 2 (summer 1975), p. 61.

32. Jacques Lacan, *The Four Fundamental Concepts of Psycho-Analysis*, trans. Alan Sheridan (Middlesex: Penguin Books, 1979), p. 107. Something should be added here about one of Lacan's most famous formulations, "man's desire is the desire of the Other," which would seem, once again, to diminish any notion of agency associated with the subject. The "Other" here refers to the locus of speech, discourse, language, the unconscious. Desire may be the effect of a condition imposed on the subject by which he must "make his need pass through the defiles of the signifier," but a desiring subject is one who can be conceptualized as residing within the realm of language and who attains an active relation to the signifier. The formulation "man's desire is the desire of the Other" thus indicates "man's" privileged relation to language. See Jacques Lacan, "The Direction of the Treatment and the Principles of Its Power," *Écrits: A Selection*, trans. Alan Sheridan (New York: W.W. Norton, 1977), p. 264. Compare, "There is woman only as excluded by the nature of things which is the nature of words, and it has to be said that if there is one thing they themselves are complaining about

enough at the moment it is well and truly that—only they don't know what they are saying, which is all the difference between them and me." "God and the *Jouissance* of The Woman," *Feminine Sexuality*, p. 144.

33. Lacan, *Écrits*, p. 257. In reference to Freud's analysis of a hysteric who dreams of another woman's desire, Lacan states, "One should try and count the number of substitutions that operate here to bring desire to a geometrically increasing power." The hysteric's desire, precisely because it is so displaced and convoluted—so distanced from any "real" object— becomes representative of all desire, and this is why the Freudian exploration of the unconscious begins with the hysteric. But curiously, because the hysteric comes to represent and exemplify desire, she loses access to it. For Lacan later in this same analysis claims, "To be the phallus, if only a somewhat thin one. Was not that the ultimate identification with the signifier of desire?" (p. 202). The woman's goal is to *be* the phallus (*the* signifier of desire) rather than to *have* it.

34. Lacan, "Guiding Remarks for a Congress on Feminine Sexuality," in *Feminine Sexuality*, p. 97.

35. For examples of the activation of Freudian and Lacanian psychoanalysis in theories of spectatorship see Metz, "The Imaginary Signifier"; Mulvey, "Visual Pleasure and Narrative Cinema"; Jean-Louis Baudry, "The Apparatus," trans. Jean Andrews and Bertrand Augst, *Camera Obscura*, no. 1 (fall 1976), pp. 104–26; Baudry, "Ideological Effects of the Basic Cinematographic Apparatus," *Film Quarterly*, vol. 28, no. 2 (winter 1974–75), pp. 39–47; Stephen Heath, "Lessons from Brecht," *Screen*, vol. 15, no. 2 (summer 1974), pp. 103–28.

36. Sigmund Freud, *Beyond the Pleasure Principle*, trans. and ed. James Strachey (New York: W.W. Norton, 1961), pp. 8–11.

37. See, for example, Christian Metz, "The Fiction Film and Its Spectator: A Metapsychological Study," *The Imaginary Signifier: Psychoanalysis and the Cinema*, trans. Celia Britton, Annwyl Williams, Ben Brewster, and Alfred Guzzetti (Bloomington: Indiana University Press, 1977), p. 112.

38. See Heath, "Lessons from Brecht." Metz's analysis of fetishism in "The Imaginary Signifier" is somewhat different than Heath's, focusing on the frame and technological fetishism. Mulvey's analysis of fetishism in "Visual Pleasure and Narrative Cinema" explicates its consequences for sexual difference. See also O. Mannoni, *Clefs pour l'imaginaire ou l'autre scène* (Paris: Editions du Seuil, 1969).

39. Metz, "The Imaginary Signifier," p. 51.

40. Ibid., pp. 48–51.

41. See Irigaray, *This Sex Which Is Not One*, pp. 23–33.

42. Luce Irigaray, *Speculum de l'autre femme* (Paris: Les Éditions de Minuit, 1974), p. 93. My translation.

43. Ibid.

44. Sigmund Freud, "Fetishism," *Sexuality and the Psychology of Love*, ed. Philip Rieff (New York: Collier Books, 1963), p. 216.

45. Sigmund Freud, *The Interpretation of Dreams*, trans. and ed. James Strachey (New York: Avon Books, 1965), p. 183.

46. Sigmund Freud, *Group Psychology and the Analysis of the Ego*, trans. James Strachey (New York: Bantam Books, 1960), p. 48.

47. Ibid., p. 49.

48. Sigmund Freud, "The Economic Problem in Masochism," in *General Psychological Theory*, ed. Philip Rieff (New York: Collier Books, 1963), p. 193.

49. Sigmund Freud, "A Child is Being Beaten," in *Sexuality and the Psychology of Love*, ed. Philip Rieff (New York: Collier Books, 1963), p. 128.

50. Freud's explanation for this sexual transformation is quite interesting and worth quoting in full: "When they [girls] turn away from their incestuous love for their father, with its genital significance, they easily abandon their feminine role. They spur their 'masculinity

complex' (v. Ophuijsen) into activity, and from that time forward only want to be boys. For that reason the whipping-boys who represent them are boys too. In both the cases of day-dreaming—one of which almost rose to the level of a work of art—the heroes were always young men; indeed women used not to come into these creations at all, and only made their first appearance after many years, and then in minor parts" (Ibid., pp. 119–20). The positioning of the male as protagonist of the fantasy clearly makes a strict parallel between the "Child is Being Beaten" fantasy and the woman's film impossible. Nevertheless, the sexual transformation of female into male in the fantasy does parallel the de-eroticization of the female body in the masochistic women's films and the consequent loss of the "feminine" category of spectacle.

51. Ibid., p. 114.

52. Ibid., p. 128.

53. Stephen Heath, "Family Plots," *Comparative Criticism*, vol. 5 (Cambridge University Press, 1983), p. 329.

54. Sigmund Freud, *Studies on Hysteria, The Standard Edition of the Complete Psychological Works of Sigmund Freud*, vol. 2 (London 1955), p. 160. Quoted by Heath, "Family Plots," p. 318.

55. See Juliet Mitchell, *Psychoanalysis and Feminism* (New York: Vintage Books, 1974); Mitchell and Rose, *Feminine Sexuality*; and Jacqueline Rose, "Femininity and Its Discontents," *Feminist Review*, no. 14 (summer 1983), pp. 5–21.

56. Kristeva, *Powers of Horror*, p. 67.

57. Fredric Jameson, "Reification and Utopia in Mass Culture," *Social Text*, vol. 1, no. 1 (winter 1979), p. 131.

58. See Elaine Marks and Isabelle de Courtivron, eds., *New French Feminisms* (Amherst: The University of Massachusetts Press, 1980), pp. 107–10 and Irigaray, *This Sex Which Is Not One*, pp. 170–92.

59. Irigaray, *This Sex Which Is Not One*, p. 84. Also, see pp. 172–73.

60. Claude Lévi-Strauss, *The Elementary Structures of Kinship*, trans. James Harle Bell, John Richard von Sturmer, and Rodney Needham (Boston: Beacon Press, 1969), p. 496.

61. Ibid.

62. Fredric Jameson, "Pleasure: A Political Issue," *Formations of Pleasure* (London: Routledge and Kegan Paul, 1983), p. 4.

63. Charles Eckert, "The Carole Lombard in Macy's Window," *Quarterly Review of Film Studies*, vol. 3, no. 1 (winter 1978), p. 4.

64. Jeanne Allen, "The Film Viewer as Consumer," *Quarterly Review of Film Studies*, vol. 5, no. 4 (fall 1980), p. 482.

65. Quoted in Eckert, "Carole Lombard," p. 5.

66. Michèle Le Doeuff, "Pierre Roussel's Chiasmas: from imaginary knowledge to the learned imagination," *Ideology and Consciousness*, no. 9 (winter 1981–82), p. 46.

67. See Stuart Ewen, *Captains of Consciousness: Advertising and the Social Roots of the Consumer Culture* (New York: McGraw-Hill, 1976).

68. Judith Mayne, "Immigrants and Spectators," *Wide Angle*, vol. 5, no. 2 (1982), p. 34.

69. Allen, "Film Viewer as Consumer," p. 487.

70. Ibid., p. 486.

71. Eckert, "Carole Lombard," p. 4.

72. Ibid., p. 10.

73. Carl Laemmle, "The Business of Motion Pictures," in *The American Film Industry*, ed. Tino Balio (Madison: The University of Wisconsin Press, 1976), p. 163.

74. Ibid., p. 162.

75. Eckert, "Carole Lombard," p. 19. Also, Stuart Ewen claims that in the 1920s, "the home, the arena of consumption, was central to the woman's world and consequently only

a small percentage of advertising appears to have been directed at the male population," Ewen, p. 151.

76. Eckert, "Carole Lombard," pp. 19–20.

77. Handel, *Hollywood Looks at Its Audience*, p. 101.

78. Susan M. Hartmann, *The Home Front and Beyond: American Women in the 1940s* (Boston: Twayne Publishers, 1982), p. 200.

79. Ferdinand Lundberg and Marynia F. Farnham, M.D., *Modern Woman: The Lost Sex* (New York: Harper, 1947).

80. The press books for 1940s films which I examined are available in the collection of the Doheny Library at the University of Southern California.

81. Rachel Bowlby, *Just Looking: Consumer Culture in Dreiser, Gissing, and Zola* (New York: Methuen, 1985), p. 32.

82. Wolfgang Schivelbusch, *The Railway Journey: Trains and Travel in the 19th Century*, trans. Anselm Hollo (New York: Urizen Books, 1977), pp. 184–85.

83. Jameson, "Reification and Utopia," p. 133.

84. Walter Benjamin, "The Work of Art in the Age of Mechanical Reproduction," in *Illuminations*, trans. Harry Zohn, ed. Hannah Arendt (New York: Schocken Books, 1969), p. 223.

85. Schivelbusch, *Railway Journey*, p. 48.

86. Benjamin, "Mechanical Reproduction," p. 222.

87. Ibid., p. 223.

88. As Miriam Hansen has pointed out to me, the alignment of the opposition between distance and closeness with that between fetishism and nonfetishism does tend to reduce the dynamics of proximity and distance operating within fetishism itself. One could undoubtedly also argue that narcissism presupposes a similar dialectic, invoking the inevitable distance between the desiring subject and the mirror image. Nevertheless, my point is that fetishism ultimately enables the maintenance of a distance—for the fetishist, "having" and "being" are separable. The fetishist's relation to the object is always doubly mediated: through the constitution of a substitute object and the "knowledge" that the woman "really" does lack the phallus. Narcissism implies no knowledge whatsoever—rather, it signifies full investment in an illusion.

89. Ewen, *Captains of Consciousness*, p. 47.

90. See Ewen, *Captains of Consciousness*, p. 39.

91. Benjamin, *Charles Baudelaire: A Lyric Poet in the Era of High Capitalism*, trans. Harry Zohn (London: New Left Books, 1973), p. 55.

92. Guy Debord, *Society of the Spectacle* (Detroit: Black and Red, 1977), section 62.

93. Irigaray, *This Sex Which Is Not One*, p. 177.

94. Michael Renov, "From Fetish to Subject: The Containment of Sexual Difference in Hollywood's Wartime Cinema," *Wide Angle*, vol. 5, no. 1 (1982), p. 17. For another very interesting analysis of the construction of sexual difference in the 1940s, see Dana Polan, *Power and Paranoia: History, Narrative, and the American Cinema, 1940–1950* (New York: Columbia University Press, 1986).

95. Kuhn, *Women's Pictures*, p. 191.

96. Molly Haskell, *From Reverence to Rape: The Treatment of Women in the Movies* (Baltimore: Penguin Books, 1974), pp. 163–64.

97. See, for instance, Andrea S. Walsh, *Women's Film and Female Experience* (New York: Praeger, 1984). Walsh divides the woman's film of the 1940s into three categories: the maternal dramas, the career woman comedies, and the films of "madness, suspicion, and distrust." Walsh's general approach to the woman's film is quite problematic, for it rests on the assumption that women's "experience" and popular consciousness in the 1940s are somehow reflected by or represented in the films, and that the films therefore offer the analyst a privileged access to that experience. This leads, in the actual analysis of the films, to an emphasis on plot and characterization and, ultimately, a stress on the strength and/or weakness

of the female characters as a measure of potential feminist or antifeminist meaning. Theories of the cinematic apparatus and the unconscious aspects of spectatorship are totally neglected.

98. Renov, "From Fetish to Subject," p. 20.

99. Gerald M. Mayer, "American Motion Pictures in World Trade," *The Annals of the American Academy of Political and Social Science*, vol. 254 (November 1947), p. 34.

### 2. *Clinical Eyes: The Medical Discourse*

1. Michel Foucault, *The Birth of the Clinic: An Archaeology of Medical Perception*, trans. A.M. Sheridan Smith (New York: Pantheon, 1973), p. x.

2. Phyllis Chesler, *Women and Madness* (New York: Avon Books, 1972), p. 75.

3. The films discussed in this chapter include: *Dark Victory* (Edmund Goulding, 1939); *A Woman's Face* (George Cukor, 1941); *The Cat People* (Jacques Tourneur, 1942); *Now, Voyager* (Irving Rapper, 1942); *Guest in the House* (John Brahm, 1944); *Lady in the Dark* (Mitchell Leisen, 1944); *Dark Mirror* (Robert Siodmak, 1946); *A Stolen Life* (Curtis Bernhardt, 1946); *The Locket* (John Brahm, 1946); *Shock* (Alfred Werker, 1946); *Possessed* (Curtis Bernhardt, 1947); *Johnny Belinda* (Jean Negulesco, 1948); *The Snake Pit* (Anatole Litvak, 1948); *Beyond the Forest* (King Vidor, 1949); *Whirlpool* (Otto Preminger, 1949).

4. Foucault, *Birth of the Clinic*, pp. 165–66.

5. Sigmund Freud and Joseph Breuer, *Studies on Hysteria*, trans. and ed. James Strachey (New York: Avon Books, 1966), p. 38.

6. Foucault, *Birth of the Clinic*, pp. 121–22.

7. Future references to the look of the doctor will make use of the term "gaze" despite Foucault's very important distinction, in this context, between the glance and the gaze. I continue to utilize "gaze" due to its connotative relation to temporality. While the glance is rapid, punctual, momentary, gaze implies a sustained process of looking which more accurately describes the strategy of the films. For my purpose, the most significant aspect of Foucault's distinction is its correlation with the opposition surface/depth.

8. Louis Althusser and Étienne Balibar, *Reading Capital* (London: New Left Books, 1970), p. 26.

9. Geoffrey Nowell-Smith, "Minnelli and Melodrama," *Screen*, vol. 18, no. 2 (summer 1977), p. 117.

10. Althusser and Balibar, *Reading Capital*, p. 86.

11. Irving Schneider, M.D., "Images of the Mind: Psychiatry in the Commercial Film," *American Journal of Psychiatry*, Vol. 134, no. 6 (June 1977), p. 615.

12. See, for instance, Lawrence S. Kubie, "Psychiatry and the Films," *Hollywood Quarterly*, vol. 2, no. 2 (January 1947), pp. 113–17 and Franklin Fearing, "Psychology and the Films," *Hollywood Quarterly*, vol. 2, no. 2 (January 1947), pp 118–21.

13. See the pressbooks for *Dark Mirror* (International Pictures, 1946) and *Sleep My Love* (United Artists, 1948).

14. Marc Vernet, "Freud: effets spéciaux—Mise en scène: U.S.A.," *Communications*, no. 23 (1975), p. 229.

15. Ibid., p. 233.

16. The analysis of *The Cat People* which follows owes a great deal to discussions I had with Deborah Linderman about the film in the spring of 1983.

17. See Colin MacCabe, "Realism and the Cinema: Notes on Some Brechtian Theses," *Screen*, vol. 15, no. 2 (summer 1974), pp. 7–27.

18. Samuel Weber, *The Legend of Freud* (Minneapolis: University of Minnesota Press, 1982), p. 47.

19. Jacques Derrida, *Writing and Difference*, trans. Alan Bass (Chicago: The University of Chicago Press, 1978), p. 230.

20. Sigmund Freud, *Dora: An Analysis of a Case of Hysteria,* ed. Philip Rieff (New York: Collier Books, 1963), pp. 70–71.

21. Freud and Breuer, *Studies on Hysteria,* p. 42.

22. Ibid., pp. 64–65.

23. Ibid., p. 66.

24. Ibid., p. 47.

25. Ibid., p. 56.

26. In *Home of the Brave,* a black soldier is also given an injection ("narcosynthesis") which motivates the flashback structure of the film. However, not only does his status as a black insure that, like a woman, he is culturally marginalized, but he is implicitly "feminized" in various ways throughout the film, particularly in his relation to the doctor.

27. Michel Foucault, *Madness and Civilization: A History of Insanity in the Age of Reason,* trans. Richard Howard (New York: Random House, 1965), p. 94.

28. Ibid., p. 108.

29. See Joan Copjec, "Flavit et Dissipati Sunt," *October,* no. 18 (fall 1981), pp. 21–40.

30. Susan Sontag, *Illness as Metaphor* (New York: Farrar, Straus and Giroux, 1977–78), pp. 20–21.

31. Ibid., p. 28.

32. Foucault, *Madness and Civilization,* p. 88.

33. See Sontag, *Illness as Metaphor,* pp. 56–57 and Barbara Ehrenreich and Deirdre English, *Complaints and Disorders: The Sexual Politics of Sickness* (New York: The Feminist Press, 1973), pp. 38–44.

34. Foucault, *Madness and Civilization,* pp. 269, 278.

35. Ibid., pp. 271–72.

36. Ibid., p. 274.

37. The social and moral function of the doctor figure in these films is evidenced by the fact that when *Johnny Belinda* was remade as a TV movie in 1982, the doctor was replaced by a Vista volunteer.

38. Sontag, *Illness as Metaphor,* p. 58.

39. Sigmund Freud, *Inhibitions, Symptoms and Anxiety,* trans. Alix Strachey (New York: W. W. Norton, 1959), p. 69.

40. Sigmund Freud, "A Case of Chronic Paranoia," *The Standard Edition of the Complete Psychological Works,* vol. 3 (London: The Hogarth Press and the Institute of Psychoanalysis, 1962), p. 175.

41. Foucault, *Madness and Civilization,* p. 154.

42. See Laura Mulvey, "Afterthoughts . . . Inspired by *Duel in the Sun,*" *Framework,* nos. 15, 16, 17 (summer 1981), p. 13 and my article, "Film and the Masquerade: Theorising the Female Spectator," *Screen,* vol. 23, nos. 3, 4 (September, October 1982), pp. 74–87.

43. Foucault, *Madness and Civilization,* pp. 153–54.

### 3. *The Moving Image: Pathos and the Maternal*

1. The lack of a mother also connotes the precise opposite—an absolute sadness—as in the blues song, "Sometimes I feel like a motherless child . . . ," which signifies a state of complete loss of identity, homelessness, etc. The lack of a father, or illegitimacy, on the other hand, signals the impairment of identity, not its obliteration.

2. Peter Brooks, *The Melodramatic Imagination: Balzac, Henry James, Melodrama, and the Mode of Excess* (New Haven: Yale University Press, 1976), p. 15.

3. Ibid., pp. 41, 48.

4. See, for instance, Claude Beylie, "Propositions sur le mélo," *Les Cahiers de la Cinematheque: Pour Une Histoire du Mélodrame au Cinéma,* no. 28, pp. 7–11. Peter Brooks in *The Melodramatic Imagination* also refers to the cinema as a whole as a continuation of the melodramatic stage tradition, particularly in its use of music.

5. Thomas Elsaesser, "Tales of Sound and Fury: Observations on the Family Melodrama," *Monogram*, no. 4 (1972), pp. 2–15 and Griselda Pollock, Geoffrey Nowell-Smith, and Stephen Heath, "Dossier on Melodrama," *Screen*, vol. 18, no. 2, (summer 1977) pp. 105–19.

6. Elsaesser, "Tales of Sound and Fury," p. 2.

7. Robert Bechtold Heilman, *Tragedy and Melodrama: Versions of Experience* (Seattle: University of Washington Press, 1968), p. 86.

8. Elsaesser, "Tales of Sound and Fury," p. 10.

9. Nowell-Smith, "Dossier on Melodrama," p. 115.

10. Ibid., p. 116.

11. Elsaesser, "Tales of Sound and Fury," p. 9.

12. Jacques Goimard, "Le mélodrame: le mot et la chose," *Les Cahiers de la Cinematheque: Pour Une Histoire du Mélodrame au Cinema*, no. 28, p. 51. My translation.

13. Films discussed in this chapter include: *Stella Dallas* (King Vidor, 1937); *That Certain Woman* (Edmund Goulding, 1937); *The Great Lie* (Edmund Goulding, 1941); *Blossoms in the Dust* (Mervyn LeRoy, 1941); *Lydia* (Julien Duvivier, 1941); *Now, Voyager* (Irving Rapper, 1942); *Tender Comrade* (Edward Dmytryk, 1943); *Watch on the Rhine* (Herman Shumlin, 1943); *Since You Went Away* (John Cromwell, 1944); *Mildred Pierce* (Michael Curtiz, 1945); *To Each His Own* (Mitchell Leisen, 1946); *Tomorrow Is Forever* (Irving Pichel, 1946); *Letter from an Unknown Woman* (Max Ophuls, 1948); *Johnny Belinda* (Jean Negulesco, 1948); *My Foolish Heart* (Mark Robson, 1949); *The Reckless Moment* (Max Ophuls, 1949).

14. Christian Viviani, "Who Is Without Sin? The Maternal Melodrama in American Film, 1930–39," *Wide Angle*, vol. 4, no. 2 (1980), p. 7.

15. Two other feminist analyses of *Stella Dallas* with somewhat different overall emphases are E. Ann Kaplan, "The Case of the Missing Mother: Maternal Issues in Vidor's *Stella Dallas*," *Heresies*, no. 16, pp. 81–85 and Linda Williams, " 'Something Else Besides a Mother': *Stella Dallas* and the Maternal Melodrama," *Cinema Journal*, vol. 24, no. 1 (fall 1984), pp. 2–27.

16. Viviani, "Who Is Without Sin?" p. 15.

17. Ibid., p. 15.

18. Williams, "Something Else Besides a Mother," p. 2.

19. For a fuller discussion of this process, which she refers to as trait-stripping, see Anne Norton, "Maternal Metaphors in Politics: Three Studies," unpublished manuscript.

20. Wartime "Rosie the Riveter" imagery is also denaturalized, but in a different way—through an emphasis on its exceptionality, its incompatibility with or reversal of existing norms of femininity.

21. See Barbara Ehrenreich and Deirdre English, *For Her Own Good: 150 Years of the Experts' Advice to Women* (Garden City: Anchor Books, 1979), p. 220.

22. The mother who escapes these excesses—e.g., Ann Hilton (Claudette Colbert) in *Since You Went Away*—is abstracted and idealized until she becomes a symbol for something beyond the maternal—America in its unity and identity. The film constantly flirts with the possibility of Ann having an extramarital affair with Tony (Joseph Cotten), but is ultimately quite explicit about the impossibility of such a liaison—it would tarnish the ideal image of Mrs. Hilton.

23. Monique Plaza, "The Mother/The Same: Hatred of the Mother in Psychoanalysis," *Feminist Issues*, vol. 2, no. 1 (spring 1982), p. 88.

24. Brooks, *Melodramatic Imagination*, p. 36.

25. Luce Irigaray, "And the One Doesn't Stir Without the Other," trans. Hélène Vivienne Wenzel, *Signs*, vol. 7, no. 1 (autumn 1981), pp. 60–67.

26. Julia Kristeva, *Powers of Horror* (New York: Columbia University Press, 1983). *Powers of Horror* will be discussed more fully in chapter 5.

27. Julia Kristeva, "Maternité selon Giovanni Bellini," *Polylogue* (Paris: Éditions du Seuil, 1977), p. 409. My translation.

28. Ibid.

29. Films like *Psycho* (and other more contemporary horror films) indicate the underside of this, the terror attached to the maternal, the repression of the mother's other aspect as outlined in *Powers of Horror*.

30. Brooks, *Melodramatic Imagination*, pp. 67–68.

31. Ibid., p. 66.

32. *Encyclopédie*; s.v. "Geste" (Paris, 1757), quoted in Brooks, *Melodramatic Imagination*, p. 66.

33. See Claudia Gorbman, "The Drama's Melos: Max Steiner and *Mildred Pierce*," *The Velvet Light Trap: Review of Cinema*, no. 19 (1982), pp. 35–39, for an illuminating analysis of the music Max Steiner composed for a number of women's pictures including, in particular, *Mildred Pierce*.

34. Martha Wolfenstein and Nathan Leites, *Movies: A Psychological Study* (New York: Atheneum, 1970), p. 133.

35. Ibid.

36. Elsaesser, "Tales of Sound and Fury," p. 10.

37. Ibid., p. 14.

38. Franco Moretti, *Signs Taken For Wonders: Essays in the Sociology of Literary Forms*, trans. Susan Fischer, David Forgacs, David Miller (London: New Left Books, 1983), p. 159.

39. Ibid., p. 160.

40. Ibid., p. 162.

41. Sigmund Freud, "Femininity," *The Standard Edition of the Complete Psychological Works of Sigmund Freud*, ed. James Strachey (London: The Hogarth Press and the Institute of Psycho-analysis, 1964), p. 134.

42. Members of the *Framework* editorial board, "The Reckless Moment" and "The Family in 'The Reckless Moment,' " *Framework*, no. 4 (autumn 1976), pp. 17–24.

43. Elisabeth Saxony Holding, "The Blank Wall," *Ladies' Home Journal* (October 1947), pp. 37–223.

44. Beylie, "Propositions sur le mélo," p. 7. My translation.

### 4. The Love Story

1. The films discussed in this chapter include: *Intermezzo* (Gregory Ratoff, 1939); *When Tomorrow Comes* (John Stahl, 1939); *The Letter* (William Wyler, 1940); *Kitty Foyle* (Sam Wood, 1940); *Waterloo Bridge* (Mervyn Le Roy, 1940); *Back Street* (Robert Stevenson, 1941); *Lydia* (Julien Duvivier, 1941); *Now, Voyager* (Irving Rapper, 1942); *Leave Her to Heaven* (John Stahl, 1945); *The Enchanted Cottage* (John Cromwell, 1945); *Love Letters* (William Dieterle, 1945); *Humoresque* (Jean Negulesco, 1946); *Deception* (Irving Rapper, 1946); *The Strange Love of Martha Ivers* (Lewis Milestone, 1946); *Daisy Kenyon* (Otto Preminger, 1947); *Letter from an Unknown Woman* (Max Ophuls, 1948); *The Heiress* (William Wyler, 1949); *My Foolish Heart* (Mark Robson, 1949); *Madame Bovary* (Vincente Minnelli, 1949).

2. Linda Williams, "When the Woman Looks," in *Re-vision: Essays in Feminist Film Criticism*, ed. Mary Ann Doane, Patricia Mellencamp, and Linda Williams (Frederick, Md.: University Publications of America and The American Film Institute, 1984), p. 83.

3. Roland Barthes, *A Lover's Discourse*, trans. Richard Howard (New York: Hill and Wang, 1978), p. 14.

4. Group µ (J. Dubois, P. Dubois, F. Edeline, J.M. Klinkenberg, P. Minguet), "Iro-

nique et iconique," *Poétique: revue de théorie et d'analyse littéraires*, no. 36 (Novembre 1978), p. 436. My translation.

5. Peter Wollen, "Godard and Counter Cinema: *Vent d'Est*," in *Readings and Writings: Semiotic Counter-Strategies* (London: Verso Editions and New Left Books, 1982), p. 83.

6. Christian Metz, "The Cinema: Language or Language System?" in *Film Language: A Semiotics of the Cinema*, trans. Michael Taylor (New York: Oxford University Press, 1974), p. 67.

7. This is literally true. There is a point-of-view shot clearly attributed to Helen as she sinks in the water, bubbles rising to the surface and seaweed floating by.

8. Stephen Heath, "The Question Oshima," *Ophuls*, ed. Paul Willeman (London: British Film Institute, 1978), p. 76.

9. Luce Irigaray, "La 'Mécanique' des fluides," *Ce sexe qui n'en est pas un* (Paris: Les Éditions de Minuit, 1977), p. 106. My translation.

10. Roland Barthes, *S/Z: An Essay*, trans. Richard Miller (New York: Hill and Wang, 1974), p. 204.

11. Ibid., p. 262.

12. Pascal Bonitzer, "Partial Vision: Film and the Labyrinth," trans. Fabrice Ziolkowski, *Wide Angle*, vol. 4, no. 4 (1981), p. 62.

13. Julia Kristeva, "Women's Time," trans. Alice Jardine and Harry Blake, *Signs: Journal of Women in Culture and Society*, vol. 7, no. 1 (1981), p. 17. Kristeva is very careful to avoid labeling this obsessional linear time as masculine in order to oppose it to a "hysterical" and therefore feminine cyclical or monumental time. But she does recognize affinities between this binary opposition of temporalities and a certain culturally constructed understanding of sexual difference. Tania Modleski, in a very provocative analysis of *Letter from an Unknown Woman* ("Time and Desire in the Woman's Film," *Cinema Journal*, vol. 23, no. 3 [spring 1984], pp. 19–30) attempts to undermine such a binary opposition by proposing a third type of relation to time—a more playful, creative, imaginative relation to time which is neither obsessional nor hysterical. Although I agree with Modleski that the binarism can be quite suffocating at the level of theorizing female desire, I do not believe that the woman's investment in imagination or her "joyful" evocation of reminiscences in *Letter from an Unknown Woman* is a viable alternative. The reasons for this will become clear in my discussions of repetition and imagination later in this chapter.

14. Barthes, *Lover's Discourse*, p. 14.

15. Modleski, "Time and Desire," p. 22. See also Heath, "The Question Oshima," p. 81.

16. Barthes, *Lover's Discourse*, pp. 13–14.

17. Sigmund Freud, "Femininity," *The Standard Edition of the Complete Psychological Works of Sigmund Freud*, ed. James Strachey (London: The Hogarth Press and the Institute of Psycho-analysis, 1964), p. 132.

18. Barthes, *S/Z*, p. 160 (italics in Barthes).

19. In this respect, the film is very close to the novel and some of the phrases from Mason's voice-over testimony are drawn directly from it (e.g., "persecuted ladies fainting in lonely pavilions," "horses ridden to death on every page," "gentlemen brave as lions, gentle as lambs," etc.). See Gustave Flaubert, *Madame Bovary*, ed. and trans. Paul de Man (New York: W.W. Norton, 1965), p. 26.

20. *The Enchanted Cottage* diverges somewhat from the other films discussed here since it represents the imagination in a more positive light. Furthermore, both the man and the woman are presented as ugly or distorted in some way, and both imagine the other to be more beautiful/handsome than they really are. The point of the film is that love gives them a special "sight" which is not accessible to ordinary people. However, it is extremely significant that Laura is represented as ugly from birth (her distortion is essential), whereas Oliver's

disfiguring is accidental (he is injured in the war). The film also asserts very strongly that one can live a fantasy as long as one recognizes the distinction between the fantastic and the real.

21. *Système physique et moral de la femme*, quoted by Michèle Le Doeuff, "Pierre Roussel's Chiasmas: from imaginary knowledge to the learned imagination," *Ideology and Consciousness*, no. 9 (winter 1981–82), p. 44.

22. Pam Cook, "Melodrama and the Women's Picture," *The Gainsborough Melodrama*, ed. Sue Aspinall and Sue Harper (London: British Film Institute, 1983), p. 16.

23. See Barthes, *A Lover's Discourse*, pp. 63, 93.

24. Modleski, "Time and Desire," pp. 26–27.

25. Quoted by Stuart Ewen, *Captains of Consciousness* (New York: McGraw-Hill, 1977), p. 48.

26. Sigmund Freud, *The Interpretation of Dreams*, trans. and ed. James Strachey (New York: Avon Books, 1965), p. 184.

27. Hélène Cixous, "The Laugh of the Medusa," *New French Feminisms*, ed. Elaine Marks and Isabelle de Courtivron (Amherst: The University of Massachusetts Press, 1980), p. 255.

28. Claire Johnston, "Femininity and the Masquerade: Anne of the Indies," in *Jacques Tourneur* (London: British Film Institute, 1975), p. 40.

29. Stephen Heath, "Family Plots," *Comparative Criticism*, vol. 5 (Cambridge University Press, 1983), p. 318.

30. Ferdinand Lundberg and Marynia F. Farnham, M.D., *Modern Woman: The Lost Sex* (New York: Harper, 1947), p. 3.

### 5. Paranoia and the Specular

1. The films belonging to the paranoid cycle which are discussed in this chapter include: *Rebecca* (Alfred Hitchcock, 1940); *Suspicion* (Alfred Hitchcock, 1941); *Jane Eyre* (Robert Stevenson, 1944); *Dark Waters* (Andre de Toth, 1944); *Experiment Perilous* (Jacques Tourneur, 1944); *Gaslight* (George Cukor, 1944); *Undercurrent* (Vincente Minnelli, 1946); *Shock* (Alfred Werker, 1946); *Dragonwyck* (Joseph Mankiewicz, 1946); *The Spiral Staircase* (Robert Siodmak, 1946); *The Two Mrs. Carrolls* (Peter Godfrey, 1947); *Sleep My Love* (Douglas Sirk, 1948); *Secret Beyond the Door* (Fritz Lang, 1948); *Caught* (Max Ophuls, 1949).

2. Although it is not necessarily the case that the violence exercised by the man on the woman takes place within the context of marriage, the husband/wife axis is present in all but three of the fourteen films considered in this chapter. In those instances where a marriage is not involved (*The Spiral Staircase, Dark Waters, Shock*), the woman is nevertheless in a position of dependence with respect to the aggressor(s).

3. Thomas Elsaesser, "Tales of Sound and Fury," *Monogram*, no. 4 (1972), p. 11.

4. Norman N. Holland and Leona F. Sherman, "Gothic Possibilities," *New Literary History*, vol. 8, no. 2 (winter 1977), p. 279.

5. Ibid., p. 281.

6. Joanna Russ, "Somebody's Trying to Kill Me and I Think It's My Husband: The Modern Gothic," *Journal of Popular Culture*, vol. 6, no. 4 (spring 1973), p. 666.

7. There is at least one notable exception. Diane Waldman in her unpublished dissertation, "Horror and Domesticity: The Modern Gothic Romance Film of the 1940s," University of Wisconsin—Madison, 1981, claims that these films constitute a subgenre of the woman's film.

8. These examples are all taken from those given in Russ's article cited above, although she does not discuss this prevalence of an intent masculine gaze in the novels.

9. Press book for *Secret Beyond the Door*, Universal Pictures, 1947.

10. See Christian Metz, *The Imaginary Signifier: Psychoanalysis and the Cinema*,

trans. Celia Britton, Annwyl Williams, Ben Brewster, and Alfred Guzzetti (Bloomington: Indiana University Press, 1977), pp. 42–57.

11. Jacques Lacan, *Écrits: A Selection*, trans. Alan Sheridan (New York: W.W. Norton, 1977), p. 16.

12. Ibid., p. 22.

13. Anika Lemaire, *Jacques Lacan*, trans. David Macey (London: Routledge & Kegan Paul, 1977), p. 179.

14. Jacqueline Rose, "Paranoia and the Film System," *Screen*, vol. 17, no. 4 (winter 1976/7), pp. 85–104.

15. Laura Mulvey, "Visual Pleasure and Narrative Cinema," *Screen*, vol. 16, no. 3 (autumn 1975), pp. 6–18.

16. Sigmund Freud, *The Standard Edition of the Complete Psychological Works*, vol. 12, trans. and ed. James Strachey (London: The Hogarth Press, 1958), p. 72.

17. Ibid., p. 47.

18. Ibid., p. 32.

19. Ibid., p. 71.

20. J. Laplanche and J.B. Pontalis, *The Language of Psychoanalysis*, trans. Donald Nicholson-Smith (New York: W.W. Norton, 1973), p. 351.

21. Julia Kristeva, "Psychoanalysis and the Polis," *Critical Inquiry*, vol. 9 (September 1982), p. 82.

22. The close relation between paranoia and epistemology is emphasized by both Freud and Lacan. Freud, in "On Narcissism: An Introduction," indicates a kinship between the speculation of paranoia and that of philosophy: "The lament of the paranoiac shows also that at bottom the self-criticism of conscience is identical with, and based upon, self-observation. That activity of the mind which took over the function of conscience has also enlisted itself in the service of introspection, which furnishes philosophy with the material for its intellectual operations. This must have something to do with the characteristic tendency of paranoiacs to form speculative systems." *General Psychological Theory*, ed. Philip Rieff (New York: Collier Books, 1963), pp. 76–77. Lacan frequently refers to the "paranoid structure of knowledge." See, for example, "Aggressivity in Psychoanalysis," in *Écrits*, p. 17.

23. Freud, "Negation," *The Standard Edition of the Complete Psychological Works*, vol. 19, p. 237.

24. Freud, *Sexuality and the Psychology of Love*, ed. Philip Rieff (New York: Collier Books, 1963), pp. 97–106. For an intriguing analysis of this short case history in relation to feminist theory see Naomi Schor, "Female Paranoia: The Case for Psychoanalytic Feminist Criticism," *Yale French Studies*, no. 62 (1981), pp. 204–19.

25. Freud, *Sexuality and the Psychology of Love*, p. 103.

26. Ibid., pp. 103–4.

27. Guy Rosolato, "Paranoia et scène primitive," in *Essais sur le symbolique* (Paris: Éditions Gallimard, 1964), pp. 199–241.

28. Ibid., p. 201.

29. Ibid., p. 202.

30. B.D. Lewin, "Sleep, the Mouth, and the Dream Screen," *Psychoanalytic Quarterly*, vol. 15 (1946), pp. 419–34.

31. Rosolato, "Paranoia et scène primitive," p. 225. My translation.

32. Ibid., pp. 202, 200. My translation.

33. Julia Kristeva, *Powers of Horror: An Essay on Abjection*, trans. Leon S. Roudiez (New York: Columbia University Press, 1982), p. 44.

34. Pascal Bonitzer, "Here: The Notion of the Shot and the Subject of the Cinema," *Film Reader*, no. 4 (1979), p. 113.

35. Russ, "Somebody's Trying to Kill Me," p. 685 (italics in Russ).

36. Press book for *Dark Waters*, United Artists, 1944.

37. Diane Waldman analyzes the films in relation to what she terms the "fear of the familiar" (the uncanny), "familiar" here defined as both "recognizable" and "of the family." See Waldman, "Horror and Domesticity," p. 17.

38. Thierry Kuntzel, "The Film-Work, 2," *Camera Obscura*, no. 5 (spring 1980), p. 9.

39. Pascal Bonitzer, *Le regard et la voix* (Paris: Union Générale d'Éditions, 1976), p. 105. My translation.

40. Kuntzel, "Film Work, 2," p. 10.

41. André Bazin, *What Is Cinema?* vol. 2, trans. Hugh Gray (Berkeley: University of California Press, 1971), p. 37.

42. Sigmund Freud, *The Standard Edition of the Complete Psychological Works*, vol. 17, p. 226. Although it is clear that the translation in English of *unheimlich* as "uncanny" poses difficulties in the appropriation of Freud's analysis, the word "canny" nevertheless has a wide range of meanings, many of which can easily and fruitfully be articulated with that analysis. Among the most provocative meanings listed by the *OED* are: 1) Knowing, sagacious, judicious, prudent; wary, cautious. 3) Skilful, clever, 'cunning.' *Canny wife*: 'wise woman,' midwife; hence *canny moment*: moment of childbirth. 8) Quiet, easy, snug, comfortable, pleasant, cosy. 9) Agreeable to the eyes or perception. . . .

43. Freud, *Standard Edition*, vol. 17, p. 245.

44. Samuel Weber, "The Sideshow, or: Remarks on a Canny Moment," *MLN*, vol. 88, no. 6 (December 1973), p. 1112.

45. Ibid., p. 1113.

46. Ibid., p. 1133.

47. For an excellent analysis of the representation of women in the horror film see Linda Williams, "When the Woman Looks," in *Re-vision: Essays in Feminist Film Criticism*, ed. Mary Ann Doane, Patricia Mellencamp, and Linda Williams (Frederick, Md.: University Publications of America and The American Film Institute, 1984), pp. 83–99.

48. "Something to Be Scared Of" is the title of the second chapter of Kristeva's *Powers of Horror*.

49. Kristeva, *Powers of Horror*, pp. 1–2.

50. Kristeva, "Psychoanalysis and the Polis," p. 90.

51. Williams, "When the Woman Looks," p. 88.

52. For a more extensive analysis of the function of the portrait in these films in relation to contemporary understandings of the opposition between illusionism and modernism in art, see chapter 4 of Waldman's dissertation ("The Portrait and Modes of Representation").

53. For an elaboration of this difficulty in the mother-daughter relationship, see Luce Irigaray, "And the One Doesn't Stir without the Other," trans. Hélène Vivienne Wenzel, *Signs*, vol. 7, no. 1 (autumn 1981), pp. 60–67 and Nancy Chodorow, *The Reproduction of Mothering* (Berkeley: University of California Press, 1978).

54. Tania Modleski, *Loving with a Vengeance: Mass-Produced Fantasies for Women* (Hamden: Archon Books, 1982), pp. 70–71. For other analyses of gothic literature in relation to mother-daughter separation anxieties see Holland and Sherman, "Gothic Possibilities" and Claire Kahane, "Gothic Mirrors and Feminine Identity," *The Centennial Review*, vol. 24, no. 1 (1980), pp. 43–64.

55. The veiling or repression of the narrative's obsession with the maternal in comparison with the explicit concern with the paternal can be seen in the fact that these portraits represent actual fathers (men whose actual role in the film is that of father), while the female portraits are representations of maternal *figures* (metaphorical mothers).

56. Kristeva, *Powers of Horror*, p. 58.

57. Ibid., p. 62.

58. Ibid., pp. 62–64.

59. Ibid., p. 80.

60. Stephen Heath, *Questions of Cinema* (London: Macmillan, 1981), pp. 47–48.

61. See François Truffaut, *Hitchcock* (New York: Simon and Schuster, 1967), p. 102.

62. Stephen Jenkins, "Lang: Fear and Desire," in *Fritz Lang: The Image and the Look*, ed. Stephen Jenkins (London: British Film Institute, 1981), p. 104.

### 6. *Female Spectatorship and Machines of Projection:* Caught *and* Rebecca

1. Sigmund Freud, *Three Case Histories* (New York: Collier Books, 1963), p. 149.

2. Julia Kristeva, *About Chinese Women*, trans. Anita Barrows (New York: Urizen Books, 1977), p. 29.

3. The figure is Franzi, Ohlrig's rather slick public relations man and secretary who is endowed with characteristics stereotyped as homosexual. Thus, an intensification of the representation of male binding (as in the predominantly male audience of Ohlrig's cinema) immediately precedes the threatening laugh of the only female spectator present.

4. The sequence is composed of fifty shots; this brief analysis covers only twenty-five of these.

5. Jacqueline Rose, "Paranoia and the Film System," *Screen*, vol. 17, no. 4 (winter 1976–77), p. 86.

6. Freud, "A Case of Paranoia Running Counter to the Psychoanalytical Theory of the Disease," in *Sexuality and the Psychology of Love* (New York: Collier Books, 1963), p. 104.

7. See J. Laplanche and J. B. Pontalis, *The Language of Psychoanalysis*, trans. Donald Nicholson-Smith (New York: W. W. Norton, 1973), pp. 349–56. Laplanche and Pontalis define projection as having a sense "comparable to the cinematographic one: the subject sends out into the external world an image of something that exists in him in an unconscious way. Projection is here defined as a mode of *refusal to recognize (méconnaissance)*. . . ."

8. Parveen Adams, "Representation and Sexuality," *m/f*, no. 1, pp. 66–67.

9. An acknowledgment of the difficulties with the ending of *Caught* can be found in Ophuls's remarks about the film: "I worked for MGM. I made *Caught*, which I quite like. But I had difficulties with the production over the script, so that the film goes off the rails towards the end. Yes, the ending is really almost impossible, but up until the last ten minutes it's not bad." Paul Willeman, ed., *Ophuls* (London: British Film Institute, 1978), p. 23.

10. In the generic subcategory to which *Caught* and *Rebecca* belong, the "paranoid" woman's film, there are frequently two major male characters, one evil or psychotic, the other good and heroic. The woman, as in Lévi-Strauss's fable of the constitution of society, is exchanged from one to the other. In *Rebecca* this is not quite the case. Nevertheless, Maxim is a composite figure and therefore incorporates both character types—both sane and insane, rich but with middle-class tastes (e.g., the Joan Fontaine character). At the end of the film, Fontaine finds a harmonious reunification with the sane Maxim, whose strongest symbol of wealth—Manderley—burns to the ground.

11. The vicious quality of such a gesture is mitigated by the fact that Rebecca, in contradistinction to the Joan Fontaine character, is isolated as the evil, sexually active woman.

### 7. *The Shadow of Her Gaze*

1. Luce Irigaray, *Speculum of the Other Woman*, trans. Gillian C. Gill (Ithaca: Cornell University Press, 1985), p. 193.

2. See Michel Foucault, *The History of Sexuality*, vol. 1, trans. Robert Hurley (New York: Pantheon Books, 1978).

3. Sigmund Freud, *The Interpretation of Dreams*, trans. James Strachey (New York: Avon Books, 1965), p. 183.

4. M. M. Bakhtin, *The Dialogic Imagination: Four Essays*, trans. Caryl Emerson and Michael Holquist, ed. M. Holquist (Austin: University of Texas Press, 1981), p. 394.

5. Ibid., pp. 397–98.

6. Janice Radway, *Reading the Romance: Women, Patriarchy, and Popular Litera-*

*ture* (Chapel Hill and London: The University of North Carolina Press, 1984). See also Andrea S. Walsh, *Women's Film and Female Experience 1940–1950* (New York: Praeger, 1984).

7. John Brenkman, "Mass Media: From Collective Experience to the Culture of Privatization," *Social Text*, no. 1 (winter 1979), p. 105.

8. Silvia Bovenschen, "Is There A Feminine Aesthetic?" *New German Critique*, no. 10 (winter 1977), p. 129.

9. Roland Barthes, *Mythologies*, trans. Annette Lavers (New York: Hill and Wang, 1972), p. 135.

10. Irigaray, *This Sex Which Is Not One*, trans. Catherine Porter (Ithaca: Cornell University Press, 1985), p. 76.

# BIBLIOGRAPHY

Allen, Jeanne. "The Film Viewer as Consumer." *Quarterly Review of Film Studies*, vol. 5, no. 4 (fall 1980), pp. 481–499.

Althusser, Louis and Balibar, Étienne. *Reading Capital*. Translated by Ben Brewster. London: New Left Books, 1970.

Bakhtin, M. M. *The Dialogic Imagination: Four Essays*. Translated by Caryl Emerson and Michael Holquist. Edited by Michael Holquist. Austin: University of Texas Press, 1981.

Barthes, Roland. *Camera Lucida: Reflections on Photography*. Translated by Richard Howard. New York: Hill and Wang, 1981.

———. *Image/Music/Text*. Translated by Stephen Heath. New York: Hill and Wang, 1977.

———. *A Lover's Discourse*. Translated by Richard Howard. New York: Hill and Wang, 1978.

———. *Mythologies*. Translated by Annette Lavers. New York: Hill and Wang, 1972.

———. *S/Z: An Essay*. Translated by Richard Miller. New York: Hill and Wang, 1974.

Baudry, Jean-Louis. "The Apparatus." Translated by Jean Andrews and Bertrand Augst. *Camera Obscura*, no. 1 (fall 1976): pp. 104–26.

———. "Ideological Effects of the Basic Cinematographic Apparatus." Translated by Allan Williams. *Film Quarterly*, vol. 28, no. 2 (winter 1974–75), pp. 39–47.

Bazin, André. *What Is Cinema?* Vol. 2. Translated by Hugh Gray. Berkeley: University of California Press, 1971.

Benjamin, Walter. *Illuminations*. Translated by Harry Zohn. Edited by Hannah Arendt. New York: Schocken Books, 1969.

———. *Charles Baudelaire: A Lyric Poet in the Era of High Capitalism*. Translated by Harry Zohn. London: New Left Books, 1973.

Benveniste, Émile. *Problems in General Linguistics*. Translated by Mary Elizabeth Meek. Coral Gables: University of Miami Press, 1971.

Beylie, Claude. "Propositions sur le mélo." *Les Cahiers de la Cinematheque: Pour Une Histoire du Mélodrame au Cinéma*, no. 28, pp. 7–11.

Bonitzer, Pascal. "Here: The Notion of the Shot and the Subject of the Cinema." *Film Reader*, no. 4 (1979), pp. 108–19.

———. "Partial Vision: Film and the Labyrinth." Translated by Fabrice Ziolkowski. *Wide Angle*, vol. 4, no. 4 (1981), pp. 56–63.

———. *Le regard et la voix*. Paris: Union Générale d'Éditions, 1976.

Bovenschen, Silvia. "Is There A Feminine Aesthetic?" *New German Critique*, no. 10 (winter 1977), pp. 111–37.

Bowlby, Rachel. *Just Looking: Consumer Culture in Dreiser, Gissing and Zola*. New York: Methuen, 1985.

Brenkman, John. "Mass Media: From Collective Experience to the Culture of Privatization." *Social Text*, vol. 1, no. 1 (winter 1979), pp. 94–109.

Brooks, Peter. *The Melodramatic Imagination: Balzac, Henry James, Melodrama, and the Mode of Excess*. New Haven: Yale University Press, 1976.

Chafe, William H. *The American Woman: Her Changing Social, Economic, and Political Roles, 1920–1970*. New York: Oxford University Press, 1972.

Chesler, Phyllis. *Women and Madness*. New York: Avon Books, 1972.

Chodorow, Nancy. *The Reproduction of Mothering*. Berkeley: University of California Press, 1978.

Cixous, Hélène. "The Laugh of the Medusa." *New French Feminisms*. Edited by Elaine Marks and Isabelle de Courtivron. Amherst: The University of Massachusetts Press, 1980, pp. 245–64.

Cook, Pam. "Melodrama and the Women's Picture." *The Gainsborough Melodrama*. Edited by Sue Aspinall and Sue Harper. London: British Film Institute, 1983.

Copjec, Joan. "Flavit et Dissipati Sunt." *October*, no. 18 (fall 1981), pp. 21–40.

Coward, Rosalind. *Female Desire: Women's Sexuality Today*. London: Paladin Books, 1984.

Cowie, Elizabeth. "Fantasia." *m/f*, no. 9 (1984), pp. 71–105.

———. "Woman as Sign." *m/f*, no. 1 (1978), pp. 49–63.

Debord, Guy. *Society of the Spectacle*. Detroit: Black and Red, 1977.

de Lauretis, Teresa. *Alice Doesn't: Feminism, Semiotics, Cinema*. Bloomington: Indiana University Press, 1984.

———. "Oedipus Interruptus." *Wide Angle*, vol. 7, nos. 1–2 (1985), pp. 34–40.

Derrida, Jacques. *Writing and Difference*. Translated by Alan Bass. Chicago: The University of Chicago Press, 1978.

Doane, Mary Ann. "Film and the Masquerade—Theorising the Female Spectator." *Screen*, vol. 23, nos. 3–4 (September-October 1982), pp. 74–88.

———. "*Gilda*: Epistemology as Striptease." *Camera Obscura*, no. 11 (1983), pp. 7–27.

Doane, Mary Ann; Mellencamp, Patricia; and Williams, Linda, eds. *Re-vision: Essays in Feminist Film Criticism*. Frederick, Md.: University Publications of America and The American Film Institute, 1984.

———. " '. . . when the direction of the force acting on the body is changed.': The Moving Image." *Wide Angle*, vol. 7, nos. 1–2 (1985), pp. 42–58.

———. "Woman's Stake: Filming the Female Body." *October*, no. 17 (summer 1981), pp. 23–36.

Eckert, Charles. "The Carole Lombard in Macy's Window." *Quarterly Review of Film Studies*, vol. 3, no. 1 (winter 1978), pp. 1–22.

Ehrenreich, Barbara and English, Deirdre. *Complaints and Disorders: The Sexual Politics of Sickness*. New York: The Feminist Press, 1973.

———. *For Her Own Good: 150 Years of the Experts' Advice to Women*. Garden City: Anchor Books, 1979.

Elsaesser, Thomas. "Tales of Sound and Fury: Observations on the Family Melodrama." *Monogram*, no. 4 (1972), pp. 2–15.

Erens, Patricia, ed. *Sexual Stratagems: The World of Women in Film*. New York: Horizon Press, 1979.

Ewen, Stuart. *Captains of Consciousness: Advertising and the Social Roots of the Consumer Culture*. New York: McGraw-Hill, 1976.

Fearing, Franklin. "Psychology and the Films." *Hollywood Quarterly*, vol. 2, no. 2 (January 1947), pp. 118–21.

Fischer, Lucy. "The Image of Woman as Image: The Optical Politics of *Dames*." *Film Quarterly*, vol. 30, no. 1 (fall 1976), pp. 2–11.

———. "The Lady Vanishes: Women, Magic, and the Movies." *Film Quarterly*, vol. 33, no. 1 (fall 1979), pp. 30–40.

———. "Two-faced Women: The 'Double' in Women's Melodrama of the 1940s." *Cinema Journal*, vol. 23, no. 1 (fall 1983), pp. 24–43.

Flitterman, Sandy. "*Guest in the House*: Rupture and Reconstitution of the Bourgeois Nuclear Family." *Wide Angle*, vol. 4, no. 2 (1980), pp. 18–27.

———. "Montage/Discourse: Germaine Dulac's *The Smiling Madame Beudet*." *Wide Angle*, vol. 4, no. 3 (1980), pp. 54–59.

————. "Woman, Desire and the Look: Feminism and the Enunciative Apparatus in Cinema." *Theories of Authorship.* Edited by John Caughie. London: Routledge & Kegan Paul, 1981.

Flitterman, Sandy and Suter, Jacquelyn. "Textual Riddles: Woman as Enigma or Site of Social Meanings? An Interview with Laura Mulvey." *Discourse*, no. 1 (1979), pp. 86–127.

Foucault, Michel. *The Birth of the Clinic: An Archaeology of Medical Perception.* Translated by A. M. Sheridan Smith. New York: Pantheon Books, 1973.

————. *The History of Sexuality.* Translated by Robert Hurley. Vol. 1. New York: Pantheon Books, 1978.

————. *Madness and Civilization: A History of Insanity in the Age of Reason.* Translated by Richard Howard. New York: Random House, 1965.

————. "What is an Author?" in *Language, Counter-memory, Practice.* Translated by Donald F. Bouchard and Sherry Simon. Ithaca: Cornell University Press, 1977.

Framework Editorial Board, "The Reckless Moment" and "The Family in 'The Reckless Moment.' " *Framework*, no. 4 (autumn 1976), pp. 17–24.

Freud, Sigmund. *Beyond the Pleasure Principle.* Translated and edited by James Strachey. New York: W. W. Norton, 1961.

————. "A Case of Paranoia Running Counter to the Psychoanalytical Theory of the Disease." *Sexuality and the Psychology of Love.* Edited by Philip Rieff. New York: Collier Books, 1963.

————. "A Child is Being Beaten." *Sexuality and the Psychology of Love.* Edited by Philip Rieff. New York: Collier Books, 1963.

————. *Dora: An Analysis of a Case of Hysteria.* Edited by Philip Rieff. New York: Collier Books, 1963.

————. "The Economic Problem in Masochism." *General Psychological Theory.* Edited by Philip Rieff. New York: Collier Books, 1963.

————. "Fetishism." *Sexuality and the Psychology of Love.* Edited by Philip Rieff. New York: Collier Books, 1963.

————. *Group Psychology and the Analysis of the Ego.* Translated by James Strachey. New York: Bantam Books, 1960.

————. *Inhibitions, Symptoms and Anxiety.* Translated by Alix Strachey. New York: W. W. Norton, 1959.

————. *The Interpretation of Dreams.* Translated and edited by James Strachey. New York: Avon Books, 1965.

————. *The Standard Edition of the Complete Psychological Works of Sigmund Freud*, 24 vols. Translated and edited by James Strachey. London: The Hogarth Press Limited, 1953.

————. *Three Case Histories.* New York: Collier Books, 1963.

Freud, Sigmund and Breuer, Joseph. *Studies on Hysteria.* Translated and edited by James Strachey. New York: Avon Books, 1966.

Friedberg, Anne. "On H.D., Woman, History, Recognition." *Wide Angle*, vol. 5, no. 2 (1982), pp. 26–31.

Goimard, Jacques. "Le mélodrame: le mot et la chose." *Les Cahiers de la Cinematheque: Pour Une Histoire du Mélodrame au Cinema*, no. 28, pp. 17–66.

Gorbman, Claudia. "The Drama's Melos: Max Steiner and *Mildred Pierce*." *The Velvet Light Trap: Review of Cinema*, no. 19 (1982), pp. 35–39.

Groupe μ (J. Dubois, P. Dubois, F. Edeline, J.M. Klinkenberg, P. Minguet). "Ironique et iconique." *Poetique*, no. 36 (Novembre 1978), pp. 427–42.

Handel, Leo A. *Hollywood Looks At Its Audience: A Report of Film Audience Research.* Urbana: The University of Illinois Press, 1950.

Hartmann, Susan M. *The Home Front and Beyond: American Women in the 1940s.* Boston: Twayne Publishers, 1982.

Haskell, Molly. *From Reverence to Rape: The Treatment of Women in the Movies*. Baltimore: Penguin Books, 1974.

Heath, Stephen. "Difference." *Screen*, vol. 19, no. 3 (autumn 1978), pp. 51–112.

———. "Family Plots." *Comparative Criticism*, vol. 5. Cambridge University Press, 1983, pp. 317–31.

———. "Lessons from Brecht." *Screen*, vol. 15, no. 2 (summer 1974), pp. 103–28.

———. "The Question Oshima." *Ophuls*. Edited by Paul Willeman. London: British Film Institute, 1978, pp. 75–87.

Heilman, Robert Bechtold. *Tragedy and Melodrama: Versions of Experience*. Seattle: University of Washington Press, 1968.

Higham, Charles and Greenberg, Joel. *Hollywood in the Forties*. New York: Paperback Library, 1970.

Holland, Norman N. and Sherman, Leona F. "Gothic Possibilities." *New Literary History*, vol. 8, no. 2 (winter 1977), pp. 279–94.

Irigaray, Luce. "And the One Doesn't Stir Without the Other." Translated by Hélène Vivienne Wenzel. *Signs*, vol. 7, no. 1 (autumn 1981), pp. 60–67.

———. *Ce sexe qui n'en est pas un*. Paris: Les Éditions de Minuit, 1977.

———. *Speculum de l'autre femme*. Paris: Les Éditions de Minuit, 1974.

———. *Speculum of the Other Woman*. Translated by Gillian C. Gill. Ithaca: Cornell University Press, 1985.

———. *This Sex Which Is Not One*. Translated by Catherine Porter. Ithaca: Cornell University Press, 1985.

Jacobs, Lea. "*Now, Voyager*: Some Problems of Enunciation and Sexual Difference." *Camera Obscura*, no. 7 (1981), pp. 89–109.

Jameson, Fredric. "Pleasure: A Political Issue." *Formations of Pleasure*. London: Routledge and Kegan Paul, 1983, pp. 1–13.

———. "Reification and Utopia in Mass Culture." *Social Text*, vol. 1, no. 1 (winter 1979), pp. 130–48.

Jenkins, Stephen, ed. *Fritz Lang: The Image and the Look*. London: British Film Institute, 1981.

Johnston, Claire. "Dorothy Arzner: Critical Strategies." *The Work of Dorothy Arzner: Towards a Feminist Cinema*. London: British Film Institute, 1975, pp. 1–8.

———. "Femininity and the Masquerade: Anne of the Indies." *Jacques Tourneur*. London: British Film Institute, 1975, pp. 36–44.

———. "Women's Cinema as Counter-Cinema." *Notes on Women's Cinema*. London: Society for Education in Film and Television, 1973, pp. 24–31.

Kahane, Claire. "Gothic Mirrors and Feminine Identity." *The Centennial Review*, vol. 24, no. 1 (1980), pp. 43–64.

Kamuf, Peggy. "Replacing Feminist Criticism." *Diacritics*, vol. 12, no. 2 (summer 1982), pp. 42–47.

Kaplan, E. Ann. "The Case of the Missing Mother: Maternal Issues in Vidor's *Stella Dallas*." *Heresies*, no. 16, pp. 81–85.

———. *Women and Film: Both Sides of the Camera*. New York: Methuen, 1983.

———, ed. *Women in Film Noir*. London: British Film Institute, 1978.

Kay, Karyn and Peary, Gerald, eds. *Women and the Cinema: A Critical Anthology*. New York: E.P. Dutton, 1977.

Klinger, Barbara. "*Psycho*: The Institutionalization of Female Sexuality." *Wide Angle*, vol. 5, no. 1 (1982), pp. 49–55.

Kofman, Sarah. "Ex: The Woman's Enigma." *Enclitic*, vol. 4, no. 2 (fall 1980), pp. 17–28.

Kristeva, Julia. *About Chinese Women*. Translated by Anita Barrows. New York: Urizen Books, 1977.

———. "Maternité selon Giovanni Bellini." *Polylogue*. Paris: Éditions du Seuil, 1977, pp. 409–35.

———. *Powers of Horror: An Essay on Abjection*. Translated by Leon S. Roudiez. New York: Columbia University Press, 1982.

———. "Psychoanalysis and the Polis." *Critical Inquiry* 9 (September 1982): pp. 77–92.

———. "Women's Time." Translated by Alice Jardine and Harry Blake. *Signs: Journal of Women in Culture and Society*, vol. 7, no. 1 (1981), pp. 13–35.

Kubie, Lawrence S., "Psychiatry and the Films." *Hollywood Quarterly*, vol. 2, no. 2 (January 1947), pp. 113–17.

Kuhn, Annette. *Women's Pictures: Feminism and Cinema*. London: Routledge and Kegan Paul, 1982.

Kuntzel, Thierry. "The Film-Work, 2." *Camera Obscura*, no. 5 (spring 1980), pp. 7–72.

Lacan, Jacques. *Écrits: A Selection*. Translated by Alan Sheridan. New York: W.W. Norton, 1977.

———. *The Four Fundamental Concepts of Psycho-Analysis*. Translated by Alan Sheridan. Middlesex: Penguin Books, 1979.

Laemmle, Carl. "The Business of Motion Pictures." *The American Film Industry*. Edited by Tino Balio. Madison: The University of Wisconsin Press, 1976.

La Place, Maria. "Bette Davis and the Ideal of Consumption." *Wide Angle*, vol. 6, no. 4 (1985), pp. 34–43.

Laplanche, Jean. *Life and Death in Psycho-analysis*. Translated by Jeffrey Mehlman. Baltimore: The Johns Hopkins Press, 1976.

Laplanche, J. and Pontalis, J.B. *The Language of Psychoanalysis*. Translated by Donald Nicholson-Smith. New York: W.W. Norton, 1973.

Le Doeuff, Michèle. "Pierre Roussel's Chiasmas: From Imaginary Knowledge to the Learned Imagination." *Ideology and Consciousness*, no. 9 (winter 1981/82), pp. 39–70.

Lemaire, Anika. *Jacques Lacan*. Translated by David Macey. London: Routledge & Kegan Paul, 1977.

Lévi-Strauss, Claude. *The Elementary Structures of Kinship*. Translated by James Harle Bell, John Richard von Sturmer, and Rodney Needham. Boston: Beacon Press, 1969.

Lewin, B.D. "Sleep, the Mouth, and the Dream Screen." *Psychoanalytic Quarterly* 15 (1946), pp. 419–34.

Linderman, Deborah. "Structuring by Absence in Classical Film Texts." Ph.D. dissertation Brown University, 1983.

Lundberg, Ferdinand and Farnham, Marynia F., M.D. *Modern Woman: The Lost Sex*. New York: Harper, 1947.

MacCabe, Colin. "Realism and the Cinema: Notes on Some Brechtian Theses." *Screen*, vol. 15, no. 2 (summer 1974): pp. 7–27.

Mannoni, O. *Clefs pour l'imaginaire ou l'autre scène*. Paris: Éditions du Seuil, 1969.

Mayne, Judith. "Immigrants and Spectators." *Wide Angle*, vol. 5, no. 2 (1982), pp. 32–41.

———. "The Woman at the Keyhole: Women's Cinema and Feminist Criticism." *New German Critique*, 23 (1981): pp. 27–43.

Mellencamp, Patricia. "Spectacle and Spectator: Looking through the American Musical Comedy." *Cine-tracts*, vol. 1, no. 2 (summer 1977), pp. 27–35.

Metz, Christian. *Film Language: A Semiotics of the Cinema*. Translated by Michael Taylor. New York: Oxford University Press, 1974.

———. "History/Discourse: Note on Two Voyeurisms." Translated by Susan Bennett. *Edinburgh '76 Magazine*, no. 1 (1976), pp. 21–25.

———. "The Imaginary Signifier." *Screen*, vol. 16, no. 2 (summer 1975), pp. 14–76.

———. *The Imaginary Signifier: Psychoanalysis and the Cinema*. Translated by Celia Britton, Annwyl Williams, Ben Brewster, and Alfred Guzzetti. Bloomington: Indiana University Press, 1977.

Miller, Nancy K. "The Text's Heroine: A Feminist Critic and Her Fictions." *Diacritics*, vol. 12, no. 2 (summer 1982), pp. 48–53.

Mitchell, Juliet. *Psychoanalysis and Feminism*. New York: Vintage Books, 1974.

Mitchell, Juliet and Rose, Jacqueline, eds. *Feminine Sexuality: Jacques Lacan and the École Freudienne*. New York: W.W. Norton, 1982.

Modleski, Tania. *Loving with a Vengeance: Mass-Produced Fantasies for Women*. Hamden: Archon Books, 1982.

———. " 'Never to be thirty-six years old': *Rebecca* as Female Oedipal Drama." *Wide Angle*, vol. 5, no. 1 (1982), pp. 34–41.

———. "Time and Desire in the Woman's Film." *Cinema Journal*, vol. 23, no. 3 (spring 1984), pp. 19–30.

Montrelay, Michèle. "Inquiry into Femininity." *m/f*, no. 1 (1978), pp. 83–102.

Moretti, Franco. *Signs Taken For Wonders: Essays in the Sociology of Literary Forms*. Translated by Susan Fischer, David Forgacs, and David Miller. London: New Left Books, 1983.

Mulvey, Laura. "Afterthoughts on 'Visual Pleasure and Narrative Cinema' Inspired by *Duel in the Sun*." *Framework*, nos. 15, 16, 17 (1981), pp. 12–15.

———. "Visual Pleasure and Narrative Cinema." *Screen*, vol. 16, no. 3 (autumn 1975), pp. 6–18.

Plaza, Monique. "The Mother/The Same: Hatred of the Mother in Psychoanalysis." *Feminist Issues*, vol. 2, no. 1 (spring 1982), pp. 75–99.

Polan, Dana. *Power and Paranoia: History, Narrative, and the American Cinema, 1940–1950*. New York: Columbia University Press, 1986.

Pollock, Griselda; Nowell-Smith, Geoffrey; Heath, Stephen. "Dossier on Melodrama." *Screen*, vol. 18, no. 2 (summer 1977), pp. 105–19.

Radway, Janice. *Reading the Romance: Women, Patriarchy, and Popular Literature*. Chapel Hill: University of North Carolina Press, 1984.

Renov, Michael. "From Fetish to Subject: The Containment of Sexual Difference in Hollywood's Wartime Cinema." *Wide Angle*, vol. 5, no. 1 (1982).

Rich, B. Ruby. "In the Name of Feminist Film Criticism." *Heresies*, no. 9 (1980), pp. 74–81.

Rose, Jacqueline. "Femininity and Its Discontents." *Feminist Review*, no. 14 (summer 1983), pp. 5–21.

———. "Paranoia and the Film System." *Screen*, vol. 17, no. 4 (winter 1976/77), pp. 85–104.

Rosen, Marjorie. *Popcorn Venus: Women, Movies, and the American Dream*. New York: Coward, McCann & Geoghegan, 1973.

Rosolato, Guy. "Paranoia et scène primitive." *Essais sur le symbolique*. Paris: Éditions Gallimard, 1964, pp. 199–241.

Rupp, Leila J. *Mobilizing Women For War: German and American Propaganda 1939–1945*. Princeton: Princeton University Press, 1978.

Russ, Joanna. "Somebody's Trying to Kill Me and I Think It's My Husband: The Modern Gothic." *Journal of Popular Culture*, vol. 6, no. 4 (spring 1973), pp. 666–91.

Schivelbusch, Wolfgang. *The Railway Journey: Trains and Travel in the 19th Century*. Translated by Anselm Hollo. New York: Urizen Books, 1977.

Schneider, Irving. "Images of the Mind: Psychiatry in the Commercial Film." *American Journal of Psychiatry*, vol. 134, no. 6 (June 1977), pp. 613–17.

Schor, Naomi. "Female Paranoia: The Case for Psychoanalytic Feminist Criticism." *Yale French Studies*, no. 62 (1981), pp. 204–19.

Silverman, Kaja. "Dis-Embodying the Female Voice." *Re-vision: Essays in Feminist Film Criticism*. Edited by Mary Ann Doane, Patricia Mellencamp, and Linda Williams. Frederick, Md.: University Publications of America and the American Film Institute 1984.

———. "Masochism and Subjectivity." *Framework*, no. 12, pp. 2–9.

———. *The Subject of Semiotics*. New York: Oxford University Press, 1983.

Sontag, Susan. *Illness as Metaphor*. New York: Farrar, Straus and Giroux, 1977–78.

Turim, Maureen. "Designing Women: The Emergence of the New Sweetheart Line." *Wide Angle*, vol. 6, no. 2 (1984), pp. 4–11.

———. "Gentlemen Consume Blondes." *Wide Angle*, vol. 1, no. 1 (1976), pp. 68–76.

Vernet, Marc. "Freud: effets spéciaux—Mise en scène: U.S.A." *Communications*, no. 23 (1975), pp. 223–34.

Viviani, Christian. "Who is Without Sin? The Maternal Melodrama in American Film, 1930–39." *Wide Angle*, vol. 4, no. 2 (1980), pp. 4–17.

Waldman, Diane. "Horror and Domesticity: The Modern Gothic Romance Film of the 1940s." Ph.D. dissertation. University of Wisconsin—Madison, 1981.

Walsh, Andrea S. *Women's Film and Female Experience, 1940–1950*. New York: Praeger, 1984.

Watt, Ian. *The Rise of the Novel*. Berkeley: University of California Press, 1957.

Weber, Samuel. *The Legend of Freud*. Minneapolis: University of Minnesota Press, 1982.

———. "The Sideshow, or: Remarks on a Canny Moment." *MLN*, vol. 88, no. 6 (December 1973), pp. 1102–33.

Willeman, Paul, ed. *Ophuls*. London: British Film Institute, 1978.

Williams, Carol Traynor. *The Dream Beside Me: The Movies and the Children of the Forties*. Cranbury, N.J.: Associated University Presses, 1980.

Williams, Linda. "Film Body: An Implantation of Perversions." *Ciné-tracts*, vol. 3, no. 4 (winter 1981), pp. 19–35.

———. " 'Something Else Besides a Mother': *Stella Dallas* and the Maternal Melodrama." *Cinema Journal*, vol. 24, no. 1 (fall 1984), pp. 2–27.

———. "When the Woman Looks." *Re-vision: Essays in Feminist Film Criticism*. Edited by Mary Ann Doane, Patricia Mellencamp, and Linda Williams. Frederick, Md.: University Publications of America and The American Film Institute, 1984, pp. 83–99.

Wolfenstein, Martha and Leites, Nathan. *Movies: A Psychological Study*. New York: Atheneum, 1970.

Wollen, Peter. *Readings and Writings: Semiotic Counter-Strategies*. London: Verso Editions and New Left Books, 1982.

# INDEX